THE CASH CEILING

PRINCETON STUDIES IN
Political Behavior

Edited by Tali Mendelberg

THE CASH CEILING

WHY ONLY THE RICH RUN FOR OFFICE—
AND WHAT WE CAN DO ABOUT IT

NICHOLAS CARNES

Princeton University Press

Princeton and Oxford

Published by Princeton University Press

41 William Street, Princeton, New Jersey 08540

6 Oxford Street, Woodstock, Oxfordshire OX20 1TR

press.princeton.edu

Jacket images courtesy of Shutterstock and Dreamstime

LCCN 2018945608

ISBN 978-0-691-18200-1

British Library Cataloging-in-Publication Data is available

Editorial: Eric Crahan & Pamela Weidman

Production Editorial: Ali Parrington

Text and Jacket Design: Carmina Alvarez

Production: Erin Suydam

Publicity: Tayler Lord

This book has been composed in Gentium Plus and Trade Gothic

Printed on acid-free paper. ∞

Printed in the United States of America

10 9 8 7 6 5 4 3 2 1

For Keri,
every time she sneezes . . .

Contents

Figures and Tables

FIGURES

TABLES

Acknowledgments

I first pitched the idea for this book at a meeting in September 2008. Back then there was almost no research on the fact that politicians tend to be vastly more affluent than the people they represent, and I thought that was a serious blind spot in the field of political science. So at a meeting with my mentors, Chris Achen, Doug Arnold, and Larry Bartels, I proposed to write a manuscript that would explain both why working-class Americans almost never go on to hold public office and how that inequality affects public policy. They recommended a slightly different approach, however: spend a few years studying the second question about the *consequences* of America's white-collar government—because doing that the right way would take a lot of time and energy—and save the first question about *causes* for a future project. One of them even warned that if I tried to do both, it would "take a decade to finish the thing." And they were right: I spent several years researching and writing about the effects of white-collar government, *then* turned my attention to the causes, and my work has been so much better for it. I remain deeply grateful to Chris, Doug, and Larry for all of their support and guidance. They were even right about the timing: this book is scheduled to be released nine years and eleven months after that meeting.

I started working on this book in 2011 after I took a job as an assistant professor at Duke's Sanford School of Public Policy. Here at Duke, I've been fortunate to have many wonderful colleagues who have supported my research and my career in significant ways. Jay Hamilton advised me on the earliest iterations of this project and on many of the major decisions

I've made since then. Kristin Goss has given me suggestions and feedback on all of my research and has been an amazing support. Judith Kelley has given me detailed guidance throughout my time at Duke and provided me with comments on drafts of every chapter of this book (twice!). Anirudh Krishna has given me invaluable direction, including help navigating the final stages of this project. Bruce Jentleson has been a constant source of support and guidance. My first dean at the Sanford School, Bruce Kuniholm, stuck up for me and for this project when I really needed his help, and my second dean, Kelly Brownell, did the same, going above and beyond to support this project at crucial times. David Arrington, Belinda Keith, Zach Johnson, and Donna Jones helped me manage grants and project finances. And many other colleagues and friends gave me the moral support that helped me through the long and sometimes lonely work of writing a book, especially Carolyn Barnes, Marc Bellemare and Janet Hou, Donna Dyer, Ashley Jardina, Karen Kemp, Bob Korstad, Hugh and Kate Macartney, Fritz Mayer, Manoj Mohanan, Jay Pearson, Gunther Peck, Ken Rogerson, Deondra Rose, Nancy Shaw, Jessi Strieb and Rob Garlick, and Ashley Trice.

I'm also indebted to many friends and colleagues outside of Duke who have supported this research. My fellow Kansan and dear friend Eric Hansen provided me with encouragement and support when I needed it most, and he and I coauthored some of the research I discuss in chapter 4. I'm also deeply indebted to my long-time friend and coauthor Noam F. Lupu; Noam and I have worked together on projects related to this research since 2011, and his friendship and advice have always meant the world to me.

I owe a tremendous debt to my good friends David Broockman, Chris Skovron, and Melody Crowder-Meyer. The four of us worked together on the national surveys of citizens, candidates, and party leaders that make up the backbone of the empirical evidence in this book. I wouldn't have been able to run even one of those surveys—let alone all of them—without their support, patience, and friendship.

I'm also grateful to the many scholars and friends who were willing to listen to my ideas and give me feedback at various stages of this project, especially Quinn Albaugh, Adam Bonica, Jim Curry, Ella Foster-Molina, Amy

Fried, Elizabeth Gibson, Marty Gilens, Robert Glover, Avi Green, Jake Grumbach, Jacob Hacker, Hans Hassell, Alex Hertel-Fernandez, James Howlett, Larry Jacobs, Shamus Khan, Adam Seth Levine, Peter Loewen, Cheri Maestas, Paola Maynard-Moll, Ben Newman, Brendan Nyhan, Tracy Osborn, Ben Page, Hannah Reuter, Steve Rogers, Andy Sabl, Kay Schlozman, Fred Solt, Antoine Yoshinaka, John Zaller, and Jack Zhou. This book also benefited tremendously from the feedback I received on presentations at the American Political Science Association, the Midwest Political Science Association, and the Southern Political Science Association, and at University of California–Berkeley, University of Maine, Carolina Meadows Retirement Community, Yale University, Emory University, University of Tulsa, University of Minnesota, University of Oklahoma, Oklahoma Policy Institute, University of Wisconsin, University of North Carolina, University of Michigan, University of Toronto, Lone Star Community College, Russell Sage Foundation, University of Utah, Columbia University, Ford Foundation, Princeton University, University of Iowa, John Locke Foundation, University of Oxford, Stanford University, and University of Southern California.

I'm also deeply grateful to the many students and research assistants who contributed to this project, especially Sondra Appleson, Stephanie Tsimsis, Adam Weber, Katie Pishke, Melissa Lee, Amanda Lewellyn, Amulya Vadapalli, Mary Coyne, Bailey McCann, Arjun Arora, Ryan Smith, and the students in my spring 2015 seminar, PubPol 590s.15, "Political Ambition."

I wouldn't have been able to conduct this research without generous financial support from several sources. The DeWitt Wallace Center for Media and Democracy funded the 2012 National Candidate Study. The Russell Sage Foundation funded the 2013 National Survey of Party Leaders. And the Sanford School of Public Policy funded the 2014 National Candidate Study, the candidate training program referenced in chapter 5, and the leave time that I needed to complete this book.

I am especially indebted to the people who supported this book during its final stages, including my editor at Princeton University Press, Eric Crahan; my series editor, Tali Mendelberg, who read and commented on two full drafts of this book; Jennifer Lawless, who provided detailed feedback on the entire manuscript; my anonymous reviewers; and the editorial staff at Princeton University Press, including Ali Parrington, Pam Weidman, and Jenn Backer.

I'm also grateful to my extended family for their support: Mom; Jack and Max; Kristie and Larry; Shelly and Darren; Corey and Katie; Kim and Walter; Erica and Gray; Kurtis, Boramey, Leo, and Beaux; Kerry; Kelsey, Bradlee, and Adalyn; Jessica and Austin; Ka-Ka; Grandma Frances; Arv and Linda; Nathan, Lisa, Axel, and Jade; and Ashley and Michael. And I'm lucky to have great in-laws, too: John and Kim; Jacob; Wendy and Pat; Megan, Curtis, Everett, and Mira; Kenny; Joe and Kimmer; Mike and Mark; Tim and Judy; Nana and Poppee; Charlie and Mary; Kristen and Adam; Charlie Jr.; Markie; Allison and Bryan; Matt and Linda; MJ and Daniel; Paul and Annie; and Paulie. I love you all very much.

My greatest debts will always be to my wife and children. To Joseph and Alex: you are the light of my life, my precious sons. And to my wife and best friend, Keri: you're the beauty in my world—I'll never be able to repay you for everything you've done for me, but I promise to spend the rest of my life trying.

THE CASH CEILING

1

GOVERNMENT BY THE PRIVILEGED

In 2014, something historically unprecedented almost happened in the state of Maine. Representative Mike Michaud—who had been a factory worker when he was first elected to public office—announced that he was retiring from the House of Representatives to run for governor. Soon after, a state senator named Troy Jackson launched a campaign to fill Michaud's House seat. Jackson seemed like a natural choice: like Michaud, he was a Democrat, he had served in the state legislature, and he was endorsed by many of the state's major progressive organizations. Jackson was even a blue-collar worker: when the state legislature wasn't in session, he worked full-time as a logger upstate.

And that's what would have made the election historic. If Jackson had won, he would have become the first blue-collar worker in American history to succeed another former blue-collar worker in the same congressional seat. From 1789 to the present day, seats in the House of Representatives have changed hands more than fourteen thousand times. Former lawyers have taken over for other former lawyers. Former business owners have succeeded other former business owners. But two former blue-collar workers have never served in the same U.S. House seat back-to-back.

Despite Troy Jackson's best efforts, however, that record still stood after the 2014 election. In early May of that year, a Wall Street–backed interest group began making aggressive independent expenditures against Jackson, and in June he lost the Democratic primary. When voters in Maine's second district went to the polls in November, their choices for the U.S.

House were a university administrator and a businessman. They didn't have the option to send someone from the working class to Congress.

And, chances are, neither did you.

Working-class Americans—people employed in manual labor, service industry, or clerical jobs[1]—almost never go on to hold political office in the United States. If millionaires formed their own political party, that party would make up about 3 percent of the general public, but it would have unified majority control of all three branches of the federal government. The Millionaires Party would be the majority party in the House of Representatives and would have a filibuster-proof supermajority in the Senate. It would have a majority on the Supreme Court. It would have a record-setting majority in the president's cabinet. And it would have a commander in chief in the White House—not just a millionaire but a full-fledged *billionaire*.

If, on the other hand, working-class Americans formed their own party, that party would have made up more than half of the country since at least the start of the twentieth century. But legislators from that party (those who last worked in blue-collar jobs before getting involved in politics) would never have held more than 2 percent of the seats in Congress.[2]

This economic gulf between politicians and the people they represent—what I call *government by the privileged* or *white-collar government*—has serious consequences for our democratic process. Like ordinary Americans, politicians from different classes tend to have different views, especially on economic issues. Former workers in office tend to be more pro-worker in how they think and act, former business owners tend to be more pro-business, and so on. These differences—coupled with the fact that working-class people almost never go on to hold public office—ultimately have dramatic consequences for public policy. Social safety net programs are stingier, business regulations are flimsier, tax policies are more regressive, and protections for workers are weaker than they would be if more lawmakers came from lower-income and working-class backgrounds.[3] Government *by* the rich is often government *for* the rich, and government for the rich is often bad for everyone else.

Why, then, do we have a white-collar government in the first place? Journalists and scholars have always had hunches about what keeps working-class Americans out of office—money, ambition, free time, qualifications, and so on—but to date there's been almost no actual research on why the United States is governed by the privileged or what reformers might do about it.

This book tries to change that.

BY THE RICH, FOR THE RICH

On January 19, 2012, there was an unusual demonstration in the Moroccan Parliament. Protestors had lined up outside with signs, as groups often did on the first day of the legislative session. But this time, the demonstration had also recruited allies *inside* the building. When the prime minister took the podium and began his inaugural address, a dozen sitting members of Parliament—including some from his own party—jumped to their feet and hoisted banners denouncing one of his government's first decisions.

Their complaint? Just before the session started, the prime minister had gutted the number of women in public office.[4]

In Morocco, one of the first responsibilities of a newly elected prime minister is to appoint roughly thirty people to fill cabinet-level positions in the national government. Morocco has long been a leader in women's representation in the Arab world,[5] and the previous government's cabinet had included seven women, a record for the country. When Prime Minister Abdelilah Benkirane took office in 2012, however, he announced that his cabinet would include just one female minister, Bassima Hakkaoui, who would head the Department of Women, Family, and Social Development. The news sent shock waves through the Moroccan political community. On the first day of the new legislative session, protestors both outside and inside Parliament hoisted signs reading, "Women 1, Men 30. Is that really fair?"

At bottom, concerns about the demographic backgrounds of politicians are rooted in a principle that is probably familiar to anyone who has participated in some form of group decision making, namely, that *having a seat at the table matters*. When people get together to make important choices—whether it's a government cabinet or a corporate board or a faculty hiring committee—who gets included can often powerfully affect the outcome. When a person or a social group is left out, their views and needs are often left out, too. Legislators in the Moroccan Parliament staged a protest because being included in important decision-making bodies is worth raising hell over sometimes, especially when it comes to politics.

Inclusion in political offices is so important that scholars have developed an entire subfield devoted to studying the numerical or *descriptive representation*[6] of social groups in governing institutions. Some of this research has focused on the *causes* of descriptive representation, that is, on the factors that influence how many people from a given social group go on to hold important positions in government. Other studies have focused on the *effects* of descriptive representation, in particular on how a social group's presence in a political institution influences the group's *substantive representation*, the extent to which the group's interests are advanced in that institution.[7]

In principle, descriptive and substantive representation don't have to go hand in hand. It's at least possible that a male-dominated cabinet might still protect the interests of women or that an all-white legislature might promote the well-being of racial and ethnic minorities. In practice, however, it often matters who has a seat at the table in government. Although politicians are usually constrained by external pressures (from constituents, party leaders, interest groups, donors, and so on),[8] they often have some leeway when they make decisions. Voters, party leaders, and interest groups often have conflicting demands that leave lawmakers without clear guidance. Constituents are chronically inattentive to what policymakers do; much of the actual work involved in lawmaking happens behind the scenes, where citizens have little oversight; and lawmakers are adept at crafting legislation so that blame is difficult to trace to specific politicians. Incumbent re-election rates are high, and most officeholders feel secure enough in their positions to risk angering constituents, party leaders, or interest groups, at least some of the time.[9] In those instances, their choices often reflect their own views and opinions, which in turn tend to reflect their own lives and experiences—including the social groups they come from.

Politicians from different racial groups, for instance, tend to make different choices on race-related issues, even after controlling for other things that might influence their decisions, like the parties they belong to or the views of their constituents. Likewise, even after accounting for other factors, male and female politicians tend to make different choices on women's issues (members of the Moroccan Parliament were right to protest!); veterans and nonveterans tend to make different choices on defense issues; and religious people, parents of schoolchildren, and smokers tend to make different choices on religious issues, educational issues, and smoking issues.[10] Who wins and who loses in politics depends on many factors—who votes, who lobbies, who funds campaigns, and so on. But it also depends to a large extent on *who governs*.

And one group that almost never governs is the working class. Figure 1.1 plots the most recent and detailed data available on the percentage of working-class people in the U.S. labor force (the first bar, which was computed using data from a 2013 Census Bureau survey) and in every level and branch of government for which people keep records on the occupational backgrounds of politicians.[11] Even after deindustrialization and the information revolution, people with *working-class jobs*—which I define as manual labor, service industry, and clerical jobs—still make up a majority of the labor force. But people who work primarily in these kinds of jobs make up less than 10 percent of the average city council and less than 3 percent of the average state legislature. The average member of Congress spent less than 2 percent of his or her adult life doing the kinds of jobs most Americans go to every day. None of America's governors were blue-collar workers when they got into politics (in Maine, Michaud lost in the 2014 general

Figure 1.1. The Shortage of Politicians from the Working Class

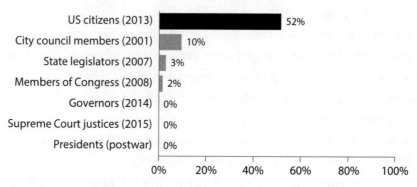

Source: U.S. Census Bureau 2013; International City/County Management Association 2001; National Conference of State Legislatures 2015; Schwarz 2014; Carnes 2011. The figure is based on data on the *primary* occupations of employed citizens, city council members, and state legislators; the *proportion* of prior occupations that were working-class jobs for members of Congress; and the *most recent* nonpolitical occupations of governors, Supreme Court justices, and presidents. For additional information, see note 11.

election), no one on the Supreme Court came from a working-class job, and at least since World War II no one from the working class has gotten into politics and gone on to become president. In most levels and branches of government in the United States, workers are as sharply underrepresented as women were in the "30 to 1" Moroccan cabinet.

This phenomenon is a remarkably durable feature of American politics. The left panel of Figure 1.2 plots the numerical representation of working-class people in Congress and state legislatures between 1961 and 2011. For comparison, the right panel plots data on the descriptive representation of *women*, another important and historically underrepresented group that makes up about 50 percent of the country. For at least the last half century, the representation of working-class people in Congress has been hovering around 2 percent; far from being a recent phenomenon, government by the privileged appears to be a rare historical constant in the United States. And it probably won't be going anywhere any time soon: as the dotted line in Figure 1.2 illustrates, the number of workers in state legislatures (which tend to foreshadow changes in federal offices) has actually fallen slightly— from 5 percent to 3 percent—over the last half century. These trends stand

FIGURE 1.2. Representation Is Improving for Some Groups, but Not the Working Class

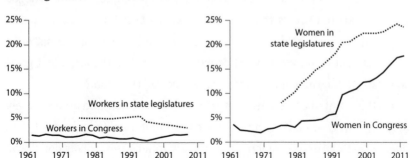

Source: ICPSR and McKibbin 1997; Carnes 2011; National Conference of State Legislatures 2015; Desilver 2015; Center for American Women and Politics 2012.

in sharp contrast to the fortunes of other historically underrepresented groups like women and racial or ethnic minorities, who have made steady progress in American political institutions over the last few decades, first at the state and local levels, then increasingly in federal offices. We've been governed by the economically privileged for generations, and that doesn't seem to be changing, even during a period of progress for other social groups that overlap substantially with the working class (compared to professionals, workers are more likely to be female and non-white).[12] To borrow a British expression, our government is getting less male and less pale, but it isn't getting less stale.

Of course, there have always been people who have argued that government by the privileged is inevitable (for instance, because voters prefer affluent candidates) or that government by the rich is necessary because the rich are better qualified. To date, however, there has never been any solid research to back these claims. (I'll return to these points in more detail in chapter 2.)

The other major argument offered in support of government by the privileged is that it doesn't matter what class of people governs. In *The Federalist #35*, Alexander Hamilton argued that workers in the United States would come to see business owners as "their natural patron[s] and friend[s]; and [workers] are aware, that however great the confidence they may justly feel in their own good sense, their interests can be more effectually promoted by the merchant than by themselves."[13] The idea has been with us ever since: every election cycle, candidates from privileged backgrounds tell voters that they want what's best for the country as a whole, that a rising tide lifts all boats, that the business of the nation is business, and so on. We all want economic prosperity, the argument goes, so what's the harm in letting affluent people call the shots?

On this point, there is actually a great deal of research, and unfortunately it's all squarely at odds with the rosy notion that a politician's social class doesn't matter. For one, Americans from different classes usually don't have harmonious views about the government's role in economic affairs. Pollsters have known for decades that public opinion is often sharply divided by class, especially on economic issues.[14] When it comes to things like the minimum wage, taxes, business regulations, unemployment, unions, the social safety net, and so on, working-class Americans tend to be more progressive or pro-worker, and more affluent Americans tend to want the government to play a smaller role in economic affairs.[15] There are exceptions, of course—blue-collar workers who vote Republican and rich professionals who care deeply about progressive economic policies—but on average, working-class Americans tend to be more liberal on economic issues and professionals tend to be more conservative. On economic policy, workers and merchants are seldom the natural friends that Hamilton hoped they would be.

The same seems to be true for people who go on to hold public office. Like ordinary citizens, politicians from different social classes tend to bring different economic perspectives with them to public office. Former House Speaker John Boehner was fond of saying that he was a small business owner at heart and that "it gave me a perspective on our country that I've carried with me throughout my time in public service." He doesn't seem to be the only one: on average, former businesspeople in government tend to think like businesspeople, former lawyers tend to think like lawyers, and (the few) former blue-collar workers tend to think like blue-collar workers. And they often behave accordingly.

These kinds of differences between politicians from different social classes have been evident in every data set I've examined since I started studying this phenomenon a decade ago. In Miller and Stokes's 1958 survey of U.S. House members, legislators from the working class were more likely to report holding progressive views on the economic issues of the day and more likely to vote that way on actual bills. The same kinds of social class gaps were evident in data on how members of Congress voted from the 1950s to the present. And in data on the kinds of bills they introduced from the 1970s to the present. And in public surveys of the views and opinions of candidates in recent elections.[16] The gaps are often considerable in magnitude: according to how the AFL-CIO and the Chamber of Commerce rank the voting records of members of Congress, for instance, legislators from the working class differ by 20 to 40 points (out of 100) from members who were business owners, even in statistical models with controls for partisanship, district characteristics, and other factors. (The same models find that the gap between workers and business owners is comparable to the gap between legislators who represent the most liberal and conservative districts and larger than the gap between male and female or white and black legislators.)[17] Social class divisions even span the two parties: among Democratic and Republican members of Congress alike, legislators from working-class jobs are more likely than their fellow partisans to take progressive or pro-worker positions on major economic issues.[18]

Other recent work on the descriptive representation of social classes has reached the same basic conclusions as my own research. Members of Congress who are wealthier have been found to be more likely to oppose the estate tax. Mayors from business backgrounds have been found to shift city resources away from social safety net programs and toward business-friendly infrastructure projects. Legislators with more education and income are less likely to support policies that would reduce economic inequality. Lawmakers with more money in the stock market are more likely to vote to raise the debt ceiling (and thereby protect the stock market).[19]

Social class divisions even show up in confidential studies of politicians' private views and beliefs. The top panel of Figure 1.3 plots data from a survey of state legislative candidates that I conducted with a team of researchers in August 2012. The survey (which was administered to each of the roughly 10,000 people running for state legislature that year and completed by close to 2,000 of them) asked a variety of questions about candidates' personal views, including several that asked whether the candidates agreed or disagreed with various statements about the government's role in economic affairs. (Readers interested in the technical details can find them in the appendix, under "Survey Details.") Figure 1.3 plots how eventual winners (that is, candidates who went on to win in November) responded to questions about four paramount economic issues: social welfare spending, government regulation of the private sector, economic inequality, and universal health care. (On all four, the graph plots the percentage of candidates who took the conservative side, whether that meant agreeing with a conservative statement or disagreeing with a liberal one.)

Viewed this way, it's easy to see that politicians from different classes truly bring different perspectives to public office: on all four issues, former workers in state legislatures were 20 to 50 percentage points more likely to take the progressive side compared to former business owners (a group that was easy to identify in surveys of both politicians and citizens—and that was generally representative of other white-collar professions).

Of course, politicians from business and working-class backgrounds differ in other ways, too; two-thirds of the workers in this sample were Democrats, for instance, compared to only one-third among the business owners. However, the gaps documented in Figure 1.3 were not simply a matter of partisanship: *within* both parties, workers were uniquely committed to policies that help the less fortunate. Republicans from the working class were 30 percentage points more likely than Republican business owners to support welfare programs, 35 percentage points more likely to support business regulations, 30 percentage points more likely to oppose economic inequality, and 65 percent more likely to support government health care. The gaps were smaller for Democrats on most items due to ceiling effects; on three of the questions, almost every Democrat in the sample took the liberal position. On the one question that generated some disagreement among Democrats, however—the item about business regulations—Democrats from the working class were 30 percentage points

FIGURE 1.3. Like Ordinary Citizens, Politicians from Different Classes Think Differently

State legislators

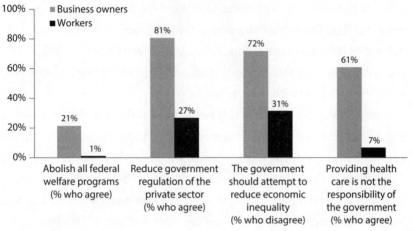

The general public

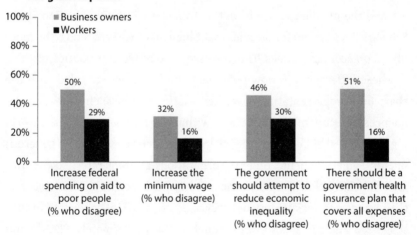

Source: Broockman et al. 2012; American National Election Studies 2014; Annenberg Public Policy Center 2004.

more likely to support business regulations than Democrats who were business owners.

The differences in Figure 1.3 were also large and significant in statistical models that controlled for a host of other characteristics of the legislator and the district, including the legislator's party, age, race, education, and gender; the state's level of legislative professionalization; and the legislative district's median income and partisanship (see Table A1.1 in the appendix). In fact, a legislator's occupation was among the best predictors of his or her views on most items, second only to party (and far better as a predictor than the district's income or the legislator's other personal characteristics like race or education). Relative to otherwise-similar politicians, elected officials from the working class really do tend to bring a more pro-worker perspective with them to public office.

Politicians aren't unique in this respect, of course. The bottom panel of Figure 1.3 plots data on how the general public answered similar questions in two 2004 surveys, the most recent I could find that asked about these issues and that also asked respondents what they did for a living (a question that many political surveys—even the American National Election Studies—stopped including on questionnaires and public data files in the early 2000s). The first and last items are from the National Election Studies, and the middle two are from the Annenberg National Election Study. Scholars have known for decades that blue-collar workers tend to be more liberal on economic issues. The same seems to be true for politicians.

These differences in how politicians think and act—coupled with the sharp underrepresentation of workers—ultimately have enormous consequences for economic policy. States with fewer legislators from the working class spend billions less on social welfare each year, offer less generous unemployment benefits, and tax corporations at lower rates. Towns with fewer working-class people on their city councils devote smaller shares of their budgets to social safety net programs; an analysis I conducted in 2013 suggested that cities nationwide would spend approximately $22.5 billion more on social assistance programs each year if their councils were made up of the same mix of classes as the people they represent. Congress has never been run by large numbers of working-class people, but if we extrapolate from the behavior of the few workers who manage to get in, it's probably safe to say that the federal government would pass far fewer pro-business policies and far more pro-worker policies if its members mirrored the social class makeup of the public.[20]

Having a seat at the table matters in U.S. politics. The shortage of politicians from the working class ultimately makes life harder for the majority of Americans from the working class (and for many economically vulnerable white-collar professionals, too).[21]

But no one really knows what's keeping the working class out of office.

BLINDED BY WEALTH

In 2010, researchers at a Delaware-based financial news firm called 24/7 Wall Street conducted a study to determine how much personal wealth each of the U.S. presidents had when they first took office. The researchers combed the historical record for data on the presidents' assets, property, and financial liabilities, adjusting their estimates along the way to account for inflation. In the end, their findings suggested that thirty-five of the forty-four individuals who had been president of the United States at that time—80 percent of commanders in chief—were millionaires by today's standards when they were sworn in.[22]

Since only a small percentage of Americans are millionaires, it would have been understandable if the authors of the study had speculated about why so many presidents were so wealthy, or contemplated how the presidents' privileged backgrounds influenced their choices in office, or even simply expressed surprise that our presidents have tended to be so much better-off than the average citizen.[23]

However, the staff of 24/7 Wall Street had a different take on their findings. In an article on Atlantic Monthly's business website, the authors of the study expressed amazement that so few presidents were millionaires: "One of the most important conclusions of this analysis," they wrote, "is that the presidency has little to do with wealth." In the face of crystal-clear evidence that politicians in the United States are vastly better-off than the people they represent, the authors concluded that there wasn't much reason to worry about government by the privileged.

Journalists and pundits—even those who write about the demographic makeup of American political institutions—often overlook the fact that we're governed by the privileged. Groups like *Roll Call* and *OpenSecrets* occasionally run one-off stories about the average wealth of members of Congress, and individual politicians sometimes come under fire for extreme displays of privilege, like when Senator John McCain couldn't remember how many houses he owned or when Senator John Edwards paid $400 for a haircut. But, in general, most media coverage of candidates and elected officials glosses over the fact that politicians are so much better-off than the people they represent. When the 113th Congress took office in January 2013, it was among the most diverse ever in terms of race, gender, sexual orientation, and religion—but also one of the least diverse in terms of occupational backgrounds and formal education, and it broke the record for the wealthiest Congress in American history.[24] The headline on CNN simply read, "Meet the 113th Congress: More Diverse than Ever."[25]

Some journalists express outright amazement that working-class Americans *ever* run for office: when a truck driver won the Democratic gubernatorial primary in Mississippi in 2015, the *New York Times* devoted an entire long-form story to his nomination, calling it a "bizarre" and "stun[ning]" development that "illustrates . . . the forlorn state of affairs for Democrats in the South."[26] In the news, white-collar government is usually taken for granted as the norm in American politics.

Unfortunately, that's how it's often treated in academic research, too. Scholars of U.S. politics have known for decades that politicians in every level and branch of government tend to outrank the people they represent by enormous margins on virtually any measure of class or social attainment. We've been urged to conduct follow-up studies on the causes and effects of white-collar government; the congressional scholar Donald Matthews was writing about the need for more research on this topic thirty years before I was born.[27] But until recently, scholars of U.S. politics—like journalists and other political observers—have tended to turn a blind eye to this important feature of the American political process.

That's beginning to change now that scholars have started to recognize the serious consequences that government by the economically privileged has for public policy in the United States (and now that more scholars have started to focus on the larger problem of political inequality). As it stands, however, we still don't know much about the *causes* of white-collar government. Why do rich people run the country? Why is it that working-class Americans almost never hold office in the United States? Why does our system of representation consistently yield such an unrepresentative group of policymakers?

To date, only a handful of studies have asked questions like these, and most have come up empty-handed. In the concluding chapter of my last book, I used public opinion data to see whether gaps in skills or qualifications could explain the shortage of workers in office. I didn't find any evidence to support that hunch. In a series of experiments embedded in public opinion surveys, Meredith Sadin tested the hypothesis that voters are biased against candidates from blue-collar jobs. She found that they weren't.[28] These kinds of studies are a start, but we're still a long way from real answers to the question of why working-class people almost never hold office in the United States.

And that represents a serious oversight in the academic literature on U.S. politics. White-collar government is a defining feature of American politics. It has major consequences for public policy and for the quality of representation in our country. We should understand where it comes from. Scholars have produced impressive research about most aspects of the democratic process in the United States, but if we can't explain why an entire class of people—the class that makes up most of the labor force—is all but excluded from every level and branch of the government, we're still missing something important.

Understanding why working-class Americans seldom govern in the United States can shed light on a host of important topics. It can help us better understand the causes of descriptive representation, that is, why some social groups hold office in large numbers and others don't. It can shed light on *candidate emergence*, the process by which people decide to run for political office.

It can also help us understand some of the most dramatic changes that are occurring in contemporary American politics. Campaign spending is soaring.

Unions and other organizations that encourage working-class political engagement are declining. These sea changes in the political landscape could have far-reaching consequences, and scholars and political observers are just beginning to understand their effects. One outcome that needs to be a part of the conversation is how these developments affect who holds office.

Understanding why so few workers govern may even help us understand what is arguably one of the most important and urgent issues in research on U.S. politics, namely, the oversized influence of the rich in American political life. In the last decade, scholars have started paying renewed attention to a wide range of economic or social class biases in the political process, thanks in large part to new evidence that politicians in the United States are vastly more responsive to the interests of affluent Americans than to the needs of the less fortunate.[29] To date, however, most of this new work on political inequality has focused on three topics. Some studies have analyzed *biases in routine forms of political participation* (e.g., how the less fortunate are less likely to follow the news and turn out to vote, or whether the public is concerned about rising economic inequality).[30] Others have focused on *inequalities in the organized pressure system* (e.g., how unions are declining, the wealthy are spending more on campaigns, and business-backed interest groups are becoming more numerous and sophisticated).[31] And a third body of research has examined *rules and strategic incentives that discourage political institutions from supporting the less fortunate* (e.g., how rules that encourage gridlock make it difficult for government to respond to rising economic inequality, or how parties have strategic incentives to direct resources to affluent constituents).[32]

Unfortunately, political inequality in the United States seems to take another important form. Whether the political process listens to one voice or another depends not just on who's doing the talking, how loud they are, or the rules of the game; it also depends on *who's doing the listening*. It's important to pay attention to inequalities in who pressures government from the outside—either through routine forms of political participation or through larger organized efforts—and to institutional rules that bias what the government does. But inequalities in who runs government can

bias public policy in favor of what the rich want, too. If we want to understand why affluent Americans wield more political influence than lower-
income and working-class citizens, we won't have the whole story until we
understand why so few lower-income and working-class citizens go on to
hold public office.

Perhaps most importantly, understanding what keeps workers out of
office may help reformers actually *fight* political inequality. Like scholars, most activists who care about the oversized political influence of the
wealthy have historically tended to focus either on routine forms of political participation like voting or on biases in the organized pressure system.
We've heard the same basic ideas for decades: if we could reform lobbying
and campaign finance and get a handle on the flow of money in politics,
the rich wouldn't have as much of a say in government. If we could promote broader political participation, enlighten the public, and revitalize
the labor movement, the poor would have more of a say. These proposals sound great in principle; they would almost certainly help reduce the
disproportionate political influence of the wealthy. In practice, however,
they've been remarkably difficult to actually carry out. For at least the last
half century, activists have been trying to regulate lobbyists, combat soaring campaign spending, revitalize the labor movement, energize the public, and rock the vote. But every major reform effort has eventually proven
more technically and politically challenging than its supporters had initially hoped. This isn't to say that activists should give up on these wor-
thy initiatives. But if reformers want to continue making headway on the
problem of political inequality, it may help to add some new arrows to the
quiver. As Jane Mansbridge (former president of the American Political Science Association) recently noted, "When unions and parties representing
the working class become less able to represent working-class interests,
descriptive representation becomes correspondingly more important."[33] In
light of how hard it's been to correct biases in who participates, organizes,
and donates, it may be time to try correcting the bias in who governs.

But before we can do that, we need to know what's keeping working-
class people out of office in the first place.

THE CASH CEILING

Since I started working on this book, many people have shared with me their personal theories about why so few working-class Americans hold office. One of the most common explanations I've heard is *money*; people will sometimes cut me off mid-sentence to complain about how expensive elections have become. I've heard other theories, too. It's all about the decline of unions. Working Americans don't have the time or resources to run. Voters prefer affluent candidates. Working-class people aren't smart enough to govern. It's all the Republicans' fault. It's all the Democrats' fault.

These kinds of explanations are a good starting point, but none of them tells the whole story. Some are simply incorrect. Workers were underrepresented in both parties long before campaign costs skyrocketed and unions declined (see Figure 1.2). Voters don't seem to be biased against workers, and workers don't seem to suffer from serious political qualification deficits. And some forces that people almost never talk about—like biases in the largely overlooked work of *candidate recruitment*—seem to matter a great deal. Simply put, the factors keeping workers out of office are often very different from what people imagine.

In this book, I analyze every source of systematic data that I know of that can shed light on why so few working-class people run for political office, including several original surveys of candidates, party officials, and ordinary citizens, which I've been conducting over the last few years with my co-investigators David Broockman, Melody Crowder-Meyer, and Chris Skovron. My analysis also draws heavily on decades of trailblazing research on the factors that keep women and racial or ethnic minorities out of public office in the United States (although my findings suggest that the factors that keep workers out of office differ in important ways from the obstacles facing other historically underrepresented groups).

My argument in this book is that workers are less likely to hold office not because they're unqualified or because voters prefer more affluent candidates, but because workers are simply less likely to run for public office in the first place. Part of the explanation is that—as people often suspect—workers are less likely to be able to shoulder the many practical burdens associated with running, to give up the time and resources that campaigning requires. But another important piece of the puzzle is a feature of the political process that people almost never talk about, namely, that workers are less likely to be recruited and encouraged by important political elites like party officials, politicians, and interest groups. Working-class Americans are less likely to hold office for some of the same basic reasons that they're less likely to participate in politics in other ways: because often they can't, and nobody asks them.[34]

These individual-level obstacles in turn share a common—and perhaps surprising—root cause: *electoral democracy*. In the United States, elections are always costly for everyone involved, and not just in monetary terms. Voters have to get informed and show up at the polls, volunteers have to knock on doors and make phone calls, candidates have to manage complex campaigns, and political and civic leaders have to recruit and support candidates. Those most directly involved—candidates and the people who support them—shoulder the greatest personal burdens. Even simple elections require huge amounts of time and energy and take significant physical, emotional, and personal tolls on those who are brave enough to throw their hat into the ring.

As a result, resources like time, energy, and money are essentially de facto prerequisites for running for public office in the United States. People can't launch campaigns—or even be seen by political and civic leaders as serious *potential* candidates—unless they can give up hundreds of hours of their time, focus most of their energy on campaigning, and accept significant uncertainty about their future. And that, in turn, powerfully disadvantages working-class Americans, who tend to have less money, less flexible schedules, fewer well-resourced friends, and less of an appetite for taking risks. Workers seldom run for public office in the United States because they can't and no one asks them—and those outcomes are in turn the natural consequences of elections themselves.

In short, this book argues that the American political process has a built-in *cash ceiling*, a series of structural barriers and corresponding individual-level attitudes and behaviors that keep qualified working-class citizens out of our political institutions. Elections (the root cause) are inherently burdensome and uncertain, especially for candidates and the people who support them (the structural or institutional obstacles; the macro-level forces). As a result, workers find it hard to run, and elites tend not to recruit workers (the attitudinal or behavioral responses; the individual-level forces). It should come as no surprise that workers have been all but absent from public office throughout our nation's history, even as politics and society have changed in significant ways, and even as social groups that overlap substantially with the working class like women and racial minorities have begun to hold office in larger numbers. Elections naturally discourage the less fortunate. The cash ceiling—the set of structural obstacles and behavioral responses that keep working-class Americans out of office—is part of the very DNA of American politics.

But DNA isn't destiny. Workers seldom have the time and energy to run for public office and political and civic leaders seldom encourage them, but these symptoms of America's cash ceiling can be treated. In the long run, many of the familiar pillars of the progressive reform agenda would probably help: if we could get the money out of politics, promote broader political participation, and revitalize labor unions, workers might hold office in larger numbers. However, understanding how the cash ceiling works also suggests several possibilities that could deliver results much faster, ideas like *political scholarships* targeting workers and *candidate recruitment and training programs* for qualified working-class Americans. These kinds of interventions aren't on many reformers' radars right now, but pilot efforts suggest that they have tremendous potential. The cash ceiling is probably here to stay—campaigns and elections will always be uniquely challenging for working-class Americans—but there are many promising new options on the horizon for reformers who want the working class to have a seat at the table in American government.

In the chapters that follow, I lay out the evidence for each part of this argument. In chapter 2, I begin by identifying the stage in the candidate entry process that screens working-class people out. Along the way, I also test two common ideas about the underrepresentation of workers, namely, that workers seldom hold office because they aren't fit to govern and because voters prefer affluent candidates. Chapter 2 shows that these ideas don't hold water: workers aren't underrepresented in public office because they're less qualified or because voters dislike them, they're underrepresented because they just don't run in the first place.

But why? Chapter 3 begins to answer this question by exploring the personal or micro-level factors that discourage qualified workers from running for public office. Using surveys of citizens, candidates, and political party leaders, I show that workers are less likely to run for public office because they don't have the free time or the economic security to do so and because they're seldom encouraged by political and civic leaders. These factors differ from what we often hear: for instance, it isn't just the high monetary costs of campaigns that discourage workers (those costs deter workers and professionals alike, actually), it's the high *personal* costs associated with campaigning—burdens like taking time off work and losing out on income during the race—that seem to make running for elected office impossible for many qualified workers.

Chapter 4 then asks where these patterns come from, that is, it explores the structural features of our political process that drive the individual-level differences documented in chapter 3. Elections themselves appear to be the root cause. Workers' personal anxieties about campaigning are understandable responses to the challenges inherent in modern campaigns; using aggregate-level data on who runs and wins in states and cities, I show how the burdens associated with large-scale elections make it all but impossible for working-class people to hold office. Elections take a toll on the political and civic leaders who recruit and support new candidates, too; using data on county-level party leaders, I show how the challenges associated with modern campaigns force many elites—Republicans and Democrats alike—to fall back on social shortcuts that lead them to pass over qualified workers. These findings illustrate the serious hurdles that workers are up against in the twenty-first century: campaigns are becoming more complex and time-consuming, unions and other worker-oriented organizations are declining, and that's making it even harder for workers to run for office and to be taken seriously by political and civic leaders.

So what can reformers do? Chapter 5 discusses the practical implications of these findings; it uses what we've learned about America's cash ceiling to sort through the various reform proposals that observers have floated throughout the years. Some are essentially pipe dreams: they would work, but they are completely infeasible (like quotas for working-class politicians or replacing democratic elections in the United States with government by lottery). Others are long shots, ideas that would probably help, but would take decades to execute and would require massive changes to American society (like revitalizing the labor movement, reducing economic inequality, or expanding access to higher education). And some seem sensible at first but don't actually square with what we know about America's cash ceiling or with data on what happens when they've been attempted (like raising politicians' salaries—workers seldom run because of the burdens associated with *campaigning*, not the salaries associated with holding office —or publicly financing elections—which helps professionals just as much as workers, and doesn't fundamentally change how time-consuming and burdensome it is to run for public office). The interventions that seem to have the most promise are reforms that *specifically target working-class people* and that *directly address the resource and recruitment gaps* that elections naturally create—reforms like political scholarships, seed money programs, and candidate training programs. If activists want to do something about America's cash ceiling, the best approach seems to be to recruit qualified workers, help them overcome practical hurdles, train them, support their campaigns, and send them on their way.

Programs like these seem to have more potential than many reformers realize, both as ways to address America's cash ceiling and also as rare opportunities to make forward progress on the larger problem of political inequality. Chapter 6 discusses the growing body of research on the oversized political influence of the upper class in American politics and the somewhat checkered recent history of conventional political equality reforms like campaign finance laws, lobbying regulations, and programs to increase voter turnout. Whereas these kinds of programs have encountered numerous practical and political roadblocks, pilot efforts to recruit and support working-class candidates have been remarkably successful. Activists who want to give the less fortunate more of a say in American politics have always had a curious blind spot when it comes to helping the less fortunate *hold office*. It may be time for that to change. If reformers want to continue moving the needle on the problem of political inequality, one of their best bets may be to start paying attention to America's cash ceiling.

Before going any further, however, a few brief observations about this book are in order. First, although this research draws a great deal of inspiration from the literature on the shortage of other historically underrepresented social groups, especially women, my argument about America's cash ceiling differs significantly from what scholars have found when they've asked why so few politicians are women, people of color, and so on. In sharp contrast to research on the gender gap in political ambition, for instance, there doesn't seem to be a social class gap in ambition; workers seldom run not because they don't want to, but because they lack the resources and because political and civic leaders are less likely to see them as viable candidates (see chapter 3). The structural forces behind these individual-level outcomes are different, too; the barriers that keep workers out of office are fundamentally different from the legal prohibitions and voter prejudices and socialization experiences that have kept women and racial or ethnic minorities out of our political institutions (see chapters 2 and 4). For qualified workers, there is another obstacle in the path to office, namely, the natural burdens associated with how democratic elections work. The contrast between the representation of workers and other underrepresented groups is itself quite telling: although most women and people of color have working-class jobs, the recent increase in officeholding among women and people of color has not been accompanied by an increase in working-class officeholding (see, for instance, Figure 1.2). That is, women and minorities are going on to hold office in larger numbers, but only if they come from white-collar backgrounds.[35] There is something unique about the working class that discourages officeholding, and the goal of this book is to understand what it is. This book draws on and attempts to engage with research on women and people of color, but of course class isn't gender and class isn't race. It should come as no surprise that our political process's cash ceiling has different contours than its glass ceiling.

What may be more surprising is that, second, this book's core argument doesn't have much of a place for ideology or partisanship. Parties and other civic *organizations* play an important role; political elites often have a hard time seeing qualified workers as viable candidates. But it is a role they play regardless of where they fall on the ideological spectrum: Republican and Democratic party leaders alike tend to have dim views about working-class candidates (see chapter 3). Although it might be tempting to imagine that Democratic voters or leaders would be more favorably inclined toward working-class candidates—because the Democratic Party has historically been the party of unions and workers—this book doesn't find any evidence to support that hunch. Qualified workers do, in fact, tend to more hold progressive views (see Figure 1.3) and more often identify as Democrats (see chapter 3), but the Democratic Party writ large is not a uniquely favorable environment for working-class candidates—Democratic voters (see chapter 2) and elites (see chapter 3) aren't any more likely than Republicans to support working-class candidates. The factors that keep workers out of office run deeper than partisanship and ideology; they are a part of the basic fabric of American democracy, the realities of campaigns and elections that affect every candidate, regardless of party or ideology.

Third, so far this chapter has discussed wealthy or affluent politicians and white-collar or professional politicians more or less interchangeably (and, likewise, sometimes alternated between talking about lower-income and working-class Americans). In the chapters that follow, my data and analysis will focus primarily on *occupation-based* measures of social class—what a person does for a living—not on measures based on income or wealth. (I typically focus on the main occupation a person has outside of politics, or in the case of full-time elected officials, the last occupation they had when they first ran for public office.) Occupation, income, and wealth are highly correlated, of course: white-collar professionals tend to be richer and tend to take home higher salaries. However, there are a few important reasons to focus on occupational data in this analysis. Income and wealth can sometimes be misleading. A cashier at Walmart and a PhD student at Princeton earn about the same annual salaries, but it probably wouldn't be right to say that they belong to the same social class. Likewise, wealth data can lead us astray, especially when people with significant financial resources put up their assets as collateral in order to take out new loans, which can make someone who lives a luxurious lifestyle appear on paper to have low or even negative net worth. Most scholars who study class recommend simply focusing on what people do for a living, which is a highly reliable way to gauge their place in the economy, their expected lifetime earnings, and how they tend to feel about a wide range of economic policies (see also note 1). Throughout this book, I focus not on low-income or low-wealth Americans, but specifically on working-class Americans, people employed in manual labor, service industry, or clerical jobs[36]—although obviously there is a great deal of overlap between these groups.

Fourth, this book's arguments are not limited to any one level or type of elected office in the United States. The nature of elections discourages working-class Americans from running, and that reality matters at the federal level, the state level, and the local level. Of course, elections for higher offices tend to be more burdensome and should therefore be *more* discouraging to workers—and this variation gives us opportunities to test this book's arguments (see chapter 4). But the basic features of America's cash ceiling are present in elections for every level and branch of government, even in races for offices like school board and city council.

As such, and fifth, in an effort to leave no stone unturned, the analysis in this book draws on every available source of relevant federal, state, and local data. Information about the occupational backgrounds of politicians and candidates and the qualifications and aspirations of ordinary citizens can be hard to come by, but each chapter of this book makes the most of what's out there, drawing on multiple data sets and sometimes moving quickly between them. Chapter 2, for instance, analyzes national surveys that measure the political qualifications of workers, then complements that analysis with data on the performance of cities governed by large numbers of workers (because city councils are the only political institutions in the United States where workers make up majorities). Chapter 2 goes on to study voter preferences at the national, state, and local levels (finding the same thing at all three), then shows that workers seldom run at the state and local levels (because these are the levels for which reliable data on candidates' social classes exist). The remaining chapters follow a similar approach: they use every available source of data on citizens, candidates, and civic leaders. Chapter 3's analysis of the role of practical resources and political ambition draws on national surveys of workers and data on state legislatures; its analysis of recruitment, however, focuses on both the local and state levels (finding the same thing in both). Chapter 4 uses data on federal, state, and local officials (finding the same basic patterns across all three). Chapter 5 focuses primarily on state-level data, since many of the reforms that have been attempted (like campaign finance regulations) have happened at the state level. To help readers keep track of the many data sets in this book, Table 6.1 reviews the book's main arguments, summarizes the data sets used most often in the book, and lists the figures that correspond to each argument and data set to provide a sort of bird's-eye view of the many analyses presented here. The "Survey Details" section of the appendix also provides detailed information about each of the original surveys conducted for this book.

Finally, my primary focus in this book will be on contemporary U.S. politics, that is, on the question of why so few working-class Americans hold office today. The historical antecedents of the modern cash ceiling are important, too, of course. But as a first cut at this question, this book will focus on the causes of government by the privileged in the present day.

The first step is understanding where, exactly, working-class Americans are screened out of the pipeline of new politicians.

Politicians in the United States are much better-off than the people they represent.
- *If millionaires formed their own party, the Millionaires Party would control all three branches of the federal government.*

Our white-collar government biases economic policy in favor of what the privileged want.
- *It matters who governs—so much, in fact, that Moroccan politicians protested attacks on women's representation.*

Scholars and journalists almost never ask why we're governed by the privileged, though.
- *One study found that 80 percent of U.S. presidents were millionaires and concluded that they weren't that rich.*

This book uses data to shed light on the *cash ceiling*, the individual attitudes and behaviors that keep working-class Americans from holding office and the larger structural forces behind them.
- *People have lots of pet theories, but many of them are wrong or incomplete. If we want to understand this phenomenon, we need to look at real data.*

My findings suggest that so few workers hold office simply because so few run. Elections are by their very nature extremely personally burdensome for candidates and those around them. Qualified workers often can't afford to launch campaigns and aren't seen by political and civic leaders as serious potential candidates.
- *Why do so few workers hold office? Because many qualified workers can't run, and because nobody asks them.*

The bottom line: Politicians in the United States have always been vastly better-off than the people they represent, and that has serious consequences for public policy. This book asks why we're governed by the privileged. It outlines the factors that keep working-class Americans out of our political institutions—what I call the *cash ceiling*—and describes the reforms that could help get more workers into office.

2

THE CONVENTIONAL WISDOM (IS WRONG)

John Parker wasn't new to politics when he ran for governor of North Carolina in 1920. Parker had earned a BA from the University of North Carolina in 1907 and a law degree in 1908, and had then spent his twenties and thirties building a successful legal practice in Monroe and Wilmington. Along the way, he had quickly become one of the state's most prominent Republicans. In 1910, Parker was nominated by the GOP to run for Congress, and in 1916 he was nominated for attorney general. When the Republican Party chose Parker to run for governor in 1920, it was hardly his first rodeo.

So when John Parker trashed African Americans on the campaign trail, he probably knew exactly what he was doing.

In April 1920—shortly after receiving his party's nomination—Parker gave a formal acceptance speech in Greensboro. In his remarks (which his campaign also distributed widely in hard copy), he digressed at length to warn listeners about an "evil and danger" that was poised to take the country by storm: African Americans were starting to vote and hold public office in significant numbers. "The Negro," Parker warned, "does not desire to enter politics. The Republican Party of North Carolina does not desire him to do so. We recognize the fact that he has not yet reached the stage in his development when he can share the burdens and responsibilities of government." In Parker's view, African Americans weren't capable of participating in politics, they knew it, and people who followed politics knew it, too. "The participation of the Negro in politics," he concluded, "is not desired by the wise men in either race or by the Republican party of North Carolina."[1]

Today, most Americans would regard Parker's remarks as shocking, offensive, immoral, and just plain factually wrong. But less than a century ago—around the time my grandmother was born—ideas like these were part of mainstream political thought in the United States. Of course, not everyone thought that African Americans were unfit to vote or hold office. But the idea was so widespread that many politicians didn't think twice about invoking it on the campaign trail.

In Parker's case, for instance, his Greensboro acceptance speech didn't draw any significant criticism during his campaign for governor, and he came close to winning the race (earning 43 percent of the popular vote, more than the Republican nominee who came before him in 1916 and the one who came after him in 1926). And although Parker lost his bid for governor in 1920, his political career continued its steady ascent: in 1923, he was appointed special assistant to the attorney general of the United States, and the next year he was elected Republican National Committeeman from North Carolina. Parker later served as a judge for the U.S. Court of Appeals, a delegate to the Republican National Convention, a representative on the Nuremberg Courts that tried the Nazis, a member of the United Nations International Law Commission, and a trustee of the University of North Carolina. The NAACP publicized his remarks about African Americans as part of their successful campaign to oppose his nomination to the Supreme Court in 1930,[2] but overall Parker did remarkably well for himself. When he passed away in 1958, Parker was the most senior appellate judge in the United States, and to this day, the highest award given by the North Carolina Bar Association is the John J. Parker Memorial Award. Just a few generations ago, an aspiring leader could brazenly slander African Americans for being unfit to "share the burdens and responsibilities of government" and go on to have a dazzlingly successful career in U.S. politics.

When people want to justify excluding a social group from some part of the political process, they often use the same line of reasoning that John Parker used in 1920. Whether it's African Americans or women or young people, opponents of inclusion tell the same basic story. They argue that the underrepresented group doesn't participate in politics because its members aren't qualified. They claim that if the group ever got involved in government affairs, terrible things would happen. They note that, thankfully, the group in question knows that it isn't really up to the task, and the relevant gatekeepers know it, too. They conclude that that's why the underrepresented group stays out of politics, and that we should all be happy about it. The story is always the same: *African Americans/Women/Whatever group I dislike aren't qualified to vote/hold office/speak their minds*, and they know it, and *party leaders/voters/politicians* know it—and that's good because if they ever got into politics, they'd ruin everything.

The working class is no exception. Historically, the John Parker line of reasoning has probably been the single most common argument people have offered to justify the fact that working-class Americans almost never go on to hold public office. When Anti-Federalists criticized the Constitution on the grounds that it would lead to a white-collar government,[3] Alexander Hamilton argued in *The Federalist #35* that working-class people "will commonly be disposed to bestow their votes upon merchants and those whom they recommend. We must therefore consider merchants as the natural representatives of all these classes of the community."[4] The idea has been part of American political thought ever since. Today, Pulitzer Prize–winning journalists assert that "voters repeatedly reject insurrectionist candidates who parallel their own ordinariness . . . in favor of candidates of proven character and competence." Wealthy campaign donors say that "the baby sitters, the nail ladies . . . they don't understand what's going on, . . . they don't understand how the systems work." Internet message boards warn against letting "career burger flippers, janitors, [and] production-line workers" have too much political power and note that, "gratefully, most voters (even the ones flipping the burgers) are smart enough to vote for people with better qualifications than their own." Political campaigns claim that "voters [want leaders] with real-world private sector experience[, not] a candidate who has no investments." Presidential aspirants argue that their opponents can't hold "office without the basic qualification [of running] a business."[5] Since the Founding, there have always been people who have said that workers don't govern because they don't have what it takes, they know it, and voters and political leaders know it, too. There have always been people who have warned that if workers ever held office in large numbers, they would ruin the country.

These ideas have even occasionally been embraced by academic researchers, often in subtle ways. Scholars of *elite theory*, for instance, have argued for decades that "all social order is necessarily hierarchical, and [that political] leadership is a specialization necessitated by the division of labor in all societies."[6] Others have invoked Parker-style arguments about the working class in studies where the researchers needed to measure the quality of a leader but only had data on the leader's income or education level. Statements like "we use education as a proxy for the skill level of candidates" and "[we assume] that 'political' and 'market' skills are correlated" have appeared in research on topics ranging from political selection and gender quotas to legislative compensation, leader survival, and voter turnout.[7]

Even academics who don't actively study topics like these sometimes confess that they think working-class people are unfit to govern. At a conference in 2012, one of my fellow panelists asked the audience point-blank, "We don't really want some Joe six-pack coming out of his garage and running for state legislature, do we?" In 2013, the editor of a major academic news site rescinded a blog post I had coauthored because, he argued, "the very nature of being a politician creates a professional bias" due to "the legal/technical bias of legislating" and because "some of the worst legislators in the US today—i.e., the Tea Party—come from more working class backgrounds." (For what it's worth, people who identified with the Tea Party actually tend to be disproportionately rich and well educated.)[8] In 2016, an anonymous journal reviewer argued, "I don't understand why the lack of blue collar workers in [C]ongress is a problem. . . . Office-holding and campaigning require skills, and we have every reason to think that not all people are equally adept at those skills."[9]

Why do so few workers hold office? We often hear—even from experts— that it's because, to borrow John Parker's expression, workers are unfit to share the burdens and responsibilities of government, and everybody knows it.

This line of reasoning is probably the closest thing there is to a conventional wisdom about the factors keeping working-class Americans out of office. And it could be true—it could be that workers seldom hold office because there aren't many qualified workers out there, and thankfully voters know better than to cast their ballots for blue-collar Americans.

Then again, John Parker–style arguments have never fared well historically: there has never been an instance in our nation's history when significantly increasing the political participation of an underrepresented group has made the United States worse off. When our country extended voting rights to landless whites, and African Americans, and women, and eighteen-year-olds, critics always claimed that the new group wasn't ready for politics and that including them would have dire consequences, but history never bore out those dire predictions.[10] Likewise for the recent increases in the number of women and people of color who hold political office; opponents have always warned that underrepresented groups make dangerously bad politicians, and they've never been right so far.

Moreover, the political observers who have questioned whether workers can govern have never actually offered any direct evidence to support the conventional wisdom. *There has never been a single published study showing that workers are underrepresented in public office because they're less qualified or less likely to win elections.* Scholars sometimes point to research on how lower-income and working-class people are less likely on average to pay attention to politics or participate in elections and public affairs, but there's never been a published study linking those engagement gaps to gaps in political officeholding, nor has there even been a published study that has found that voters dislike working-class candidates.[11]

There is another potential explanation, moreover, that the conventional wisdom ignores, another step in the candidate entry process that could help explain why workers (or any social group) are underrepresented in public office. It could be that workers seldom go into government because they aren't qualified or because they lose elections, but it could also be that qualified workers simply *choose* not to run in the first place.

I have two aims in this chapter. My first goal is do what the proponents of the conventional wisdom about workers never do, namely, test their ideas using actual data on U.S. politics. Supporters of white-collar government have raised significant concerns, and they deserve to be taken seriously. If working-class Americans really are unqualified or unappealing to voters, then the enduring numerical underrepresentation of workers might be an important and useful feature of our democratic process. John Parker–style arguments have always been wrong when they've been applied to other social groups, but if this time is different—if workers really would ruin the country if they started holding office in large numbers—we should know.

My other aim in this chapter is to begin answering this book's larger research question: *Why are working-class people virtually absent from American political institutions?* To test the Parker-style conventional wisdom, we essentially have to identify the point in the candidate entry process at which working-class people are screened out—is it that they aren't qualified, they don't run, or they don't win? That's also a logical first step in the process of understanding why workers are underrepresented in public office in general. To understand why a social group seldom holds office, scholars often first try to determine where exactly they're being filtered out (and then determine what exactly is filtering them out at that stage). Testing Parker-style arguments about the working class is important in its own right, but it's also a useful way to begin the investigation at the heart of this book. If we want to understand America's cash ceiling, the first thing we need to do is locate it.

WHERE DO POLITICIANS COME FROM?

It may seem like a serious oversimplification, but it's important to keep in mind throughout this book that *running for political office is really, really hard.* Elections take time, energy, and resources. Even at the state and local levels, candidates begin working part- or full-time on their campaigns months and years in advance, often while continuing to work at their day jobs.

They spend evenings and weekends forming exploratory committees and campaign committees, building contact lists, asking people to donate time and money, meeting with community leaders and party officials, talking to journalists, buying advertisements, attending public debates, planting yard signs, and meeting face to face with voters. They lose sleep, they chug coffee, they miss their kids, they fight with their significant others. They do it because it's important to them, and some of them love the ride, but elections by their very nature demand that even the most eager candidates make enormous personal sacrifices when they throw their hat into the ring.

In light of the many hurdles involved in what scholars call the *candidate entry process*, it probably shouldn't come as much of a surprise that the numerical or descriptive representation of social groups is often sharply unequal. Any industry that has significant barriers to entry will tend to favor people who have social and economic advantages in other aspects of life. Running for office is no different: it's hard to break into politics, and as a result, the people who do it have historically tended to be the people who have the most power: men, whites, the rich, and so on.

But what *specifically* keeps any given social group out of office? One useful way to think about the causes of descriptive representation (and underrepresentation) in public office is what I call the *Qualified-Run-Succeed Model*, or just the *QRS Model*. I'm by no means the first person to propose this way of thinking about descriptive representation—Lawless and Fox outline the same basic logic in their work on the shortage of women in office, for instance[12]—but it sometimes gets lost in discussions about descriptive representation, which often focus on other frameworks for thinking about the shortage of people in public office (like the *supply and demand model*, which I'll discuss in a moment). The QRS Model has been a powerful way for scholars to think about the shortage of other historically underrepresented groups in public office, and it's worth reiterating here.

When scholars make a serious effort to understand why a social group is numerically underrepresented in political institutions, they usually don't begin by presuming that the group is incompetent or unworthy. Instead, the best researchers start by trying to identify the stage in the candidate entry process at which the group is screened out.[13] The idea is simply that the descriptive representation of any social group—that is, the number of lawmakers who are from that group—can be thought of as the result of a winnowing process, a series of steps that each screen out more and more people from the group in question. First, some people from the group won't be *Qualified* to hold office, either because they aren't legally eligible or because they don't have the skills necessary for public service. Of those who are qualified, most won't *Run*. And of those who run, many won't *Succeed*, that is, they won't win their elections. If a social group is disproportionately screened out at any stage—if people from that group are less likely than others to be qualified or to run or to win—the group will be underrepresented in public office relative to its numbers in the population as a whole. According to the QRS Model, if we want to understand why a social group is numerically underrepresented, the first step is to understand where exactly they're being screened out (and then we can ask why).

Women and racial or ethnic minorities—the groups that have been the focus of most research on descriptive representation to date—appear to face hurdles at all three stages. Both groups experience modest inequalities in the Qualifications that promote success in politics. (Scholars sometimes refer to differences in qualifications as *supply-side explanations*, explanations that "suggest that the outcome reflects [some quality of the] applicants wishing to pursue a political career.")[14] And both groups face even more challenges at the Running and Succeeding stages: unsupportive party and interest group leaders, biased voters, and institutional arrangements that disadvantage women and minorities.[15] (Scholars often refer to these as *demand-side explanations*, explanations that attribute the shortage of a social group to external forces that discourage qualified members of the group from running for office or from winning when they run.) Every step of the way, women and people of color face significant barriers to descriptive representation; scholars have identified not one but *many* glass ceilings.

It's not out of the question, then, that workers seldom hold office either because there aren't many qualified workers out there or because the workers who run get shot down by voters. In theory at least, both prongs of the Parker-style conventional wisdom are consistent with the widely accepted model that scholars use to think about the shortage of social groups in public office.

There is some indirect evidence on these points, too. In the general public, white-collar professionals tend to perform better on measures of cognitive ability,[16] for instance. If professionals are smarter than workers, it might stand to reason that they're more qualified to hold public office, which might explain why so few workers get into politics. Likewise, there are signs that we should take the voter bias version of the conventional wisdom seriously, too: research on social psychology has consistently found that people tend to exhibit prejudices against lower-income and working-class Americans.[17] If they bring biases like those into the voting booth, it might be true that workers seldom hold office because voters simply prefer more affluent candidates.

Then again, the QRS Model also highlights a third possibility. When a social group is underrepresented, it doesn't have to be because the group is less qualified or less likely to win elections. It could also be that the qualified members of that group are just less likely to run for public office.

It's not hard to imagine numerous reasons why a qualified blue-collar worker might be less likely to run for public office than an equally qualified white-collar professional. The worker might not have enough free time. She might not be able to go without income during a campaign. She might not want to be a politician; she might not see politics as a way to make the world a better place. She might worry (rightly or wrongly) that she doesn't stand a chance of winning. She might not receive as much support from the political establishment.

Workers might be underrepresented because they aren't good enough and voters know it. Or it might be that the potential working-class candidates who are out there are just less likely to throw their hat into the ring. Running for political office in a democracy like ours is really, really hard, after all.

So which is it?

ARE WORKERS UNFIT TO GOVERN?

On a cold Tuesday in December 2008, the owners of a window factory in Chicago called Republic Windows and Doors informed their employees —240 machine operators and line workers—that the company would be closing for good at the end of the week. In just three days, they announced, every worker in the plant would be out of a job.

The news came as a shock, especially with the holidays just a few weeks away, and the workers' union scrambled to organize a meeting with management in the hopes of getting employees severance pay or at least compensation for any vacation time workers had accrued. But the plant's owners wouldn't return the union's calls.

So at the end of the day on Friday, December 5, the workers staged a rare form of political protest: they simply refused to go home. They stayed at their posts, demanding that management hear them out. The employees of Republic Windows and Doors had just started the first major *factory occupation* in the United States in decades.

The protest was an instant sensation. Within a day or so, supporters were marching day and night outside the factory. When the organizers put on a candlelight prayer vigil, a crowd of hundreds showed up. Local news stations planted journalists outside the factory, and national media outlets started covering the demonstration. Sympathetic politicians began discussing legal action against the factory's owners (who had violated federal regulations that require companies to give workers several weeks of notice before shuttering a plant). President Obama even voiced his support for the protest.

On December 10, management caved: the owners of the factory offered each of their 240 workers a severance package of about $7,000 and two months of health insurance. The employees unanimously accepted.

But they were hardly out of the woods. A few months later, the plant was bought by a California-based energy company, and most of the workers who had occupied the factory in December went back to work. In March 2012, however, the new owners announced that they would be shuttering the factory, again with little notice. The workers staged another protest, and within hours management offered a reasonable severance package: they would keep the plant open for 90 days to give their employees time to find new jobs.

But when the 90-day extension was up, something unexpected happened. The workers didn't find new jobs. They didn't occupy the plant, either. They didn't protest, or ask politicians for help, or file for unemployment. Instead, the workers purchased the window factory from their employers and started running it themselves.

During their 90-day grace period, the factory's 200-some employees organized a grassroots fundraising effort that generated $520,000 in cash, enough to buy most of the equipment in the plant, and they took out business loans to purchase the rights to the company. The week the plant was scheduled to close, its employees put in a $1.2 million bid to buy the company they had worked for. The owners accepted, and the workers hauled their factory to another location, piece by piece. Their company, New Era Windows, opened a few months later, and it's been in business ever since.

The only things the workers didn't bring with them were their bosses. All of the management-level positions in New Era Windows were staffed from within the pool of manual laborers who had worked in the factory when it was bought out. As the company's website explains, "Everyone decided enough was enough. If we want to keep quality manufacturing jobs in our communities, perhaps we should put in charge those who have the most at stake in keeping those jobs—the workers."[18]

One of the two prongs of the conventional wisdom about the shortage of working-class people in our political institutions is that workers seldom hold office because they just aren't qualified for the job. They can vote, they can volunteer for campaigns, they can organize, they can protest. But actually running things—actually governing—is a task better left to the professionals.

Is that really true? Is there hard evidence that workers aren't qualified for public office? Or could it be that many working-class Americans are just as capable of making the leap into campaigning and governing as the factory workers who made the leap into financing and managing New Era Windows?

The first challenge in answering these questions—and one of the first red flags that should make us skeptical about John Parker–style arguments about how workers aren't qualified to govern—is that there's no actual definition of what it means to be qualified to hold political office in the United States. We have clear guidelines about who is *legally eligible*. (The Constitution dictates, for instance, that only natural-born citizens over age thirty-five who have lived in the United States for fourteen years can be president.) But we don't have universally accepted lists of the traits or skills that make someone a *good* politician.

People have always had lots of ideas, of course. The Founding Fathers, for instance, thought that being qualified meant being wise and committed to the public good. But when we try to operationalize those ideas—pin down what they mean and how we can measure them—the task quickly becomes an impossible philosophical-scientific quagmire. How do we prioritize different traits? Which qualities are absolutely essential requirements for holding office, and which are just gravy? Is there a threshold that separates people who are fit and unfit, or do we just want people with more of the qualities we care about? And how do we measure the traits we identify—how do we quantify *qualified*?

Questions like these are impossible to answer in a truly definitive way. American political thought will probably never converge on a precise, measurable, universally accepted list of the traits and characteristics that make someone fit to govern. And that's fine in and of itself: everyone is entitled to their own answers to complex moral questions and their own judgments about whether specific individuals are fit to govern.

The lack of a consensus definition causes problems, however, when researchers need to answer empirical questions about our system of government. Without a precisely articulated, measurable definition of *qualified*, it's hard to know, for instance, whether implementing a new reform would lead to a more qualified candidate pool on election day, or whether high-quality candidates avoid running for office in certain kinds of races, or whether a social group that seldom holds office is underrepresented because its members are unqualified.

Some political scientists have worked around this problem by developing *proxy measures*, indirect measures of whether a person is qualified for office. Some have used *past political experience* as a proxy for quality, on the assumption that people who have held office in the past are probably better at campaigning and governing than people who haven't, at least on average. Other studies have assumed that people who work in the *pipeline professions* that supply most politicians—like law and business—tend to be more qualified. Some scholars have also recently started using *education* as a proxy for leader quality.

Unfortunately, none of these approaches will work for the questions at issue in this book. Using past political experience as a proxy for quality would make good sense if our goal were to measure whether, for instance, more qualified candidates tend to win more votes. But if our goal is to determine whether a social group that rarely holds office is less qualified, using past experience in office as a proxy for candidate quality is essentially a tautology. We'd be asking, "Are workers less likely to hold office because they seldom hold office?" Likewise for profession- and education-based quality proxies; if we defined being fit for public office as being an attorney or a business owner or having an advanced degree, we would just be *assuming* that workers are less qualified, not testing that hunch. (The education proxy is also problematic in itself: more educated leaders don't actually appear to better at campaigning or governing. To the contrary, cross-national data suggest that college-educated leaders don't tend to govern over more prosperous nations, don't pass more bills, don't tend to do better at the polls, and are no less likely to be corrupt.)[19] If we want to know whether working-class citizens are less qualified for public office, we need a different approach, one that doesn't measure a person's qualifications based on occupation, education, or prior experience in campaigns and government.[20]

One alternative is to try to systematically measure the traits or characteristics that citizens value in politicians, then measure whether working-class Americans are less likely to have those traits. Rather than trying to reason our way to a definition of what it means to be fit for office in some absolute or philosophical sense, why not just ask the people who choose our leaders how they define a good politician, then see how the working class stacks up? This approach isn't bulletproof, of course; we can always quibble with the traits that other people say they value, and those traits might change from time to time or place to place. But if there isn't much hope that political thinkers will ever agree on a universal definition of what it means to be qualified—and if we can't use the standard experience, education, or occupation proxy measures—a new *what-the-people-say-they-want* proxy may be the best alternative.

That proxy won't be exactly the same as the list of traits that *win elections*. Political scientists already know a great deal about the characteristics that predict whether a candidate will win or lose—party, incumbency, favorability, name recognition, and so on.[21] But those characteristics aren't necessarily the same as the list of traits that people truly value in a politician. In elections, voters can only choose between the options on the ballot. Those options may be over-qualified (maybe only highly qualified people run, so that if we compared winners and losers, we would overlook some baseline characteristics that all qualified candidates have). Or they may be under-qualified (maybe voters never really get to vote for people they consider truly qualified and instead just pick the lesser of two evils, in which case election results wouldn't really tell us anything about the qualities voters actually want). Knowing what traits predict a higher vote margin isn't the same as knowing what people really value in a politician. If we want to know that, we need a more direct approach.

Most research on voting and public opinion understandably focuses on how people evaluate the candidates on their ballots, not what they want from a politician in the abstract. So in 2013 and 2014, I worked with three other political scientists—David Broockman, Chris Skovron, and Melody

Crowder-Meyer—to field original surveys that asked broader questions about what people look for in a politician. The surveys focused on two groups that are extremely important in the candidate selection process: voters and political party leaders. In the fall of 2013, we sent online and paper surveys to all of the 6,000 or so chairs of every county-level branch of the Republican and Democratic parties nationwide. About one in five sent back completed surveys, and thankfully there were no apparent biases in response rates: Republicans and Democrats completed the survey at almost identical rates (18 and 17.9 percent, respectively), as did men and women (18.2 and 18.5 percent, and 16.5 percent among respondents with unknown genders), leaders in different regions, and leaders in counties where Obama's margin was large, small, or negative. (Readers interested in the technical details can find them in the appendix, under "Survey Details.") After completing the party leader survey, in January 2014 we worked with a survey firm to run a follow-up study that asked similar questions to a nationally representative sample of about 1,200 citizens.

Both surveys included a wide range of questions, including items that asked what qualities party leaders and voters would want in an ideal politician. The most important was a question that simply asked respondents to describe the ideal candidate in an open-ended fashion, without specifying a level of office or branch of government. (Later on, the surveys also asked respondents to rate different attributes on simple scales and to evaluate hypothetical candidates with different characteristics—these follow-up measures produced the same basic results.)[22] Our open-ended questions differed a little depending on the audience: in the party leader survey, the question asked, "In a perfect world, what personal qualities would all of your party's political candidates have? Please list as many as you would like." In the public opinion survey, the question was, "In an ideal world, what personal qualities would all political candidates have? Please list as many as you would like." The question only appeared on the paper version of the party leader survey (due to a programming error), but of the county-level party leaders who took the survey on paper, 234 (or 84 percent) listed at least one characteristic. Of the 1,240 people who completed the public opinion follow-up survey, 1,157 (93 percent) had something to say about their ideal candidate. With the help of research assistants, we then grouped these responses into categories, adding more new categories as we read through the list of responses. By our count, party leaders and voters listed 37 different kinds of traits that they look for in an ideal candidate.

And—perhaps somewhat remarkably—the traits they listed most often were almost exactly the same. Figure 2.1 plots the percentages of party leaders (left panel) and ordinary citizens (right panel) in each survey who listed each of the 37 characteristics we identified. Strikingly, five of the top six traits mentioned in both surveys were exactly the same qualities. According to both party leaders and the general public, an ideal politician is honest, intelligent, confident, hardworking, and personable. Ordinary citizens also prioritized being understanding (it was their second most common answer), and party leaders also prioritized speaking skills (it was the fifth most common answer they gave) and ideology (added together, the categories *liberal, conservative,* and *loyal to the party* were among their most common responses). But in general the two groups clearly shared a core concept of what it means to be qualified for political office. Both party leaders and voters felt that an ideal politician had the kinds of characteristics that predict success in most kinds of leadership roles: honesty, intelligence, friendliness, work ethic, and confidence.

These qualities seemed to be the most important to voters and party leaders even when they were asked to consider other characteristics. Figure 2.2 plots how party leaders (top panel) and ordinary citizens (bottom panel) responded to a question later in the survey that asked (again without specifying a level or branch of government), "In your opinion, how important is it that a nominee for elected office from your party have the following qualifications? (check one per row: Not important, Somewhat important, Very important)." The question then listed a variety of personal characteristics, professional traits, and life circumstances, including three of the most common traits people had mentioned earlier in the open-ended question: assertiveness, work ethic, and being personable.

FIGURE 2.1. In an Ideal World, What Would Politicians Be Like?

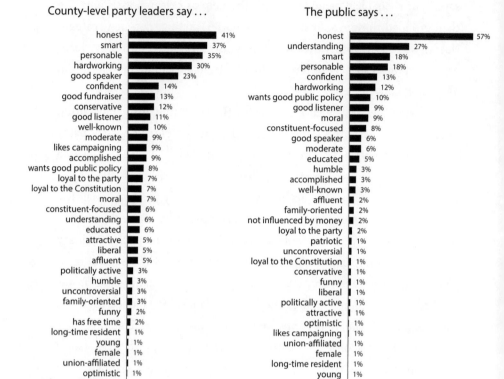

County-level party leaders say . . .

honest	41%
smart	37%
personable	35%
hardworking	30%
good speaker	23%
confident	14%
good fundraiser	13%
conservative	12%
good listener	11%
well-known	10%
moderate	9%
likes campaigning	9%
accomplished	9%
wants good public policy	8%
loyal to the party	7%
loyal to the Constitution	7%
moral	7%
constituent-focused	6%
understanding	6%
educated	6%
attractive	5%
liberal	5%
affluent	5%
politically active	3%
humble	3%
uncontroversial	3%
family-oriented	3%
funny	2%
has free time	2%
long-time resident	1%
young	1%
female	1%
union-affiliated	1%
optimistic	1%
not influenced by money	1%
patriotic	1%

The public says . . .

honest	57%
understanding	27%
smart	18%
personable	18%
confident	13%
hardworking	12%
wants good public policy	10%
good listener	9%
moral	9%
constituent-focused	8%
good speaker	6%
moderate	6%
educated	5%
humble	3%
accomplished	3%
well-known	3%
affluent	2%
family-oriented	2%
not influenced by money	2%
loyal to the party	2%
patriotic	1%
uncontroversial	1%
loyal to the Constitution	1%
conservative	1%
funny	1%
liberal	1%
politically active	1%
attractive	1%
optimistic	1%
likes campaigning	1%
union-affiliated	1%
female	1%
long-time resident	1%
young	1%
good fundraiser	0%
has free time	0%

Source: Broockman et al. 2013, 2014a.

Note: Bars report the percentages of respondents in surveys of county-level party leaders (left panel) and the general public (right panel) who mentioned the qualities listed here when asked an open-ended question about what the ideal candidate would be like. Percentages are rounded to the percentage point; items with a reported value of 0 percent were mentioned by a small number of respondents.

As Figure 2.2 illustrates, these three traits once again emerged as the most important, even when we showed party leaders and citizens other candidate characteristics that might have slipped their minds during the open-ended question. Being assertive was among the most important to both party leaders and citizens, and being hardworking and personable were by far the most important characteristics to both groups. Somewhat remarkably, responses differed little by party: the shares of Republicans

Figure 2.2. Which Qualifications Are Most Important?

In your opinion, how important is it that a nominee for elected office from your party have the following qualifications? (% of **party leaders** who said "Very important")

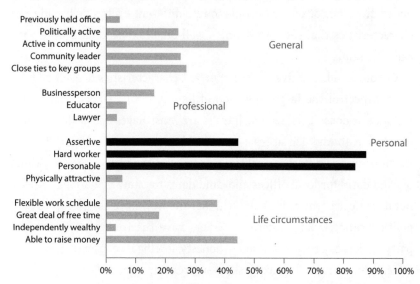

In your opinion, how important is it that a nominee for elected office from your party have the following qualifications? (% of **citizens** who said "Very important")

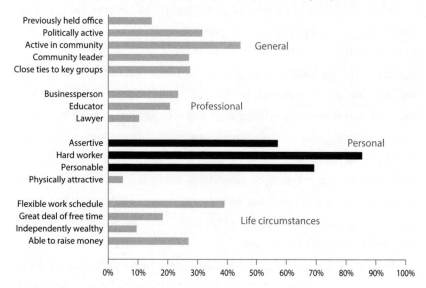

Source: Broockman et al. 2013, 2014a.

and Democrats who reported that each of these three items was "very important" were always within five percentage points of each other (in both the party leader and general public surveys). Whether we asked open-ended questions or pushed people to rate different traits side by side, the characteristics that seem to define a well-qualified candidate were basically the same.

Of course, a list of five or six important characteristics doesn't address every aspect of the larger question of how to define leader quality (for instance, it doesn't tell us which traits are must-haves and which are just nice to have). And it is at least conceivable that voters and party leaders might prioritize different qualities somewhat differently when they think of candidates for local offices and candidates for state or national offices. But if we need a way to measure whether the working class is unfit to hold political office, asking whether workers have the traits that voters and party leaders say they most value—honesty, intelligence, friendliness, work ethic, confidence, and speaking skills—is probably a good place to start.

Now, in defense of the people who have applied the John Parker argument to the working class, if we were to go out and measure these kinds of qualities in the general public, working-class Americans would probably tend to score a little lower on at least some of them. The most obvious is intelligence: lower-income and blue-collar workers are less likely to perform well on standard measures of cognitive ability, like IQ tests (although these tests are also sometimes criticized for being biased against the less fortunate).[23] Working-class people are also more likely to experience anxiety about public speaking,[24] and it's not hard to imagine that traits like confidence and being outgoing or personable might follow suit. Less affluent people also tend to score lower on most measures of participation in civic and political life,[25] which some critics point to as evidence that workers wouldn't make great politicians.

Then again, with some qualities, there are actually signs that working-class people are *more* likely to be fit for office. Honesty, for instance, tends to be higher among the less fortunate. One series of studies found that more affluent people were more likely to lie in negotiations, cheat to increase their chances of winning a prize, take valuable things from other people, endorse unethical behavior at work, and break the law while driving.[26] Honesty—the #1 trait that both voters and party leaders look for in a politician—may actually be more common among working-class Americans.

Moreover, the social class gaps in the traits that favor professionals would have to be truly staggering to account for the virtual absence of working-class people in public office. Workers make up less than 3 percent of the typical state legislature and less than 2 percent of Congress—if we really believed that the social class makeup of our political institutions simply reflected differences in qualifications, we would have to believe that workers only make up 2 to 3 percent of the intelligent, honest, hardworking, personable people in America. Could the distribution of good qualities really be that skewed? Should we really believe that almost none of the decent people in this country are working-class people?

Actual data on working-class Americans tell a very different story. When my research team fielded our national survey of the general public in 2014, we already knew which traits party leaders had said a politician should have (and we suspected that ordinary citizens would want many of the same kinds of traits). Armed with that information, we included several items on our general public survey that asked respondents to evaluate themselves, that is, that asked them to rate whether they had the personal characteristics that party leaders want in a politician (without telling them that that was what we were doing).

Of course, this approach had an obvious drawback: people tend to evaluate themselves favorably. But there was still lots of variation in most of the measures—many people were willing to say that they weren't very assertive or very outgoing or especially good at public speaking.

However, those people weren't overwhelmingly from working-class jobs. In fact, on most measures of the qualities that party leaders and voters want in a politician, working-class respondents tended to rate themselves about as favorably as their white-collar counterparts. Figure 2.3 plots responses to a block of questions that began, "Do any of the following

Figure 2.3. Workers Are about as Likely to Say They Have the Qualities We Look For

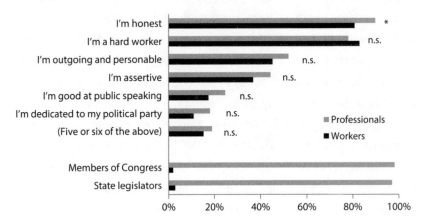

Source: Broockman et al. 2014a.

Note: Bars report the percentages of respondents in our survey of the general public who checked each of the options listed here when asked, "Do any of the following statements describe you? (check all that apply)." Statistical significance is denoted as follows: *$p < 0.05$, n.s. not significant.

statements describe you? (check all that apply)." Respondents were then shown several statements that included things like "I'm honest," "I'm a hard worker," and "I'm dedicated to my political party." (Unfortunately, we didn't ask about being intelligent or understanding.)

Looking at Figure 2.3, the first pattern worth noting is that the different items elicited substantially different answers overall. Regardless of class, more than 75 percent of respondents rated themselves hardworking and honest, but only about 15 to 20 percent said that they were good at public speaking or dedicated to their political party. Most other items fell somewhere in between. The people who completed the survey seemed perfectly willing to admit that they didn't have many of the traits people want in a politician.

When it came to class, however, there were gaps, but they were tiny compared to what we would expect if workers really were unfit to govern. (To help put the gaps in responses in perspective, I've also plotted the percentage of members of Congress and state lawmakers from working-class and white-collar jobs at the bottom of the figure.) Workers were less likely to say that they were outgoing and good at speaking, for instance, but only by seven percentage points. The biggest gap in professionals' favor—checking the box for "I'm honest"—was just eight percentage points.

When I computed the percentage of respondents who checked five or six of the six boxes—the share who seemed *extremely* promising—the gap was tiny: 15 percent of workers and 18 percent of white-collar professionals fit the bill. On this measure (and indeed on most of the measures in these figures) *workers made up close to half of the politically qualified people in the survey.* (And the social class gaps in these survey responses were essentially the same—small and usually not statistically significant—in regression models that controlled for a host of other characteristics of the respondent, including party, ideology, gender, race, marital status, and whether the respondent had children; see Table A2.1 in the appendix.)

Yes, workers are a little less likely to have the traits voters and political elites want in a politician, but not by enough to explain why they almost never hold office. Workers were almost as likely as professionals to check five or six of the boxes in Figure 2.3; in contrast, they make up less than 2 percent of the people in Congress. In this survey, a shortage of qualifications simply didn't seem to be the most important explanation for the virtual absence of workers in our political institutions. (Of course, workers might still *perceive* themselves as less qualified; I'll take up that point in chapter 3.)

The same was true when we asked a series of questions about political participation. Figure 2.4 plots how workers and white-collar professionals responded to a block of items that asked them to think about their civic engagement in the previous few years. Qualified workers were about as likely to report regularly voting, volunteering for civic groups and community organizations, and working in and around politics. There were modest social class gaps of seven or eight percentage points in the shares of respondents who reported regularly contacting elected officials, volunteering for campaigns, contacting elected officials, or donating money to political causes, but, again, these differences were nowhere near as large as the gaps in who actually goes on to hold office. (And, again, the small or nonexistent gaps in Figure 2.4 were essentially the same in regression models that controlled for a host of other characteristics of the respondent, including

FIGURE 2.4. Workers Are about as Likely to Say They Participate in Politics

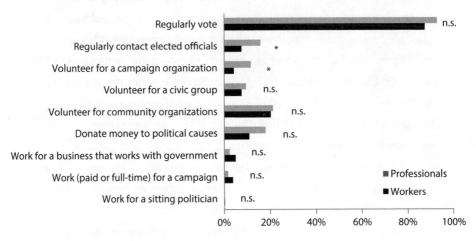

Source: Broockman et al. 2014a.

Note: Bars report the percentages of respondents in our survey of the general public who checked each of the options listed here when asked, "In the last few years, have you done any of the following? (check all that apply)." Statistical significance is denoted as follows: *$p < 0.05$, n.s. not significant.

party, ideology, gender, race, marital status, and whether the respondent had children; see Table A2.2 in the appendix.)

In sharp contrast to John Parker–style arguments about the working class, our 2014 survey data didn't produce much evidence that workers as a social group are unqualified to hold public office—or even that social class gaps in qualifications are a major factor in the underrepresentation of the working class. If workers held office in proportion to the qualities they reported in this survey, they would make up close to half of our politicians, not one in fifty.

And our 2014 survey wasn't alone. Figure 2.5 plots data on the percentages of workers and professionals with the qualities voters and party leaders say they want, this time using data from the General Social Survey, or GSS, one of the oldest and most respected surveys of social life in the United States. In 2006, the GSS asked respondents a series of questions about their personal qualities. Many mirrored items that party leaders and the general public value in a politician.

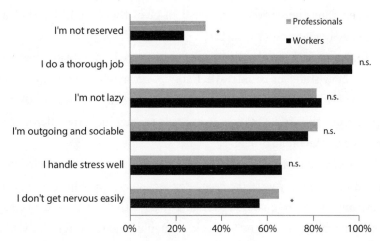

FIGURE 2.5. In the GSS, Workers Seem Just as Qualified, Too

Source: Smith, Marsden, and Hout 2015.

Note: Statistical significance is denoted as follows: *p < 0.05, n.s. not significant.

As in our 2014 survey, in the 2006 GSS, working-class respondents were about as likely as professionals to say that they had the qualities people want in a politician. They were about as likely to report that they were thorough and not lazy (in other words, hardworking), that they were outgoing and sociable (or personable), and that they handle stress well (confident). There were gaps in a few measures, like not being reserved or not getting nervous easily. However—like in Figures 2.3 and 2.4—the gaps were tiny compared to the enormous gulf in who actually goes on to hold office.

At most, the social class differences documented here could only be very partial explanations for the underrepresentation of the working class. And they are a far cry from the kinds of gaps we would expect if we believed the old argument that working-class Americans are unfit to govern. Different social classes simply don't seem to differ all that much on the traits people want in a politician.

Of course, the characteristics that voters and party leaders say they want in a politician may not be an exhaustive list of the traits that make a good leader. Someone can be honest and intelligent and hardworking but still screw up when you put them in charge. Workers look good on paper—and far better than the conventional wisdom gives them credit for—but are they really ready to run the factory?

A final approach scholars have used to measure leader quality has been to study how states or countries actually perform when different leaders take over.[27] If some individuals or social groups really are better or worse at governing, the argument goes, we should see significantly different outcomes when they hold office.

This *performance-based* proxy for quality is a useful way to double-check the findings from my *what-the-people-say-they-want* proxy. If working-class Americans really are qualified to hold office (as the survey evidence suggests), then places governed by workers should tend to perform as well as places governed by professionals. If, on the other hand, workers are less qualified in some way that national surveys don't pick up on—if the interests of workers really "can be more effectually promoted by the merchant than by themselves"—then places governed by large numbers of working-class people should tend to be worse off relative to places governed by the usual white-collar crowd. What happens when workers actually hold office in large numbers?

The only places in American politics where we can find out are cities. Congress has never had more than a few people from working-class jobs, and even state legislatures are governed almost exclusively by professionals (the highest recorded percentage of working-class state lawmakers I've ever encountered was Maine's 19 percent working-class state legislature in 1979). In cities, on the other hand, working-class people sometimes hold office in large numbers. In some cities, workers even make up a majority of the city council. When they do, does chaos follow?

It doesn't seem to. Figure 2.6 analyzes Trounstine's data on government and finances in American cities,[28] which combine information from four waves of Municipal Form of Government surveys (the only available source of systematic data on the occupational backgrounds of city officials) with city finance data from the U.S. Census Bureau's Census of Governments and data on other city characteristics from the decennial Census. I focus here on data from 1996 and 2001, the years when the Form of Government surveys included detailed occupational measures: in these two years, the survey asked respondents (city clerks) to record the number of city council members who fell into each of 11 occupational categories.[29] Using these data, I identified the cities governed by majority working-class city councils in 1996 *for which Trounstine also had follow-up data on how the city was performing in 2001* (there were 63 in all). For comparison, I also examined how cities led by majority white-collar city councils in 1996 were performing five years later (there were 2,152).

Figure 2.6 plots four simple measures of how the health of the city changed: the population, the city's revenue, the city's spending on schools, and the city's debt. (To help put the gaps between professional- and worker-run cities in perspective, I've scaled the vertical axis on each graph so that it's the size of one standard deviation of the change variable in question.)

No meaningful differences were evident in any of these measures: by 2001, cities that were run by majority working-class city councils in 1996 had grown and changed at roughly the same rates as cities that had been governed by mostly professional city councils. Both kinds of cities expanded on average—a typical professional-run city added just over 1,600 new residents, and a typical worker-run city added over 2,000 new residents. Both raised more and spent more on schools, with professional-run cities raising and spending slightly more, though not by much. And both took on more debt, with cities run by workers taking on slightly less. None of the gaps documented in Figure 2.6 was substantively large, and none was statistically significant. (I also separately compared cities that switched from majority white-collar to majority worker councils between 1996 and 2001 to cities that had majority white-collar councils in both years; again, I found no statistically significant or substantively meaningful gaps in the measures in Figure 2.6.)

Of course, it could be that the cities with majority working-class councils differed in some other way—perhaps they were stronger and more vibrant communities—that offset the "damage" done by their working-class city councils. To check for that possibility, I estimated follow-up regression

FIGURE 2.6. Cities Governed by the Working Class Do Just Fine

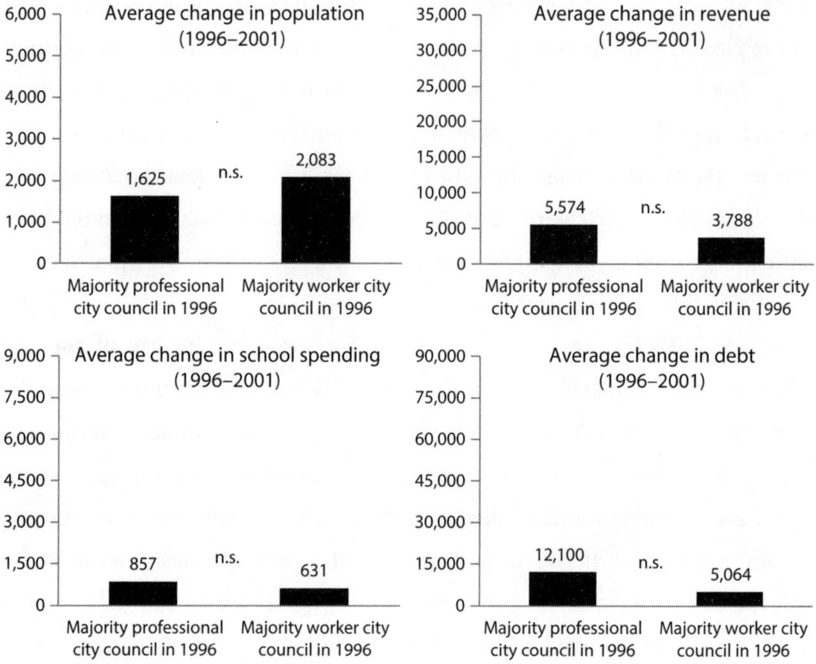

Source: Trounstine and Valdini 2008.

Note: Statistical significance is denoted as follows: n.s. not significant.

models that related changes in each of the four outcome variables in Figure 2.6 to an indicator for cities with majority working-class councils in 1996 and a list of control variables.[30] The complete results are available in Table A2.3 in the appendix, but the basic conclusion was the same as in Figure 2.6: in the one setting in U.S. politics where we can observe what happens when working-class people hold office in large numbers, they seem to perform just as well as white-collar professionals.

The old idea that working-class Americans are unfit to govern simply doesn't square with actual data on U.S. politics. It doesn't square with survey data on who has the qualities voters and party leaders say they want in a politician. It doesn't square with data on how working-class politicians perform in office. Working-class Americans score lower on some measures of their qualifications, but the gaps aren't even close to enough to explain the phenomenon of white-collar government in the United States. The first prong of the John Parker argument doesn't seem to apply to workers. People have always justified the political exclusion of social groups they dislike by saying that those groups are unfit to participate in civic life, and they've always been wrong. This time seems to be no exception. Like the men and women who took over New Era Windows, working-class Americans seem perfectly capable of running things themselves.

If we want to understand why so few working-class Americans hold public office, we should probably focus our attention elsewhere. The Qualifications stage of the QRS Model doesn't seem to explain much in this case: on most measures, workers made up 40 to 50 percent of qualified people. Our cash ceiling seems to be located elsewhere in the candidate entry process; something other than a shortage of qualifications appears to be keeping working-class Americans out of public office.

Is it voters?

DO VOTERS DISLIKE WORKERS?

Donald Matthews—a University of Washington political scientist who passed away in 2007—is arguably the father of modern research on white-collar government.[31] Today, Matthews is better known for his 1960 book *U.S. Senators and Their World*, which vividly describes the formal and informal "folkways" of the U.S. Senate. But long before he was writing about folkways, Matthews was doing pioneering research on the popular "log-cabin-to-White-House ideal" and arguing that national lawmakers were "hardly 'common men.' "[32]

In 1954, Matthews published a book titled *The Social Background of Political Decision Makers* (and a companion article that ran in *Public Opinion Quarterly*) in which he outlined how national lawmakers in the United States were disproportionately drawn from well-off families, elite colleges, and high-status occupations. He urged other scholars to follow up, to study whether politicians from different social classes behaved differently in office. He continued working on the topic himself, too; in *U.S. Senators and*

Their World, Matthews argued that the personal backgrounds of politicians were among the most important factors in how they adapted to the folkways of the Senate. (Quoting a former senator, he noted that "a man doesn't change a whole lot just because he has been elected to the Senate. If he's been a small-town lawyer, or a banker, or a businessman he is going to think and act like one when he gets to the Senate.") Matthews continued to advocate research on class and legislative conduct for decades, even as interest in the topic declined. In the 1980s, he forcefully criticized scholars of legislative politics for not doing more: "Does it make any difference whether legislators are better educated [and] enjoy higher social status . . . than the people they represent? The research literature has yet to answer that question."[33]

Although Matthews was primarily interested in the effects of government by the privileged, he also occasionally speculated about the *causes*. And one of the ideas he floated was that working-class people seldom hold office because that's the way voters want it. In *The Social Background of Political Decision Makers*, Matthews encouraged readers not to interpret the overrepresentation of the privileged as evidence of "any kind of conscious plot." Instead, he argued, there were probably simpler explanations. It is "understandable in a society with an accepted stratification system," he wrote, "for the electorate to choose men with high social status to represent them in the decision-making process. . . . Rightly or wrongly the lawyer is thought to be a better man than the factory worker. Thus when the factory worker votes for the lawyer he is voting for a man who is what he would *like* to be."[34]

Why do so few working-class people hold office? Donald Matthews—the first modern political scientist to propose a serious program of research on the social class makeup of American government—thought that voters were at least partly to blame.[35]

Political observers often attribute the shortage of working-class people in our governing institutions to the will of the people. Some, like Matthews, don't take a position on whether it's a good thing that voters prefer affluent candidates: "*Rightly or wrongly* the lawyer is thought to be a better man than the factory worker." Others point to voters as part of a John Parker–style criticism of the dangers of working-class government. *Thankfully* voters prefer affluent candidates *because working-class Americans would make lousy politicians.*

Like the first prong of the conventional wisdom (the idea that workers are unfit to govern, or that they're screened out at the Qualifications stage of the QRS Model of candidate entry), there isn't actually much hard evidence to support the second prong (the idea that voters dislike workers, or that they're screened out at the Succeed stage). To the best of my knowledge, there has never been a single published study that has suggested that voters are significantly biased against candidates from the working class.

That said, it's still an idea that we need to take seriously. Historically, voters have often been at least partly to blame for keeping underrepresented groups like women and people of color out of office.[36] It's not inconceivable that the same might be true for workers, that voters might prefer professionals to candidates from the working class.

We know from research on prejudice, for instance, that Americans—even working-class Americans—subscribe to many negative stereotypes about the less fortunate (like that they're lazy) and many positive stereotypes about people who are well-off (like that they're smart and hardworking).[37] People also sometimes engage in what economists call "statistical discrimination"—when we're unsure about a person's intelligence or ability, we sometimes make guesses based on what we know about the social groups the person comes from.

If Americans bring these kinds of biases with them into the voting booth, they could be among the factors that screen workers out and ultimately give rise to our white-collar government. If some voters are prejudiced against the working class, if some guess that working-class candidates are less qualified, or if some simply prefer affluent candidates for other reasons, that might help explain why so few working-class Americans hold office. Maybe workers just can't win elections.

Of course, the very fact that so few workers hold office isn't a guarantee that voters prefer affluent candidates (although many political observers often assume as much). It's possible that white-collar candidates are the only ones who Succeed in elections, but as the QRS Model reminds us, it's also possible that white-collar candidates are the only ones who Run.

Moreover, the case that voters prefer affluent candidates isn't as solid as it might seem at first glance. Prejudices and negative stereotypes don't just apply to the less fortunate; there are also negative stereotypes about affluent people and professionals that could come into play during an election. The well-off are often seen as cold, aloof, and out of touch.[38] Voters tend to prefer politicians who they feel understand their problems and who share their views about public policy.[39] If people feel a sense of shared identity with candidates from their social class, or if the working-class people who make up half the country worry that professional candidates don't understand their problems, share their concerns, or support their preferred policies, many voters might actually prefer candidates from humble backgrounds, other things equal.

For their part, candidates often behave as though they don't think that economic privilege is an electoral slam dunk. Wealthy and white-collar candidates routinely downplay their advantages, sometimes going so far as to engage in what the historian Edward Pessen calls "poor-mouthing"[40]—deliberately exaggerating the economic adversities they've experienced. Many worry that their good fortune could be reframed as detachment and indifference; as a national GOP strategist bluntly put it, "*Businessman problem solver good, wealthy businessman out of touch with workers bad.*"[41] Although there are good reasons to suspect that voter biases might be behind the shortage of politicians from the working class, there are also good reasons to question whether voters really are to blame.

But probably the single best reason to be skeptical that voters prefer affluent candidates is that the actual data say otherwise.

When I started researching the shortage of politicians from the working class, I couldn't find a single published study on whether voters in the United States were biased against working-class candidates. So in 2011, I took a stab at the question in my dissertation (which was later published as a book, *White-Collar Government*). Following Donald Matthews, my primary interest at that time was whether politicians from the working class behave differently in office. However, I also briefly examined the possible reasons why so few working-class Americans hold office in the first place. In the concluding chapter of my dissertation, I tested Matthews's hunch that voters prefer affluent candidates.

The brief analysis asked whether the members of Congress who had served between 1999 and 2008 who had spent more of their pre-congressional careers in working-class jobs had won their last elections by smaller margins. Contrary to the conventional wisdom, this simple exercise didn't uncover any relationship between class and election results. Members of Congress from the working class did just as well at the polls as members from other occupational backgrounds.

There were a few important problems with this analysis, of course (as I noted at the time). For one, I only had data on winners—members of Congress—not on every congressional candidate. And what that analysis was measuring wasn't really the *effect* of social class on vote margins, just the correlation between the two. The data were consistent with the idea that voters don't care about a candidate's class, but the evidence wasn't airtight. It was still possible, for instance, that voters were biased against working-class candidates, but that some workers compensated for those biases in other ways and managed to win enough votes to get into office, thereby giving the faulty appearance that there were no biases in the first place.

The next year, another political scientist, Meredith Sadin, began a series of studies that solved the most significant problems with my preliminary research. In her work, Sadin used experiments embedded in nationally representative surveys to isolate the effect of a candidate's social class. She first showed ordinary citizens a short biography of a hypothetical candidate, then asked them to evaluate the candidate on several dimensions, including how likely they were to vote for him. Unbeknownst to the subjects, Sadin randomly varied several aspects of the candidate's biography: sometimes the candidate was a blue-collar worker, and sometimes he was a successful doctor.

Sadin's findings were exactly in line with the data on vote margins in Congress: voters seemed just as willing to cast their ballots for working-class candidates as white-collar professionals.[42] And unlike my analysis of members of Congress, Sadin's work was *causally identified*: she could say with great confidence that the true effect of class on vote choice was essentially zero. Her experiments and the observational data were pointing to the same conclusion, namely, that voters aren't biased against working-class candidates.

Since then, I've done a few follow-up studies, and they've all produced the same basic result. In 2015, Noam Lupu and I ran a series of Sadin-style hypothetical candidate experiments in the United States, the United Kingdom, and Argentina.[43] To more closely simulate real-world elections, we showed voters in each country two hypothetical candidates (Sadin had shown voters just one) and asked which one they would be more likely to vote for, again randomizing several characteristics, including the candidate's social class (factory worker or business owner).

The right panel in Figure 2.7 plots the average vote margins that the hypothetical candidates in our U.S. experiments received. The typical working-class candidate performed slightly better than the typical white-collar candidate, although the gap wasn't statistically significant. Moreover, the results of our experiment were perfectly in line with my analysis of members of Congress: the center panel in Figure 2.7 plots the average vote margins of members who held office between 1999 and 2008 who spent most of their pre-congressional careers in working-class jobs and those who worked primarily in white-collar jobs. The left panel plots comparable data on the members of Congress who held office from 1945 to 1996 whose last jobs before getting into politics were professional or working-class jobs. Members of Congress had higher average vote margins overall by definition (they were all winners, so their average vote margins were higher than our hypothetical candidates, who consisted of some winners and some losers). But all three samples told the same basic story: voters seem perfectly willing to vote for working-class candidates in carefully controlled experiments and in actual elections for the U.S. Congress.

FIGURE 2.7. Working-Class Candidates Do Well in Elections

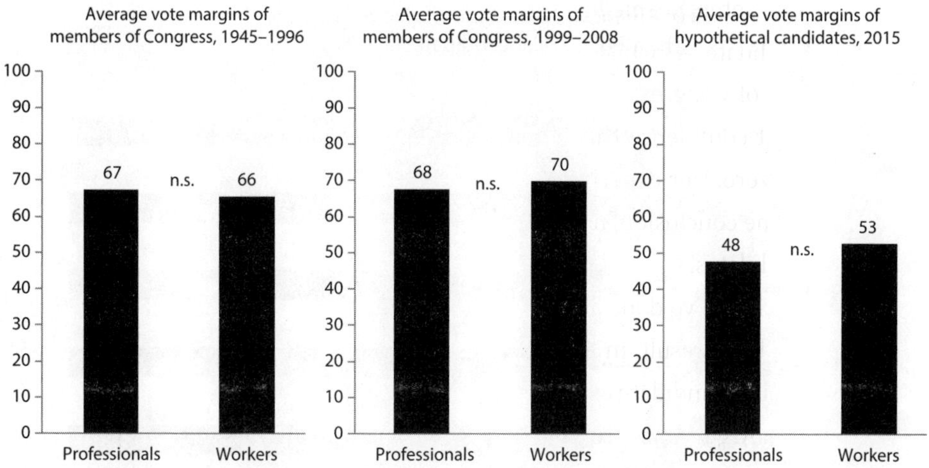

Average vote margins of members of Congress, 1945–1996	Average vote margins of members of Congress, 1999–2008	Average vote margins of hypothetical candidates, 2015

Professionals: 67   n.s.   Workers: 66
Professionals: 68   n.s.   Workers: 70
Professionals: 48   n.s.   Workers: 53

Source: ICPSR and McKibbin 1997; Carnes 2011; Carnes and Lupu 2016a.

Note: Statistical significance is denoted as follows: n.s. not significant. Samples sizes were as follows: 1945–1996: 13,352 former professionals and 153 former workers; 1999–2008: 2,663 former professionals and 17 former workers; 2015: 1,025 professionals (488 received the vote) and 975 workers (512 received the vote).

Lupu and I subjected these results to rigorous follow-up testing. We randomly varied whether the hypothetical election was for national, state, or local office. We tried splitting the sample by party (whether the candidate was portrayed as a Republican or a Democrat, Republican and Democratic voters both slightly preferred the working-class version of the candidate to an otherwise identical white-collar version), checking for anomalies in the data, and performing every other follow-up test we could think of.[44] Regardless of how we re-analyzed the data, our results were always the same. We simply couldn't find any evidence that voters were biased against working-class candidates.

I also tried another approach while working on this book. In the 2014 public opinion follow-up survey I collaborated on (the one my co-investigators and I used to see what qualities voters think an ideal politician should have), I was able to ask a nationally representative sample of Americans *point-blank* what they thought about candidates from the working class (rather than asking them to evaluate hypothetical candidates and then

FIGURE 2.8. Voters Like Working-Class Candidates

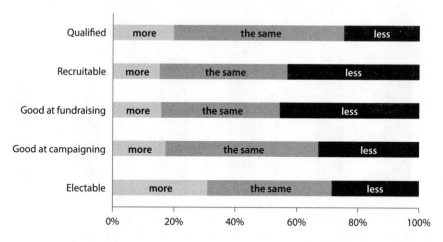

Percentages of Americans who think working-class candidates are more or less _____ than white-collar candidates.

Source: Broockman et al. 2014a.

teasing out how a candidate's class matters). The survey asked respondents directly, "In races for county and local office in your area, relative to candidates with professional backgrounds, do you think candidates from working-class backgrounds (e.g., factory workers, restaurant servers, receptionists) tend to be more or less . . ." and then listed five attributes: qualified to hold office (labeled "Qualified" in Figure 2.8), easy to convince to run ("Recruitable"), good at fundraising ("Good at fundraising"), good at campaigning ("Good at campaigning"), and preferred by voters ("Electable"). Whereas the questions about qualifications (summarized in Figures 2.1 and 2.2) were asked without reference to any particular level or branch of government, these items asked respondents to think specifically about county and local offices. Figure 2.8 plots the answers people gave.

This approach was obviously far less subtle than a hypothetical candidate experiment, but it produced the same basic result. As Figure 2.8 illustrates, respondents were realistic about the potential challenges workers would face with recruitment and fundraising, even at the local level: close to half of respondents said they thought working-class candidates would be harder to recruit and would have a harder time fundraising. But on the two measures most directly related to voter biases against workers—whether respondents personally thought that working-class candidates were less qualified to hold office (the top bar in the figure) and whether respondents thought that working-class candidates would have a hard time winning elections (the bottom bar)—the sample was essentially split: respondents were most likely to say "the same," and for every respondent who said that she thought workers were worse, there was another respondent who said workers were better. When asked a very direct question about local working-class candidates, people said that they thought workers were about as qualified and about as likely to win elections as white-collar professionals—a finding that perfectly squares with what we see in real election outcomes at the state and federal levels and in hypothetical candidate experiments at the national, state, and local levels. (And these results were remarkably consistent across the two parties; the shares of Republicans and Democrats who answered "less" to each item above were always within five percentage points of each other.) There are certainly some voters who dislike working-class candidates, but there are just as many who actually prefer them, and on balance, the two seem to roughly cancel out.

Taken as a whole, the electorate seems to be basically indifferent—voters don't think working-class candidates are superheroes, but they don't think they're unfit to govern either. And that probably helps explain why working-class candidates tend to do just fine on election day.

As it stands, these four studies—my 2011 analysis, Sadin's work, my work with Lupu, and the analysis in Figure 2.8—represent the only published research on whether voters in the United States dislike working-class candidates.[45] Obviously, it's always possible that with more work someone will uncover evidence of anti-worker biases in the electorate. But all of the available empirical evidence to date is directly at odds with the idea that voters keep workers out of office. Like the first prong of the conventional wisdom (that workers are less qualified), the second prong (that workers can't win elections) simply doesn't square with actual data on U.S. politics. There are lots of qualified workers out there, and when they run, they seem to do just fine in elections. Proponents of political exclusion have often held up voters as a shield: if a group is underrepresented in public office, it must be an expression of the public will, they say. The truth is, however, that voters—Republicans and Democrats alike—seem to like working-class candidates just fine.

With all due respect to Donald Matthews, the father of modern research on white-collar government, the electorate does not seem to choose people with high social status to represent them. That choice is made by others long before election day.

WHAT'S REALLY KEEPING WORKERS OUT?

One of my favorite reactions to the topic of this book was a brief exchange I had with the provost of Duke University in the summer of 2011. It was the week before classes began, and the president of the university had thrown a welcome party at his house for all the new professors. After about an hour, he and the provost got everyone's attention and asked all the new faculty to go around the room and say what they were researching. One woman was designing the algorithms that made high-definition TV possible. The man next to me was studying how to detect bubbles in the housing market. When it was my turn, I said something like, "I'm doing research on the fact that millionaires and white-collar professionals hold almost every political office in the country. I'm trying to understand how that affects public policy and why working-class people almost never go on to be politicians." The provost responded without missing a beat: "Of course working-class people never get into politics. They're too busy working."

We all chuckled at the remark, and the next person in the circle started his spiel. But the provost—who happened to be a distinguished political scientist—was serious. And he was basically right.

If we want to understand why so few working-class people hold office, the conventional wisdom doesn't get us very far. A social group will tend to be numerically underrepresented in public office when members of that group are less Qualified, less likely to Run, and less likely to Succeed in elections (as the QRS Model reminds us). Although people often say that working-class Americans are less qualified and less likely to win elections, those long-standing ideas don't find much support in actual data on U.S. politics. Many working-class Americans have the qualities we want in politicians, and when workers run they tend to do well in elections and in office.

By process of elimination, the Running stage would seem to be where America's cash ceiling is located. Of course, process of elimination isn't as scientifically satisfying as observing something directly.

As I mentioned earlier in this chapter, it's easy to imagine lots of reasons why qualified workers might be less likely to run for office. I'll say more about those explanations in chapters 3 and 4, but in short, there is good cause to think that in modern elections, working-class Americans are less able to shoulder the practical burdens associated with running and are also less likely to be encouraged by civic and political leaders. Running for office in a democracy like ours is really, really hard: if the less fortunate seldom hold office, we don't need to resort to Parker-style arguments about how they aren't fit to govern or can't get enough votes. There's another obvious possibility, namely, that even qualified, electable, working-class people simply choose not to run.

And that's exactly what we see in data on actual candidates. To my knowledge, there are only two data sets in the country that record the social class makeup of the entire candidate pool in a given set of elections.[46] One is the survey of state legislative candidates I analyzed briefly in chapter 1, the National Candidate Study, or NCS, which I ran with three collaborators (David Broockman, Melody Crowder-Meyer, and Chris Skovron) in 2012 and 2014. The NCS is a survey of every declared candidate for state legislature nationwide, and one of the questions it asks is what the person's main occupation is (or what it was, if the person is retired or has made politics their full-time job). About one in five state legislative candidates completed the survey in 2012 and 2014, and there weren't any obvious differences between those who took the survey and those who didn't, which makes the study a useful resource for analyzing the class backgrounds of not just people who win elections, but the entire group of people who run. (The complete technical details are listed in the "Survey Details" section of the appendix.)

The other source of systematic data is the Local Elections in America Project, or LEAP, a database of information about state and local elections compiled and regularly updated by two political scientists, Melissa Marschall and Paru Shah. The LEAP data set includes information about the more than eighteen thousand county and local elections held in California—one of the only states that requires candidates to list their occupations—from 1995 to 2011. Of course, nationwide data on the occupational backgrounds of candidates for county and local office would be even better, but those simply don't exist. The Golden State provides a one-of-a-kind window into the social class makeup of candidates for the local offices where most politicians begin their careers.

Figure 2.9 plots data on the social class makeup of state legislative candidates in 2012 and 2014 and county and local candidates in California from 1995 to 2011. In both panels, I've also plotted the percentage of working-class people in the general public. Viewed this way, it is easy to see that the underrepresentation of the working class isn't about who wins elections, but rather who runs in the first place. Working-class Americans make up just over half of the country (and as the section before last showed, on most measures, workers make up at least 40 percent of the people who have the qualities we look for in politicians). In sharp contrast, they make up less than 5 percent of candidates for state, county, and local offices. They go on to win about 5 percent of all state races nationwide and about 3 percent of county and local races in California. Most of the screening out is happening not at the Qualified or Succeed stages—it's happening when people decide whether to Run for public office.

In keeping with the idea that party and ideology are not to blame for the shortage of workers, the results in Figure 2.9 were essentially unchanged

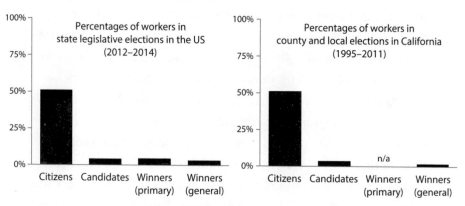

FIGURE 2.9. It's All about Who Runs

Source: Broockman et al. 2012, 2014a; Marschall and Shah 2013.

when I subset the cases by the candidate's or area's partisanship. At the state level, workers made up 4.2 percent of Democratic candidates and 4.5 percent of Republican candidates, 4.5 percent of Democratic primary winners and 4.5 percent of Republican primary winners, and 2.7 percent of Republican general election winners and 3.8 percent of Democratic general election winners. The LEAP data available to me[47] did not include information about candidates' partisanship, but when I compared counties where Obama earned less than 40 percent of the two-party vote in 2012 to counties where he earned more than 60 percent, there were essentially no differences: workers made up 4.2 percent of candidates in pro-Romney counties and 3 percent of candidates in pro-Obama counties, and workers made up 2.7 percent of winners in pro-Romney counties and 1.1 percent of winners in pro-Obama counties. The story here does not seem to be one of partisanship or ideology: Republican and Democratic voters and party leaders say they want the same things in candidates, they are just as likely to vote for workers, and workers are just as likely to run and win as Republicans or in Republican-leaning counties. Neither party is especially welcoming or unwelcoming to working-class candidates; workers rarely run in either one.

Of course, data on the social class makeup of candidates and winners can't tell us *why* so few working-class Americans run for office. Maybe workers are less likely to see politics as a desirable career move. Maybe they don't think they could actually win. Maybe workers are less likely to be encouraged to run by political elites. Or maybe they're just too busy working.

Whatever the exact reason (and I'll come back to this point in chapters 3 and 4), the findings in Figure 2.9 are perfectly in line with everything else we've seen in this chapter. Why do so few working-class people hold office? At the most basic level, the answer really is simple. It isn't because working-class people are unfit to govern or because workers don't win elections. The truth sounds far more like the explanation my provost came up with back in 2011. Working-class Americans seldom hold office because they seldom run.

In November 2015, I organized a program at Duke University for people in the Durham area who were interested in campaigning for political office. I don't work in campaigns myself, so I contacted a local nonprofit that had its own candidate training program, and they agreed to put on a nonpartisan, professional-quality "Ready to Run" event in the public policy school where I work. At eight o'clock on a Saturday morning, fifty or so people trickled into a large auditorium on the ground floor of my building for a daylong program on how to launch a career in elected political office.

The first activity of the day was a fifteen-minute session called "Help Wanted." The trainers began by asking everyone in the room a simple question: *What makes someone qualified to run for public office?* Beyond the simple legal requirements like being old enough or being a citizen, what are the traits or characteristics that someone absolutely *needs* in order to run—the "must-haves"—and what are the things that might help someone succeed in politics but aren't absolutely necessary—the "nice-to-haves"?

Hands went up all over the room. The trainers started calling on people and writing their responses on the chalkboard in two columns. After about ten minutes, the chalkboard was full:

Must-Haves	Nice-to-Haves
1. Honesty	1. Accessibility
2. Commitment	2. Compelling personal story
3. Empathy	3. Public speaking
4. Ability to raise money	4. Retired/independently wealthy
5. Connection to community	5. Past experience in public office
6. Willingness to sacrifice	
7. Cultural competence	
8. Passion for the position	
9. Common sense	
10. Self-awareness	
11. Vision for the state	

Interestingly, the qualities that the attendees listed that morning were generally consistent with the qualities that the citizens and party leaders in my surveys said that they looked for in a candidate. They were also similar to the qualities most people would want in a leader in any walk of life. Whether it's our legislatures or our workplaces or our places of worship, who doesn't want the person in charge to be honest, dedicated, and compassionate?

Importantly, no one at this candidate training program said that a person has to be from a white-collar job in order to be a good politician (and all but three of the attendees were white-collar professionals themselves). They mentioned a few traits that are likely to be a little more common among the privileged—they saw the ability to raise money as a must-have and being independently wealthy as a nice-to-have—but no one said that only professionals or affluent people are fit to govern. To the contrary, most of the attendees mentioned qualities that you can find among white-collar and working-class Americans alike.

Contrary to the conventional wisdom, working-class Americans have the qualities people look for in a politician. When they run for office, they win. When they govern, they succeed. They simply don't run that often. They are screened out at the Run stage of the Qualified-Run-Succeed Model of candidate emergence.

Indeed, despite my best efforts to recruit working-class attendees for "Ready to Run @Duke" in November 2015, almost none showed up. I called labor unions. I emailed pro-workers advocacy organizations. I tried reserving spots for Duke employees doing manual labor, service, and clerical jobs. Many people thanked me for reaching out to them. But in the end, only three of the fifty people who attended my November candidate training were employed in what I would classify as working-class jobs, about the same percentage that we see in the candidate pool nationwide.

It's time we put the John Parker–style ideas we often hear about the working class where they belong: in the garbage can of history. People have always used arguments like these to justify the political exclusion of social groups they dislike, and they've always been wrong. If we want to understand why so few working-class people hold office, the real question isn't about qualifications or elections. The real question is why so few qualified working-class Americans choose to run for public office. That's where we'll find America's cash ceiling; it stands between qualified workers and the complex undertaking of launching a campaign.

If we want to understand the personal and structural forces that keep working-class people out of American political institutions, we need to focus on the decision (not) to run for public office.

CHAPTER 2 SUMMARY

People often say that workers don't hold office because they aren't qualified, and voters know it.

- *When a social group is underrepresented, people who like it that way often resort to a John Parker-style argument, the idea that the group is excluded because they'd wreck everything if they were in charge, but thankfully everyone knows that and keeps them out, and all is well.*

There's another possibility, however: a social group will be underrepresented when people from that group are less likely to run (as the Qualified-Run-Succeed notes).

- *Running for political office is really, really hard. When a group is underrepresented, it could just be because they're choosing not to run.*

When we look at actual data, it doesn't seem to be the case that workers are unfit to govern.

- *Working-class people are often capable of running things themselves. Just ask the leaders of New Era Windows, the Chicago-based company that was purchased by its working-class employees and has been successfully managed by them ever since.*

It also doesn't seem to be the case that workers are less likely to win elections.

- *Even Donald Matthews—the father of modern research on white-collar government—thought that voters were biased against workers. But in reality, voters seem just fine with working-class candidates.*

The most important reason we have so few working-class people in political office isn't that workers are unqualified or that they lose when they run—it's that qualified workers rarely run in the first place.

- *My provost once said at a cocktail party that workers are underrepresented "because they're too busy working." His off-the-cuff remark was closer to being right than the old conventional wisdom.*

The bottom line: People often say that working-class Americans don't hold office because they aren't qualified or because voters don't want them to hold office. Neither of those arguments is true. The main reason so few workers hold office is because so few choose to run.

3

WHY DON'T WORKERS RUN?

In November 2012, I conducted a straw poll. The question was straightforward; it basically boiled down to: *Why do you think working-class people are so rare in public office in the United States?* The people I surveyed, however, were unusual. I didn't poll friends or coworkers, or post the question on social media. I put my straw poll on a survey of 1,900 candidates who had just finished running for state legislature.

A few weeks before the 2012 elections—and just after my co-investigators and I finished our first nationwide survey of state legislative candidates, the National Candidate Study—two of my collaborators began planning a short online follow-up survey scheduled for mid-November. Their goal was to learn how the candidates we had surveyed in August and September felt about politics and campaigns *after* the election was over. The questionnaire they developed was short, so I suggested adding one more item, an open-ended question about the topic of this book. What did state legislative candidates—people who know the nitty-gritty details of how elections work better than anyone—what did *they* think was keeping working-class people out of office? The final version of the question that appeared on the survey read as follows:

People from a variety of backgrounds are less likely to run for office in the United States—for example, women are less likely to run for office than are men. One regular pattern is that people who work in working-class jobs (manual labor jobs, service industry work) are relatively rare

Figure 3.1. What State Legislative Candidates Think

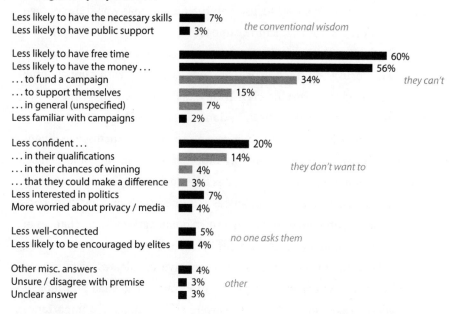

Working-class people are . . .

Less likely to have the necessary skills	7%
Less likely to have public support	3%

the conventional wisdom

Less likely to have free time	60%
Less likely to have the money . . .	56%
. . . to fund a campaign	34%
. . . to support themselves	15%
. . . in general (unspecified)	7%
Less familiar with campaigns	2%

they can't

Less confident . . .	20%
. . . in their qualifications	14%
. . . in their chances of winning	4%
. . . that they could make a difference	3%
Less interested in politics	7%
More worried about privacy / media	4%

they don't want to

Less well-connected	5%
Less likely to be encouraged by elites	4%

no one asks them

Other misc. answers	4%
Unsure / disagree with premise	3%
Unclear answer	3%

other

Source: Broockman et al. 2012.

Note: Bars report the percentages of state legislators (out of 434 who gave answers) who mentioned each type of explanation when asked why they think so few working-class Americans run for political office. The question was open-ended, and candidates could list as many explanations as they wanted. Groups of gray bars are disaggregations of the category immediately above them.

in public office in the United States. Based on your experiences deciding to run for office and in speaking to others, why do you think that is?

Of the 1,907 candidates who completed the pre-election survey, 514 responded to the post-election follow-up survey. Of those, 434 answered the open-ended question about why so few working-class Americans hold office.[1] With the help of a research assistant, I then grouped their responses into about a dozen categories. Figure 3.1 plots what they said.

The question itself primed candidates to think about the reasons so few workers *run* (it began by noting that so few women *run* for office, and it asked respondents to think about their experiences *deciding to run*). Even so, a few candidates gave John Parker–style conventional wisdom explanations that stressed that workers were unqualified or disliked by voters. However, the vast majority focused on the factors that would discourage qualified workers from launching campaigns.

As Figure 3.1 illustrates, by far the most common explanations candidates gave focused on the practical burdens associated with campaigning; many reasoned that working-class people don't have enough time to run (the single most common answer), don't have enough money to fund a campaign, and don't have enough money to support themselves financially while campaigning or holding office. Aside from time and money, the other common hunches candidates offered focused on what we might call *political ambition*; many candidates reasoned that working-class people were less confident, either in their own qualifications, their chances of winning, or their ability to make a difference in government.

As I later found out, these state legislative candidates were mostly right about the importance of practical obstacles like time and money. However—perhaps surprisingly—they were off base about the importance of confidence or ambition. And almost none of the candidates mentioned one of the most important factors keeping working-class Americans from running: they're almost never recruited.

The aim of this chapter is to begin understanding why so few working-class Americans run for political office. Chapter 1 illustrated that workers almost never hold office, and chapter 2 showed that workers almost never govern because they almost never run (*not* because they aren't qualified or because voters prefer affluent candidates). Chapters 3 and 4 answer the obvious follow-up question: If so few workers hold office mainly because so few run, why do so few run? In this chapter, I focus on the individual- or micro-level forces that discourage qualified workers, the personal concerns that weigh more heavily on working-class Americans and ultimately pull them out of the candidate pool at higher rates.

These individual-level concerns are more complicated than they might seem at first glance; my findings in this chapter (and my larger argument in this book) point to a slightly different set of obstacles than what many observers often imagine. As chapter 1 noted, democratic elections demand a lot from candidates and others involved in the race—and the costs aren't just limited to campaign money. Whether an election costs millions of dollars or involves just a few hundred yards signs, the people involved usually have to sacrifice a great deal of time, energy, and other personal resources. This built-in feature of democratic elections naturally screens out qualified workers at higher rates: even in relatively inexpensive races, workers worry far more than white-collar professionals about how running for office could affect their ability to make ends meet and keep up with the basic demands of their lives. The practical burdens associated with elections also drive political and civic leaders to recruit new candidates primarily from among white-collar professionals. These are the individual-level manifestations of what I call America's cash ceiling: in democratic elections, workers often can't afford to run, and elites rarely see them as viable candidates.

This argument differs from what many people—even candidates themselves—often say about the shortage of working-class candidates. In my account, the largely overlooked world of elite recruitment looms large, but often-cited factors like confidence and ambition aren't really part of the story. In my view, time and money are important obstacles, but money means more than just campaign donations; it also means the personal income that people have to forgo while campaigning—a powerful obstacle for the less fortunate that observers often forget when they marvel at the soaring costs of elections themselves.

This argument may be different from what we often hear, but it is squarely in line with widely accepted scholarly theories about political participation and candidate emergence, and it aligns neatly with the available data on qualified citizens, candidates, and civic leaders. In this chapter, I first discuss how candidate emergence works at the individual level, then zoom in one at a time on the three major factors that seem to influence people's decisions about whether to run for office: resources, ambition, and recruitment.

Whereas chapter 2 summarized and expanded on past research on workers' qualifications and electability, this chapter moves into uncharted territory. To my knowledge, there is no prior research on the personal considerations that keep working-class people from running for office. This chapter uses a variety of data sets to test several hypotheses inspired by the scholarship on political participation and candidate entry. This approach has limitations, of course; because the analysis relies on multiple data sets, it can be difficult to precisely compare the relative importance of different explanations on a common scale (although I can generate rough estimates) or analyze the interactions between the different forces under consideration. My goal here is to *begin* to understand the factors that keep qualified workers from running for office, but the analysis in this chapter probably won't close the case for good.

This chapter will also sideline another important consideration, namely, the larger structural or macro-level features of our society, economy, and political process that drive the individual-level differences between workers and professionals. These larger structural forces will be the subject of chapter 4, and so I will mention them only briefly in this chapter.

Finally, much of the evidence in this chapter comes from surveys that tap the views of citizens, candidates, and party leaders. In the next chapter, I will present additional data on what those actors actually *do* in the real world. For now, my goal is simply to understand what goes on in the minds of potential candidates from the working class (and the people who recruit them) that's keeping qualified workers off of our ballots.

To do that, we first need to understand what makes *anyone* run for office in the United States.

WHY WOULD ANYONE RUN?

When someone decides to run for elected office, the first thing they're usually encouraged to do is develop a *campaign plan*, a written document that lays out exactly what the candidate will need to do to succeed in his or her race. A good campaign plan outlines the central points of the candidate's message or platform. It identifies the people who will staff key leadership positions on the candidate's campaign team; these might include a finance director to oversee fundraising, a treasurer to serve as an accountant, a communications director or press secretary to supervise the campaign's interactions with the media, a field director in charge of the campaign's direct contact with voters, a political director to manage relationships with key constituency groups like seniors or college students, a volunteer co-ordinator, a scheduler, a technology manager, an office manager, a legal advisor, and a campaign manager to oversee it all. (Plans for larger campaigns might also include a get-out-the-vote coordinator, a phone bank coordinator, a canvassing director, a research director, a policy director, and a new media director. Plans for smaller campaigns, on the other hand, might drop a few roles.) A good campaign plan also describes the specific objectives a candidate will need to accomplish in order to win: how much money the campaign will need to raise, roughly when and how the campaign will spend it (usually on campaign advertisements or *paid media*), the candidate's plan for attracting media coverage (or *earned media*), and the rough schedule for the campaign's voter and interest group outreach efforts (including how to identify voters, build a base, target and persuade people who are on the fence, and get supporters to the polls on election day). A good campaign plan will also spell out the campaign's organizational structure, the communication technology it will use internally, and the schedule it will adhere to until election day. And—most important—any good plan will calculate the candidate's *win number*, the absolute number of votes the candidate estimates he or she will need to receive on election day in order to have a majority and win the seat.

Putting together a campaign plan isn't rocket science. But it isn't easy by any stretch either. It takes heaps of the two scarcest resources in life: time and energy. And it's only the tip of the iceberg: it's just the *plan* for a campaign that could drag on for months, cost thousands of dollars, and consume every spare moment of a candidate's time.

For most people, doing all this work is basically out of the question. Running for office would be a massively difficult and personally disruptive experience, of roughly the same magnitude as raising newborn triplets, climbing Mount Everest, or building an in-ground swimming pool by hand. For the vast majority of us, fundamentally altering day-to-day life in the ways campaigning requires simply isn't something we're able to do.

The rare people who actually decide to take on the task of campaigning (or any other life-altering project, for that matter) usually only do it *when the time is exactly right*. They do it when they think they can complete the job successfully (no one starts building a swimming pool if they can't afford the concrete). They do it when they feel powerfully motivated to (no one who hates swimming builds a pool). And they do it when important people encourage them to (if the homeowners' association threatens to sue, a pool probably isn't going in). Like any other monumental personal undertaking, people usually only run for office when the conditions are perfect, that is, when they can, they want to, and people encourage them.

Research on *candidate entry* or *emergence*—when, where, and why people run for public office—has historically tended to focus on three aspects of the decision to run. The first (and by far the most extensively studied) is *electoral strategy*. People who are seriously considering campaigning for public office are usually careful about it: they think hard about the benefits associated with holding office, the costs associated with running, and their chances of winning.[2] They give lots of thought to the difficulty of campaigning and the resources they would need, the time and money and energy it would require. They consider the opponent they might face, too: if a popular incumbent is planning to run for re-election, a would-be candidate might look for another office, or just postpone the campaign for a few years (especially if the incumbent is close to being forced out by term limits).[3]

But what makes someone want to be a candidate in the first place? A second line of research has focused on the causes and consequences of *political ambition*, the intrinsic desire to run for public office.[4] Some people want to become politicians; other people don't. And people with a strong drive to govern are far more likely to run (and win, and run again).[5] This *nascent* political ambition—the "embryonic or potential interest in office seeking that precedes the actual decision to enter a specific political contest," in the words of the canonical article on the subject[6]—has been the focus of some of the most important recent work on candidate entry, in particular research on the shortage of women in public office, which seems to be driven largely by ambition gaps.[7] Building on those findings, scholars have recently taken a renewed interest in the root causes of nascent ambition: whether someone generally wants to be a politician appears to reflect whether they feel qualified to hold office and whether they feel cynical about politics and government—which are in turn the results of their experiences with politics throughout their lives, especially in childhood and young adulthood (e.g., whether they discussed politics with their parents when they were growing up).[8]

A third and related line of research has emphasized the importance of *recruitment*. The vast majority of candidates report that they were first encouraged to run and supported in doing so by a local political or civic figure, like a party official, a politician, or an interest group leader. These elite actors can be extremely consequential in the larger candidate entry process: when they encourage someone to run, it can vastly increase that person's chances of doing so. And, likewise, when elites are biased against a candidate (or a whole social group), recruitment can be just as important as strategic considerations and personal ambition.[9]

As others have noted, these three major perspectives on what drives people to run for office—strategy, ambition, and recruitment—are remarkably similar to the three kinds of factors that have been the focus of most academic research on other *routine forms of political participation* like voting, volunteering for campaigns, and following the news about politics. The most widely accepted theory about why people engage in these more ordinary political acts, the Civic Voluntarism Model outlined by Sidney Verba, Kay Lehman Schlozman, and Henry Brady, stresses that Americans participate in politics when they have the resources (the time, the energy, the ability), the motivation, and the encouragement needed to do so. That is, people participate in politics when they can, they want to, and someone asks them.[10]

The similarity between this way of thinking about political participation and the theories developed (mostly independently) in the literature on candidate emergence is striking and probably deserves more attention in and of itself. Indeed, in electoral democracies *it is probably sensible to think about the decision to run for public office as essentially an extreme version of the decision to participate in politics in other ways.* Running for office is extremely difficult—maybe even more so than climbing a mountain or building a swimming pool, and certainly more so than voting or attending a campaign rally. As a result, launching a campaign is far less common than other forms of political participation. However, the decision to run still follows a similar logic. Just as people are more likely to vote or attend a campaign rally when the conditions are favorable, qualified citizens are more likely to run for public office when they have the resources (when the barriers aren't insurmountable; when the expected benefits outweigh the costs), when they want to (when they feel qualified; when they don't think politics is a waste of time), and when someone asks them (when they're encouraged and supported by people who are already established in politics).

If we want to understand why so few qualified workers choose to run for public office, these are our prime suspects. Let's begin with resources.

WORKERS CAN'T RUN

How likely do you think it is that you could take on a full-time volunteer job for the next six months, starting today? The job would involve forty to sixty hours a week of stimulating, highly involved work—but no pay. Of course, you can change your daily routine in any ways that you might need to; you can cut back on your hours at the office or even quit your job, you can ask friends and family to take on more of your personal responsibilities, you can sell your house. Whatever it takes. If you really cared about this volunteer position—if it were a once-in-a-lifetime opportunity to make the world a better place—what are the chances that you could find a way to make it work? Is it even remotely feasible?

Now imagine that you're a single mom with three young daughters. You live in a small apartment, you don't have any savings, nobody you know has any money, and the income you earn working full-time as a hotel housekeeper just barely covers your bills. Are the chances that you could take on a full-time volunteer job for the next six months better or worse?

The practical burdens associated with elections are among the most significant barriers that keep anyone—regardless of their social class—from running for public office. Even talented, qualified people won't run if they don't have enough free time, if they don't have enough money, or if they can't take time off work. They won't run if they can't raise enough campaign donations or recruit enough volunteers. They won't run when there's no chance that their campaign will ever even get off the ground. And they won't run when doing so would destroy their very way of life.

Besides John Parker–style arguments, these practical obstacles are probably the most common factors people cite when they discuss why so few working-class Americans run for political office. They were the most common in the straw poll of state legislative candidates summarized in Figure 3.1. And for good reason. Running for public office is extremely demanding: even at the state and local levels, candidates begin working part- or full-time on their campaigns months and even years in advance. And running for public office is expensive: even candidates for school board are advised to raise $5,000 or more. These barriers may not seem like much to some, but for people who don't have any free time, any spare cash, or any rich friends, they can be insurmountable obstacles.

The resources that are most often singled out as unique obstacles for workers are *time* and *money*. Time is relatively straightforward: even local elections take lots of time, and many people simply don't have enough of it to run a campaign without disrupting their lives in other ways that they aren't willing to. It isn't difficult to imagine how this obstacle might take a disproportionate toll on working-class Americans. If qualified workers are more likely to work multiple jobs, do more of their housework themselves (rather than hiring cleaners and landscapers), do more of their childcare themselves, and so on, qualified workers will tend to have less free time—and will therefore be less able to run for public office.

Money, on the other hand, is more complicated. When people talk about money as a unique burden for workers, they are often referring to two very different obstacles. "Money" sometimes refers to *campaign finances*, the money candidates raise to fund their campaigns' direct expenses. And it sometimes refers to *personal finances*, the money candidates need for themselves to pay their own bills. Both are important practical obstacles in the candidate emergence process: people won't run for office if they don't think they can raise enough campaign money, and they won't run if they don't think they can maintain some basic standard of living for themselves and their families while campaigning. Of course, campaign and personal finances can be one and the same; in many elections, a candidate can legally pay herself a salary from her campaign funds. But when it comes to the basic logic of candidate emergence, campaign finances and personal finances are usually distinct burdens: most candidates at the state and local levels never raise enough campaign money to pay themselves salaries, and even those who do usually have to spend months working on their campaigns without pay before they have enough in their coffers to start cutting themselves checks. For most qualified Americans, fundraising and lost wages are two distinct obstacles to candidate entry.

Like time, both campaign finances and personal finances could be uniquely problematic for qualified working-class Americans. Workers may not have as many rich friends to ask for seed money. Personal finances seem especially daunting: for people living paycheck to paycheck, taking time off work to campaign may simply be impossible.[11]

So which is it? In principle, qualified workers could be discouraged from running at higher rates because they don't have as much free time, because campaign fundraising is more daunting to them, and because they can't take time off work. But what actually happens in practice? Is there any evidence of an individual-level link between the practical burdens inherent in democratic elections and the shortage of candidates from the working class?

Unfortunately, most large-scale political surveys don't ask questions about how people make decisions about running for public office (because so few people do). And past research on potential candidates has tended to focus only on people from white-collar jobs (as chapter 2 noted). However, there are a few sources of data that can be used to study the links between the practical burdens associated with campaigning and the social class gap in who runs.

One is the survey of the general public that my co-investigators and I fielded in 2014. As chapter 2 noted, the survey included several items designed to see how qualified the people who completed the survey were, that is, whether they reported having the personal qualities that voters and party leaders say they look for in an ideal candidate.

The survey also included several items that asked whether respondents had the practical resources necessary to field a political campaign. Figure 3.2 plots the answers given by *high-potential respondents*, that is, people who separately reported[12] that they had at least four of the six qualities that voters and party leaders most want in a candidate: honesty, outgoingness, assertiveness, work ethic, public speaking skills, and party loyalty (unfortunately, the survey didn't include questions that measured two other popular traits, being smart and being understanding, so they are not included here).[13] The sample included 82 high-potential working-class respondents (32 percent of the workers) and 267 high-potential professional respondents (39 percent—a statistically indistinguishable share, consistent with chapter 2's discussion of qualifications; see Figure 2.3). Were concerns about time, campaign finances, and/or personal finances more common among high-potential workers?

When it came to time and personal finances, the answer seemed to be yes. One set of items on the survey asked respondents, "Imagine you were thinking about running for public office in the next few years. What would you be concerned about? (check all that apply)," then listed a variety of options, including "giving up my free time," "the need to raise lots of money," and "giving up my income or job to run for office." Figure 3.2 plots the percentages of high-potential white-collar and high-potential working-class respondents who checked each box. Of the three, income was the concern that most clearly differentiated workers and professionals: workers were

Figure 3.2. Qualified Workers Worry More about Losing Time and Income

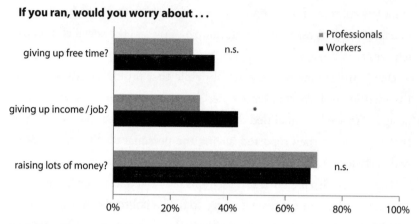

If you ran, would you worry about . . .

Source: Broockman et al. 2014a.

Note: Bars report the percentages of high-potential respondents (those who said that they had at least four of the six qualities that voters and party leaders most want in a candidate; see Figure 2.3) who indicated that each item was a concern. Of the 942 respondents who completed both the occupation and qualifications questions, there were 82 high-potential workers (32 percent of the 255 workers identified in the sample) and 267 high-potential professionals (39 percent of the 687 professionals in the sample). Statistical significance is denoted as follows: *$p < 0.05$, n.s. not significant.

thirteen percentage points more likely than professionals to say that "giving up my income or job to run for office" would deter them from running. Workers were also seven percentage points more likely to say that they would worry about giving up their free time (although that difference was not statistically significant).

Fundraising, on the other hand, was a major obstacle for workers and professionals alike. Around 70 percent of both groups said that concerns about "the need to raise lots of money" would discourage them from running for public office. Observers are right to point to campaign finance as one of the main reasons that qualified workers don't run for political office; it is more daunting to qualified workers than the prospect of losing free time or giving up their income or job. But fundraising does not appear to be *more* daunting to qualified workers than it is to qualified professionals; concerns about fundraising don't seem to help explain why qualified workers are less likely to run than other qualified citizens. Everyone hates fundraising. The concerns that are *unique* to workers seem to be more basic concerns about paying the bills and taking care of things at home. That is, the workers in this sample weren't deterred *at higher rates* than professionals by how much campaign money they might have to raise; they were deterred at higher rates by how much income and time they would have to give up.[14] (And the same basic patterns were evident in follow-up regression models that controlled for the respondent's party, ideology, race, gender, marital status, and whether the respondent had children; in these models, workers were only statistically significantly different when it came to concerns about losing income or a job; see Table A3.1 in the appendix.)

This social class gap in concerns about losing income was especially striking. Although not enormous in absolute terms, the difference between workers and professionals was large in its own right; qualified workers were 44 percent more likely to say that they would worry about losing their incomes and jobs relative to qualified professionals. Perhaps more important, this *income anxiety gap* was large by the standards of research on descriptive representation—and especially research on the shortage of working-class politicians. The gap was larger than any of the differences in qualifications or voter preferences documented in chapter 2. It was comparable in magnitude to the consequential gender gap in political ambition documented by Lawless and Fox.[15] The social class gap in income anxiety documented in Figure 3.2 is the one of the first positive findings *ever* in the larger search for an explanation for the shortage of working-class candidates.

Similar patterns were evident, moreover, in other related items on the 2014 survey. Figure 3.3 plots how high-potential working-class respondents answered a question that asked what they thought would be the most significant obstacles for *other* working-class people. "In races for county and local office in your area," the question asked, "relative to candidates with professional backgrounds, do you think candidates from working-class backgrounds (e.g., factory workers, restaurant servers, receptionists) tend to be more or less . . ." and then listed five attributes: qualified to hold office, easy to convince to run, good at fundraising, good at campaigning, and preferred by voters. (This is the same item used in Figure 2.8; here I have only plotted the percentages who answered "less.")

What was telling about this item was that it essentially asked respondents to imagine different practical obstacles that might keep working-class people out of office. For qualified workers, the question was essentially an exercise in *projection*: it asked, do you think *people like you* have a harder time than professionals with each of these tasks?

Once again, fundraising did not emerge as a *unique* obstacle for workers; only one qualified worker in five thought that workers struggle more than professionals with fundraising. By far, the biggest class-specific weakness qualified workers saw with people like themselves was not that they were worse fundraisers, but that they would be more reluctant: more than 40 percent said that workers would be harder to convince to run for public office. Of course, these qualified workers might have been thinking that other workers would be reluctant to run for reasons beyond the practical obstacles documented in Figure 3.2 (perhaps ambition?). But to the extent that this question betrayed something about qualified workers' *own* concerns about running for public office, it pointed once again to obstacles aside from fundraising itself that would pose unique challenges for qualified workers.

In some respects, of course, these findings should come as no surprise. Scholars have long pointed to inequalities in bread-and-butter personal resources as explanations for social class gaps in political participation. When the 1990 American Citizen Participation Study (the survey that gave rise to the Civic Voluntarism Model) asked people about participating in politics in routine ways, for instance, the kinds of practical obstacles documented in Figure 3.2 surfaced as major explanations for why so few workers participated. Figure 3.4 plots how professional and working-class respondents answered a question that asked them how important the demands associated with "tak[ing] care of myself and my family" were in their decision not to participate in political office. The social class gaps were strikingly similar to the differences documented in Figure 3.2.

Figure 3.3. Qualified Workers Worry More about Entering the Race than Fundraising Itself

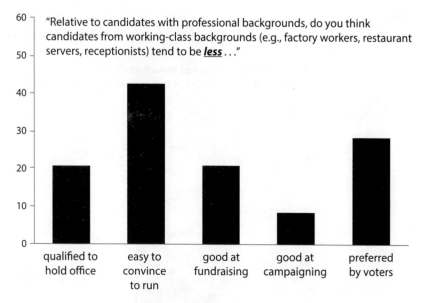

"Relative to candidates with professional backgrounds, do you think candidates from working-class backgrounds (e.g., factory workers, restaurant servers, receptionists) tend to be **_less_** ..."

Source: Broockman et al. 2014a.

Note: Bars report the percentages of the 82 working-class respondents who were identified as high-potential (those who said that they had at least four of the six qualities that voters and party leaders most want in a candidate; see Figure 2.3) who indicated that each item was a concern. The gap between "easy to convince to run" and every other measure in the graph was statistically significant at $p < 0.05$.

Twenty-five percent of white-collar respondents who didn't participate actively in politics said that their own needs and the needs of their family were a big part of the explanation. In contrast, the rate was 40 percent among working-class Americans, about 15 percentage points higher. Elections are costly for everyone involved; one important reason working-class people say they don't engage in politics—either in routine ways like voting and going to rallies or in more extreme ways like running for office—is that they simply can't do so without sacrificing the basic needs of themselves and their families.

Of course, one obvious drawback with surveys like these is that they ask people to explain their own choices or imagine how they might behave

FIGURE 3.4. Needs Were Barriers for Workers in the 1990 Citizen Participation Study, Too

Please tell me if each of these reasons is very important, somewhat important, or not at all important in explaining why you have not (recently) been active in politics and public affairs? . . .

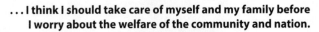

. . . I think I should take care of myself and my family before I worry about the welfare of the community and nation.

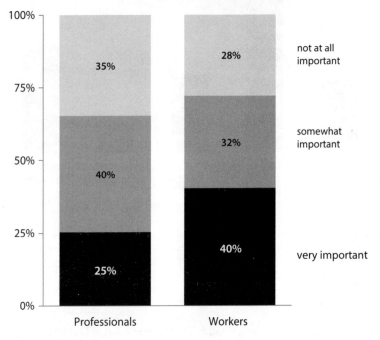

Source: Verba et al. 1990.

in the future. It's always possible, however, that people don't really know what makes themselves tick. If time and money were *really* less concerning to qualified workers, would more of them really run for office?

One way to find out is to compare places where workers earn better relative incomes—where they are less likely to be living paycheck to paycheck—to places where workers take home a smaller piece of the pie. Figure 3.5 plots the relationship between how economically disadvantaged workers are in a state relative to professionals (measured as the gap between the inflation-adjusted total income of people employed as lawyers

FIGURE 3.5. Economically Unequal States Have Fewer Workers in Their Legislatures

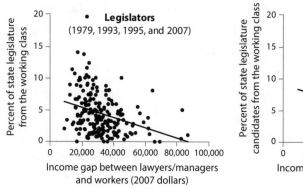
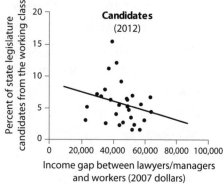

Source: Broockman et al. 2012; Flood et al. 2015; Insurance Information Institute 1979; National Conference of State Legislatures 2015.

Note: Dots represent state averages collected in 1979, 1993, 1995, and 2007 (left panel) and estimated for 2012 (right panel). The best-fit line in the left panel is statistically significant ($p <$ 0.01); the best-fit line in the right panel has roughly the same slope, but with only 29 cases, it is not statistically significant.

or managers and the income of people employed in working-class jobs, from the Census Bureau's Current Population Study) against the percentage of the state's legislature that comes from the working class (from studies conducted by the Insurance Information Institute in 1979 and the National Conference of State Legislatures in 1993, 1995, and 2007) and the percentage of state legislative *candidates* from the working class (estimated using my collaborative 2012 National Candidate Study, and only counting states that had at least one respondent candidate from the working class).

These data are only suggestive, of course—income gaps are only a rough way to approximate gaps in the capacity to take time off work and run for office—but the results in Figure 3.5 are squarely in line with what more qualified working-class respondents said in my 2014 survey.[16] Qualified workers were more likely than professionals to say that concerns about time and lost income would keep them from running. Likewise, in states where the workers earned far less than professionals (further right on the graph)—and where the social class gap in income anxiety was presumably greater—working-class people were, in fact, less likely to run (right panel) and hold office (left panel). The same was also true in regression models (available in Table A3.2 in the appendix) that controlled for standard measures of legislative professionalism (legislative salary, session length, and staff size), whether the state legislature had term limits, the demographic makeup of the state (percent black, urban, and in poverty), and the partisan makeup of the state (the Republican share of the two-party presidential vote). Even after accounting for factors like these, workers were still significantly less likely to serve in the legislature in states where the resource gap (and presumably the resource *anxiety* gap) between workers and professionals was larger.

Of course, with the data in Figure 3.5, it's always possible that the causal arrow could run the other way (having more workers in office could be *why* workers' incomes are higher), or there could be some other factor driving both working-class representation and inequality. But the data in Figure 3.5 are strongly consistent with what qualified workers reported in my 2014 survey—and with the common idea that qualified workers don't run at least in part because they *can't* run. These two data sets represent the only sources of systematic evidence that I know of that capture the extent to which practical resources discourage working-class candidates from running, and they both have the same basic message. There is certainly room for more research on these points, but the available evidence is squarely in line with the idea that the personal burdens associated with campaigning are a part of the explanation for why so few working-class Americans go on to become politicians.

However, the exact nature of the individual-level obstacles that keep workers out seems to be slightly different than what many observers often imagine. The time and money that elections naturally require are uniquely burdensome to qualified workers, but the *kind* of money that discriminates most against the working class is *not* the widely discussed cost of campaigns themselves. Working-class and white-collar candidates alike seem to dread fundraising. The kind of money that screens out workers *at higher rates* is the personal income that people have to forgo while campaigning.

Elections by their very nature take many tolls on candidates. The burdens that seem to drag workers out of the pool of potential candidates faster than professionals have more to do with time and lost income than with campaign fundraising per se.

Concerns about resources seem to be part of the answer to the question of why so few qualified workers run for office. But they don't seem to be the entire answer. Qualified workers were thirteen percentage points more likely to say that lost income would keep them from running, but workers are underrepresented in most political institutions by gaps of forty to fifty percentage points. Something else may be keeping qualified workers out of office.

What about the second major factor that drives political engagement and candidate emergence, *political ambition*? Could that be another individual-level barrier to working-class representation?

WORKERS DON'T WANT TO RUN? NOT SO FAST . . .

In the early 2000s, Jennifer Lawless and Richard Fox turned the political science research on the underrepresentation of women on its head.

In the 1980s and 1990s, scholars had started asking why so few women hold public office. Most of this early research had focused on two factors: the *incumbency advantage* and the *eligibility pool*. (In the terms used in this book, these explanations stressed structural features of the political environment—which chapter 4 will discuss—and qualifications—which chapter 2 explored.) Women weren't holding office in large numbers, researchers thought, because re-election rates were around 90 percent, which meant that opportunities for women to break into politics were few and far between.[17] And even in the late 1990s, women were still badly underrepresented in the high-level white-collar jobs that most politicians come from.[18] In time, scholars thought, women would break through more professional glass ceilings, popular incumbents would retire, women would increasingly nab their seats, and American political institutions would move slowly toward gender equality.

This conventional wisdom among scholars was overlooking something crucial, however. There were many women in high-level professions, but even when political offices opened up, women were still far less likely to run for them than similarly accomplished men. Lawless and Fox argued that scholars were missing an important piece of the puzzle, namely, *political ambition*, an intrinsic desire to seek office. Even those who are well qualified and well resourced won't run if they don't want to be politicians. When Lawless and Fox surveyed men and women working in the kinds of jobs that supply most of our political leaders—law, business, and education—they found that qualified women were less likely to *see themselves* as qualified and were therefore less likely to want to run or hold office.[19] The mainstream view that stressed opportunities and qualifications was ignoring an important reality, namely, that even qualified people with clear windows of opportunity don't volunteer for jobs they don't want.[20]

Today, the discovery of gender gaps in political ambition weighs heavily in the larger literatures on descriptive representation and candidate emergence. When people ask why *any* social group is underrepresented in public office, nascent ambition is usually a prime suspect now.[21] When scholars write about candidate entry (separate from questions about the numerical representation of social groups), the origins and consequences of ambition are once again front and center.

Against this backdrop, it is naturally tempting to blame the shortage of working-class candidates on social class gaps in ambition. Women seldom hold office because of ambition gaps, so why wouldn't we expect the same to be true for workers? We can easily come up with plausible-sounding reasons why workers might exhibit less nascent ambition: maybe they're less likely to find campaigning and governing personally appealing,[22] to see public office as a useful career move (the way a lawyer or a business owner might), to think of government as a way to make the world a better place, or to feel qualified to campaign or govern.[23] Political observers often *think* that workers have an ambition problem; many of the state legislative candidates in Figure 3.1 speculated that workers don't see themselves as qualified to campaign or to hold office—exactly the concerns that Lawless and Fox identified as the root of qualified women's reluctance to see themselves as candidates.

Then again, researchers should always be cautious when applying theories that pertain to women's underrepresentation to other historically underrepresented groups. Gender isn't class (or race, or sexual orientation, and so on). Although the general framework that scholars have used to study the underrepresentation of women—for instance, the Qualified-Run-Succeed Model—can help guide our thinking about the *potential* barriers workers might face, we cannot assume that the *specific* obstacles that keep workers out at any given stage are exactly the same as the obstacles that women or other social groups face.

This is especially true when we talk about political ambition. The gender gap in ambition is the result of powerful socialization processes, that is, how we as a society raise and educate young men and young women in fundamentally different ways.[24] These gendered processes are at work all around us: parents talk to boys and girls differently, teachers treat boys and girls differently, and even retailers steer boys and girls toward different lives. (The toy sections at stores are often divided into pink rows full of Barbies and Bratz and blue rows full of Legos and X-Men.) It is of course possible that there are analogous forces at work that discourage young working-class people from pursuing careers in politics, too. However, I don't know of any evidence on this point—and I certainly don't know of any evidence that would suggest that social class gaps in political socialization are as stark and pointed as the gender gaps in political socialization. Young women in all social classes unfortunately get subtle messages throughout their lives that say that politics is for the boys. Without some evidence of an equally pointed class gap in political socialization, it would be a mistake to simply assume that workers face the same micro-level obstacles that women face.

Indeed, actual data on political ambition tell a very different story.

Unfortunately, we cannot re-analyze the data from Lawless and Fox's well-known studies to test for an ambition gap between workers and professionals analogous to the gender gap that they discovered in the early 2000s. As chapter 2 noted, Lawless and Fox defined qualified people as individuals working in law, business, and education. This approach helped ensure that differences in ambition weren't driven by gender-based differences in professional qualifications, but it also meant that their sample didn't include any working-class respondents. We can't ask whether the workers in their study had less ambition because their study didn't have any workers in it.

Instead, to determine whether there are in fact social class gaps in nascent ambition, I again analyzed the high-potential respondents in my 2014 national survey of the general public, that is, the respondents who reported that they had four or more of the six qualities that voters and party leaders most want in an ideal candidate. Within this more qualified sample, were the workers less likely to express political ambition?

The left panel of Figure 3.6 plots how these high-potential respondents answered two questions that tapped whether they *felt* qualified (the root difference that Lawless and Fox uncovered in their work on the gender gap in ambition). One question asked, "Overall, how qualified do you feel you are to run for public office? (Very qualified, Qualified, Somewhat qualified, Not at all qualified)." Another asked, "Overall, how qualified do you feel you are to do the job of an elected official?"[25]

In general, many high-potential respondents saw themselves as high-potential: overall, 29 percent said they felt qualified or very qualified to run for political office, and 42 percent felt qualified or very qualified to hold office. (In contrast, only 16 percent and 23 percent of people who *did not have* four or more ideal-candidate qualities reported feeling qualified.)

However, the high-potential respondents who felt qualified weren't just the white-collar professionals. The left panel of Figure 3.6 plots the percentages of high-potential professionals and high-potential workers who said that they felt qualified to run for or hold public office. There were only modest differences by social class, the differences were not statistically significant, and they went in both directions: high-potential workers were about two percentage points less likely to feel qualified to hold office, but they were actually four percentage points more likely to feel qualified to run.

These social class differences were miniscule, moreover, compared to the gender gaps in the same measures. The right panel of Figure 3.6 plots

FIGURE 3.6. Qualified Workers Don't *Feel* Less Qualified

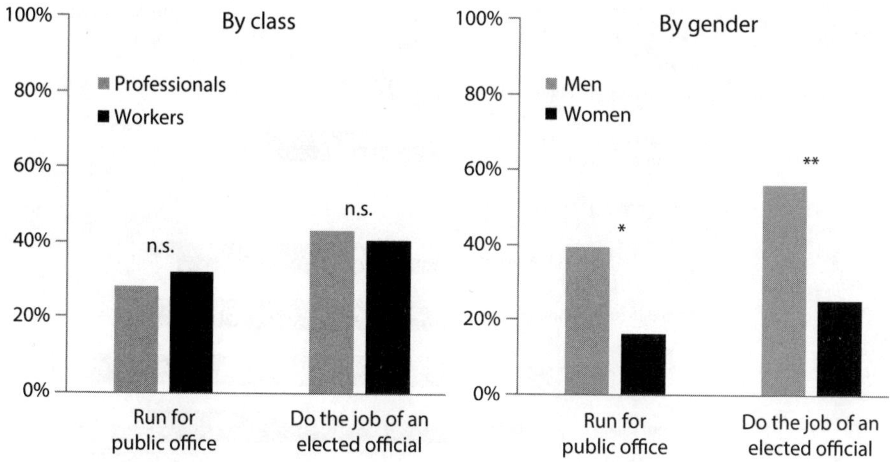

Source: Broockman et al. 2014a.

Note: Bars report the percentages of high-potential respondents (those who said that they had at least four of the six qualities that voters and party leaders most want in a candidate; see Figure 2.3) who reported that they felt qualified or very qualified to run for or hold public office. Of the 942 respondents who completed both the occupation and qualifications questions, there were 82 high-potential workers (32 percent of the 255 workers identified in the sample) and 267 high-potential professionals (39 percent of the 687 professionals in the sample). Statistical significance is denoted as follows: **$p < 0.01$, *$p < 0.05$, n.s. not significant.

responses to the same two questions, this time dividing the same respondents by gender. Just as Lawless and Fox found in the early 2000s, the more qualified women in my 2014 survey were twenty to thirty percentage points less likely to report feeling qualified to run for or hold public office (and these gaps were statistically significant at conventional levels, even in follow-up regression models that controlled for class, race, party, ideology, marital status, and having children; see Table A3.3 in the appendix). Whereas qualified workers were about as likely as professionals to say that they *felt* qualified, qualified women were far less likely than men to realize that they had political potential. There is a real and consequential gender gap in political ambition; there did not seem to be an analogous social class gap, however.

The same was true in analyses of several other questions on the survey that tapped some aspect of nascent political ambition. Figure 3.7 plots

FIGURE 3.7. Qualified Workers Don't Seem Less Interested in Running

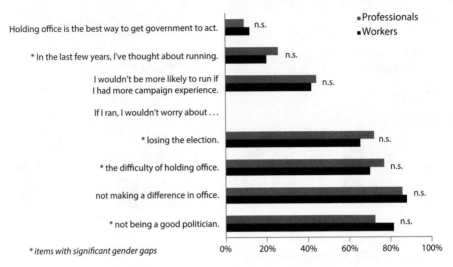

Source: Broockman et al. 2014a.

Note: Bars report the percentages of highly qualified respondents who agreed with each statement. None of the social class gaps documented in this figure were statistically significant (they are all denoted n.s. here). However, there were large and significant *gender gaps* on many of these items; those questions are denoted with asterisks to the left of the category name.

social class gaps in questions related to political efficacy ("Which of the following options do you think is the most effective way for you to get government to address a political issue? . . . Run for office and become a policymaker"), past nascent ambition ("In the last few years, have you ever thought about running for political office?"), concerns about being unqualified ("Would you be more likely to consider running for office if . . . you had more experience working in politics [e.g., on a campaign]?"), and whether respondents were worried about several aspects of running for office ("Imagine you were thinking about running for public office in the next few years. What would you be concerned about? [check all that apply]").

None of these items elicited large or statistically significant social class gaps. Once again, on about half of the measures in Figure 3.7, workers actually expressed higher levels of ambition: they were more likely to say that holding office is the best way to get government to act and that they wouldn't worry about making a difference in office or being a good politician if they ever ran.

Gender gaps (not pictured) again dwarfed social class gaps: on four of the seven items plotted in Figure 3.7, qualified women were significantly less enthusiastic about running. (The figure plots social class gaps, not gender gaps, but I've placed an asterisk to the left of the four items in the figure that elicited statistically significant gender differences.) The qualified women who responded to the survey had significant concerns about running for office: they had thought less about running in the past and they were less confident in their ability to hold office, win the election, and be good politicians. The same kinds of gaps simply weren't evident for working-class respondents: across all seven of the measures in Figure 3.7, there was never a statistically significant difference between qualified workers and qualified professionals. Social class differences in nascent political ambition simply didn't seem all that important.

State-level data tell the same basic story.[26] Figure 3.8 plots the social class makeup of each state's legislature in 1979, 1993, 1995, and 2007 (as in Figure 3.5) against estimates of the share of working-class people who were politically confident. Unfortunately, during the years covered by these data, national public opinion surveys never asked about both what a person does for a living and how interested he is in running for political office. The American National Election Studies, or NES, however, asked a question during that time frame that tapped general *political confidence*, an important precursor to political ambition. The question asked whether respondents agreed or disagreed with this statement: "Sometimes politics and government seem so complicated that a person like me can't really understand what's going on." Using responses to this item, I estimated the percentage of working-class people in each state who disagreed with this statement (pooling three waves of NES surveys for each year of state-level data in order to have large enough samples to generate state-level estimates).[27]

These estimates were only a blunt way to measure social class differences in political ambition, of course (the question wasn't perfect, and the average sample size in each state was only 203). However, the data pointed

FIGURE 3.8. When Workers Are Confident, They Still Don't Hold Office

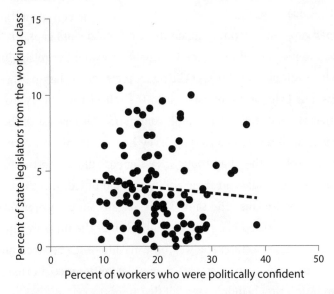

Source: Insurance Information Institute 1979; National Conference of State Legislatures 2015; American National Election Studies 2014.

Note: Dots represent state averages collected in 1979, 1993, 1995, and 2007. The best-fit line is not statistically significant.

to the same basic conclusions as my 2014 survey. There was essentially no association between working-class political confidence and working-class representation in the state legislature. The states where more workers were politically confident had no more workers in their legislatures, on average. Although prior research on gender and officeholding makes it tempting to blame the shortage of workers in office on social class gaps in ambition, my analysis didn't find any concrete evidence that political ambition is an important factor in the shortage of working-class people in American political institutions.

Of course, with more research, scholars might still find evidence of a social class gap in nascent political ambition. But as it stands, that hunch doesn't find much support, even in data sets that allow for apples-to-apples comparisons between social class and gender gaps in nascent ambition. Qualified working-class Americans seem to be about as interested in running for office as qualified white-collar professionals, at least in the ways we can measure. In places where workers are more politically confident, they are no more likely to hold office. Although many observers *think* that a shortage of confidence is to blame for the shortage of working-class candidates, there isn't any evidence to support that hunch. Differences in ambition don't seem to be among the personal considerations that keep qualified workers from running; they are not a part of America's cash ceiling, as far as the available evidence is concerned.

Does that mean that ambition doesn't matter? Of course not! Nascent ambition is a key ingredient in the decision to run for office—people don't run unless they want to—and gender gaps in ambition are crucial in explaining why qualified women so seldom run for political office. But the factors that keep women and workers from running simply aren't the same. The lesson here isn't that ambition is unimportant; it's that ambition isn't a unique barrier for qualified workers the way it is for qualified women. Although scholars studying different inequalities in the makeup of American political institutions can learn a great deal from one another's theories, this section's findings are a useful reminder that different social groups often face different obstacles on the path to political representation. Political ambition in the United States is highly *gendered*, but it isn't divided by class in the same fashion.

For workers, the bigger obstacle is something else that Lawless and Fox uncovered in the early 2000s. And it usually happens behind the curtains of American electoral politics.

WORKERS AREN'T ASKED TO RUN

A few months after Mitt Romney lost the 2012 presidential election to Barack Obama, *Politico* reported that one of Romney's opponents during the primaries—former Pennsylvania senator Rick Santorum—had "ripped" the Romney campaign in an after-hours session at a conservative leadership conference. The complaint? According to Santorum, Romney and the Republican Party should have done more to recruit working-class people into leadership positions.

Santorum illustrated his point with a brief analysis of the speakers at the 2012 Republican National Convention. "One after another," he said, "they talked about the business they had built. But not a single—not a single—factory worker went out there. Not a single janitor, waitress, or person who worked in that company! We didn't care about them. You know what? They built that company, too! And we should have had them on that stage." Santorum even came close to calling for increasing the representation of working-class Americans in public office. "Our leaders don't accurately reflect who we are," he said. "Everyone who is up here is wanting an edge for their company or their industry. We've got to get away from that."[28]

Of course, Santorum's populist appeal was probably part of a larger messaging strategy in preparation for another bid for the presidency in 2016. (And, indeed, just two years later—in May 2015—he launched his campaign.) When Santorum complained that his party didn't do enough to recruit working-class people, he was almost certainly trying to score points with Republican voters and shore up his reputation as a populist outsider.

What was striking about Santorum's remarks wasn't that he praised the working class or criticized the Washington establishment; candidates running as populists do that year in and year out. What was striking was that Santorum took aim at *patterns of elite access and recruitment*. Politicians and party leaders almost never talk about the shortage of politicians from the working class, how little people in politics do to recruit working-class Americans, or how that affects public policy. Santorum was hardly the first self-proclaimed populist to run against the establishment, but in 2013, he became one of the few high-profile candidates to ever publicly discuss how little political elites do to recruit new leaders from the working class.

People who follow politics probably don't pay as much attention to candidate recruitment as they should. *Candidate recruiters*—the people who actively try to influence who runs for public office, who can include party officials, politicians, interest group leaders, activists, and journalists—work for months and years to identify, recruit, train, and groom new candidates. Many are constantly on the lookout for talented newcomers for their *bench* or *pipeline* of emerging candidates. And these elites are powerful. When they encourage someone to run for office, they vastly increase the odds that he or she will do so.[29] True self-starters are somewhat rare, especially at the state and local levels: most candidates run only after local political figures encourage them.[30] Elections narrow the field from a few potential leaders to one winner, but long beforehand, candidate recruiters narrow the field from tens or hundreds of thousands of eligible citizens to the handful of candidates who appear on our ballots.

Even so, elections hog the media spotlight. Campaigns inspire legions of headlines. Media coverage of candidate recruitment is paltry by comparison. Of course, it's easy to understand why journalists and engaged citizens focus more on campaigns. Elections have an immediate impact on politics and government; in contrast, candidate recruitment is a slow, upstream, and uncertain process. Elections are exciting; candidate recruitment occurs mostly in one-on-one conversations and private deliberations. Campaigns have dramatic culminating events; candidate recruitment is a long process that never really stops. It's no mystery why journalists, political observers, and a busy public choose to focus more on campaigns. Candidate recruitment is to an election what the birth of a new generation of foals is to the Kentucky Derby.

That said, people who care about the makeup of our political institutions *should* be paying close attention to candidate recruitment. Political and civic leaders in the United States can powerfully influence who wins on election day by influencing who runs in the first place. Moreover, when civic leaders are *biased* against a particular social group—when they are less likely to encourage or support people from that group, even those who are well qualified—it can have significant consequences for the group's numerical or descriptive representation. People don't often think about recruiting—less than 5 percent of the state legislative candidates in my 2014 straw poll mentioned it as a reason why so few working-class Americans hold office (see Figure 3.1)—but subtle biases in candidate recruitment are often among the most significant factors keeping historically underrepresented groups out of public office.[31]

When Lawless and Fox shook up the research on women's representation over a decade ago, for instance, one of their most important discoveries was that political elites could overcome the gender gap in ambition—*if* they were willing to recruit female candidates.[32] Unfortunately, party leaders and other recruiters often underestimate qualified women, passing them over in favor of equally qualified or even less-qualified male candidates. In a survey of county-level party leaders a few years after Lawless and Fox began publishing their findings, Melody Crowder-Meyer found that these important elites often believed that female candidates didn't stand a chance in their areas—even in counties where female candidates won elections at high rates.[33] Candidate recruitment may not inspire many headlines, but it appears to be one of the main reasons why so few women run for public office.

Of course, as we saw in the last section, not every individual-level barrier to women's representation is also a barrier to working-class representation. In this case, however, it seems more likely that women and workers have something in common. There are strong theoretical reasons to think that political and civic leaders might prefer white-collar candidates—and might not see workers as serious options.

In democratic elections, candidate recruitment can be just as burdensome as campaigning. Like running for office, recruiting new candidates—identifying them, encouraging them, grooming them, and supporting them during their campaigns—takes time, energy, and resources. And like candidates, the political and civic leaders who cultivate new politicians are essentially volunteers; the work they do to support new candidates takes time and resources away from their jobs, their families, and their lives. Of course, like candidates, they care deeply about the outcome of the election. But, like people considering running for political office, their choices are often driven by the practical demands associated with democratic elections.

There are at least two ways that that could disadvantage the working class. One is social. In an effort to make finding new candidates easier, recruiters often look to their own acquaintances and friends for new talent.

And recruiters tend to be affluent and white collar themselves; local political party leaders, for instance, tend to be drawn overwhelmingly from the same kinds of high-income, professional jobs that candidates and politicians come from.[34] If political and civic leaders look to their personal contacts when they recruit new politicians, they will naturally tend to see a pool of white-collar options.

The other is strategic. When recruiters look for new candidates, they focus on people who they think will have the best chances of agreeing to run and successfully enduring the burdens associated with campaigning. In this kind of environment, it's not hard to imagine that they might see workers as less viable.[35] If they think like the state legislative candidates summarized in Figure 3.1, for instance, they might see workers as less able to run, less interested, and therefore worse at the job. In some sense, workers *are* less viable; as we saw earlier in this chapter, qualified workers have a harder time shouldering the burdens that come with campaigning.

The practical demands associated with elections create a built-in bias against qualified workers—and that bias may be amplified by the strategic demands associated with *recruiting candidates* for elections. In a democracy like ours, one important reason so few workers run may be because so few are asked.

If we want to determine whether qualified workers are less likely to be encouraged to run for public office by political elites, we will need to shift our focus from qualified citizens themselves (who we analyzed in the last two sections) to the people who recruit them. Being recruited to run for public office is extremely rare—so much so that even in my 2014 survey of the general public, there weren't enough qualified people who reported having contact with political recruiters (just sixteen respondents in all) to allow us to make meaningful generalizations.

To my knowledge, the only data set in existence that is suitable for determining whether qualified working-class Americans are less likely to be asked to run for public office is another unique survey that I conducted with my collaborators David Broockman, Melody Crowder-Meyer, and Chris Skovron. The survey—which was titled the National Survey of Party Leaders, or NSPL—was essentially a follow-up to Crowder-Meyer's earlier research on county-level political party leaders. In 2013, we worked with research assistants to compile contact information for almost all of the chairs or leaders of the roughly 6,000 county-level (or equivalent)[36] branches of the Republican and Democratic parties. We then sent postcards and pre-survey emails to each party leader, and followed up a week later with a full letter and/or email inviting the chair to complete our survey. (If both a mailing address and an email address were available, we attempted to contact party leaders both ways.) About one in five party leaders responded, and thankfully there were no apparent biases in response rates: Republicans and Democrats responded at almost identical rates (18 and 17.9 percent, respectively), as did men and women (18.2 and 18.5 percent, and 16.5 percent among respondents with unknown genders), leaders in different regions, and leaders in counties where Obama's margin was large, small, or negative. (The complete technical details are described in the appendix, under "Survey Details.") With these data, we can at least get an *indirect* view of the individual-level differences between qualified workers and qualified professionals; if candidate recruiters say they are less likely to encourage qualified workers to run, we can be fairly confident that recruitment gaps are among the personal differences that help explain why so few workers run.

The NSPL, moreover, provides an ideal window into the larger world of candidate recruitment. County-level party leaders are by no means the only political actors who recruit new candidates, of course. But in most federal, state, and local elections, party leaders are important parts of the larger community of interest groups and organizations that recruit and support new candidates. Party organizations at every level of government engage in significant candidate recruitment activities,[37] and they often powerfully influence who ultimately appears on the ballot on election day.[38] Moreover, party leaders are far easier to reliably identify and survey than the many other political and civic leaders who support new candidates. (It can be difficult to know which interest groups are involved in candidate recruitment in a given community, which sitting politicians help identify and recruit candidates, which journalists act as kingmakers, and so on.) And *county-level* political party leaders are more numerous and more willing to participate in surveys than state or federal party officials. Data on county party leaders provide us with a one-of-a-kind look inside the candidate recruitment process—and a rare opportunity to study how recruiters treat qualified workers.

The NSPL included three items designed to capture any biases party leaders might have against potential candidates from the working class and, for the sake of comparison, questions about how leaders recruited or thought about male and female candidates.[39] The first was an item in a series of simple *recall* questions; the question asked, "In the last few elections, what percentage of the following groups would you estimate were employed in working-class jobs (e.g., factory workers, restaurant servers, receptionists) at the time?" then prompted party leaders to think about the share of workers among "The potential candidates your party tried to recruit." (This item was followed by two more that asked about the share of workers among "Your party's candidates for county and local office" and "Your party's current county and local officeholders," so party leaders were almost certainly thinking of candidates for *county and local* office when they answered this recall question.) The survey also asked an analogous question about women: "In the last few elections, what percentage of the [potential candidates your party tried to recruit] would you estimate were women?" Figure 3.9 plots their responses.

When party leaders recruit new candidates, they usually ask people from white-collar jobs. Whereas working-class Americans make up over half of the general public (and close to half of the people who seem to have the qualifications citizens and party leaders say they want; see chapter 2), party leaders reported that workers made up just 28 percent of the candidates they had recently attempted to recruit (29 percent among Republicans and 27 percent among Democrats). And these estimates probably substantially overstate the actual percentages they recruited; if party leaders felt some pressure to seem inclusive—or if they simply misremembered—they may

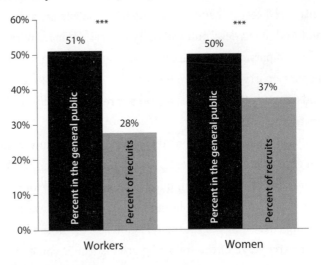

FIGURE 3.9. Party Leaders Say They Don't Recruit as Many Workers

Source: Broockman et al. 2013.

Note: Statistical significance is denoted as follows: ***$p < 0.001$.

have reported recruiting more workers than they really did. (This may well be the case; in a related item on the NSPL, party leaders estimated that workers made up roughly 30 percent of the local candidates who actually ran and won, although as chapter 1 showed, working-class people actually make up less than 10 percent of local officeholders.) Even with these potential *halo effects*, however, party leaders estimated that they recruited far fewer working-class candidates than professionals—the recruitment gap in Figure 3.9 was substantial (close to half the magnitude of the total underrepresentation of workers in most public offices) and comparable in size to the difference between the share of women party leaders recruited and their numbers in the general public. One reason so few working-class people run for political office may simply be that so few are asked: party leaders say they mostly recruit white-collar professionals.

That may in turn be because party leaders don't tend to think of workers as viable candidates. The second set of worker bias questions on the NSPL asked party leaders about their *beliefs* about how well working-class candidates perform on several tasks related to campaigning and governing:

"In races for county and local office in your area, relative to candidates with professional backgrounds, do you think candidates from working-class jobs (e.g., factory workers, restaurant servers, receptionists) tend to be [options: more, the same, less] . . . Qualified to hold office? Easy to convince to run? Preferred by voters? Good at fundraising? Good at campaigning?" Again, the survey also included an analogous question about female versus male candidates ("relative to male candidates, do you think female candidates tend to be . . .").[40]

Figure 3.10 plots the breakdown of responses, comparing how party leaders evaluated workers and women in terms of how qualified they were ("Qualified"), how easy they were to recruit ("Recruitable"), how good they were at fundraising ("Good at fundraising") and campaigning ("Good at campaigning"), and their odds of winning the election ("Electable"). On all five measures, at least a quarter of party leaders reported that they viewed working-class citizens as worse potential candidates than white-collar professionals. These important elites had especially dim views of the ease with which workers could be recruited to run for office—*more than half* reported that workers were harder to recruit than white-collar professionals—and the ease with which workers could raise money—*fully two-thirds* of party leaders believed that working-class candidates would have a harder time fundraising. These negative views about working-class candidates were at least as common as negative views about female candidates (as the bottom panel of Figure 3.10 illustrates). They were also remarkably consistent across parties: Democratic leaders were only slightly less likely to see workers as unqualified (23 percent, compared to 30 percent among Republicans), bad at fundraising (63 percent, compared to 67 percent), and bad at campaigning (28 percent, compared to 33 percent), and Democratic leaders were actually *more* likely to say that workers were hard to recruit (55 percent, compared to 52 percent) and less likely to win elections (33 percent, compared to 29). In the eyes of many political elites on both sides of the aisle, working-class Americans simply aren't viable options.

And these low opinions appear to be remarkably widespread. In follow-up analyses (reported in Table A3.4 in the appendix), I estimated regression

FIGURE 3.10. Party Leaders Have Low Opinions of Working-Class Candidates

Workers . . .

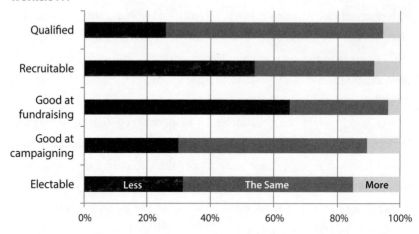

Women . . .

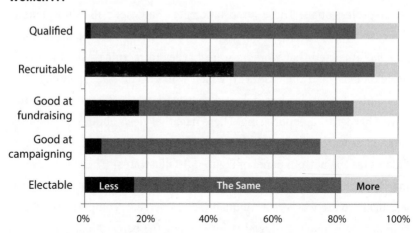

Source: Broockman et al. 2013.

models that related the measures plotted in Figures 3.8 and 3.9 to controls for a leader's party identification, gender, race, income, self-reported political ideology, the cost of elections, the percentage of seats that were "safe" for their party in their area, the party organization's resources (year-round physical office, campaign office, website, constitution, monthly meetings), whether any working-class people served on the party's executive committee, whether the party had a formal candidate recruitment program, and where party leaders reported that they usually recruited candidates (people active in elections, current officeholders, business groups, and so on). I found some evidence that when campaigns were more expensive, party leaders were more likely to report viewing workers as worse fundraisers, that parties that regularly recruited candidates from labor unions or voter lists reported recruiting more working-class candidates, and that party leaders who regularly recruited candidates recommended by donors recruited significantly fewer workers. But by far the most striking finding was that very few features of a party leader's personal background or strategic environment were related to working-class candidate recruitment. Party leaders of all stripes appear not to recruit working-class candidates.

This preference for professionals even showed up on an exercise in the NSPL designed to simulate the actual *process* of candidate recruitment. The item began, "Suppose there is a primary for an open [county board/ state legislative/U.S. House][41] seat in your county and the two individuals below are considering running. We'd like you to consider the following two potential candidates for this office." It then went on to describe "Candidate A" and "Candidate B" by displaying two side-by-side lists of the candidates' personal attributes. Unbeknownst to the party leader completing the survey, each aspect of each candidate's biography was independently generated at random: the survey supplied each candidate's name (randomizing among a set of male and female first names), age (randomizing between 43 and 47), occupation (randomizing among law, business, politics, education, and working-class jobs), experience in the party (randomizing how active the candidate had been in the party organization), life circumstances (randomizing among having free time, being a veteran, having flexible work hours, being independently wealthy, and having two young children), personal characteristics (randomizing among assertiveness, fundraising experience, work ethic, physical attractiveness, public speaking ability, and name recognition), and political ideology (randomizing among being similar to the party's typical voter, somewhat more liberal, somewhat

FIGURE 3.11. Even in Experiments, Party Leaders Exhibit Anti-Worker Preferences

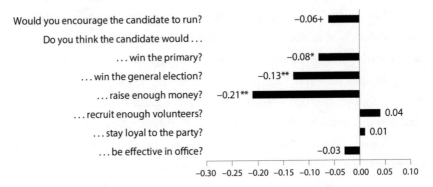

Source: Broockman et al. 2013.

Note: Bars report how much more or less likely (on a 0 to 1 scale) a party leader was to say "yes" to each of the items listed on the left when a hypothetical candidate was randomly described as having a working-class occupation (receptionist, restaurant server, or factory worker) and not a white-collar occupation (attorney, business owner, investor, lawyer, nurse, small business owner, social worker, or teacher). Statistical significance is denoted as follows: $^+p < 0.10$, $^*p < 0.05$, $^{**}p < 0.01$.

more conservative, much more liberal, and much more conservative). This approach allowed me to measure how a wide range of characteristics—including class—affected party leaders' recruitment decisions.

Figure 3.11 plots estimates of the effect of being from the working class on the odds that a potential candidate would be recruited or viewed favorably by party leaders.[42] Like Figures 3.8 and 3.9, the estimates in Figure 3.11 suggested that party leaders prefer white-collar candidates. As the first bar in Figure 3.11 illustrates, a candidate randomly described as a blue-collar worker was six percentage points less likely to be chosen for recruitment. This six-percentage-point penalty was about as large as the penalty associated with having two small children (seven percentage points) and the benefits associated with being a hard worker (five percentage points), a gifted public speaker (five percentage points), and a veteran (ten percentage points).

The main reason party leaders preferred professionals seemed to be an unshakable belief that working-class Americans have a hard time raising money and winning elections. Party leaders were just as likely to say that they believed working-class candidates could recruit volunteers, stay loyal to the party, and serve in office effectively. However, they were vastly less likely to believe that working-class candidates could raise money or win races.[43] And these beliefs persisted even after controlling for whether the candidate was active in the county party, was active in the interest groups that were important to the party, was a frequent campaign volunteer, had a great deal of free time, was assertive, was attractive, was a gifted public speaker, *or was an experienced fundraiser for a local nonprofit*. Even when presented with evidence that a working-class candidate had desirable qualities, many party leaders simply assumed that the worker would be a bad fundraiser and would struggle to win, and passed the worker over in favor of a white-collar alternative.[44]

Across the board, the party leaders who participated in the NSPL exhibited a clear preference for white-collar professionals. Many didn't see workers as viable options, even when presented with evidence that a worker might have the right stuff. Of course, qualified workers more often have serious concerns about making ends meet while they run, as we saw earlier. That point does not seem to be lost on party leaders (and probably isn't lost on the other elites involved in candidate recruitment either). Recruiting new candidates is difficult, and party leaders tend to pass over workers in favor of more familiar white-collar options.

Rick Santorum was right, and not just about the Romney campaign or the GOP. One reason so few workers run for office seems to be that so few are asked: party leaders don't seem to recruit workers or see them as serious options in modern elections.

The phenomenon does not seem to be about ideology either: party leaders on both sides of the aisle report that they don't recruit many workers and that they view workers as less capable. In the experiment summarized in Figure 3.11, Republican and Democratic leaders were remarkably consistent: every effect reported in the figure was in the same direction and had the same approximate magnitude for both parties (e.g., Democrats were 5 percentage points less likely to recruit workers, Republicans were 6 percentage points less likely; Democrats were 13 and 22 percentage points less likely to say that a worker would win and raise enough money, respectively; Republicans were 13 and 18 percentage points less likely). Although it might be tempting to imagine that one party would be a more natural home for working-class candidates based on its ideology or voter base, leaders in both parties seem to have serious reservations about working-class candidates.

Of course, the NSPL focuses not on qualified workers and professionals, but on the people who recruit them, and a particular subset of those people, namely, the leaders of the two major parties. If party leaders say they don't recruit workers, then it is probably safe to conclude that qualified workers would say the same thing (if we surveyed enough of them to make meaningful inferences), not just about party leaders, but about the larger community of organizations and stakeholders who recruit and support new candidates.

One way to test this hunch is to study people who have actually run for office. People who run tend to receive the *most* encouragement, of course. But if qualified workers really are less likely to be recruited, we might still see evidence of those kinds of biases, even among candidates.

Figure 3.12 plots data from the national survey of state legislative candidates that my collaborators and I fielded in August and September 2012 (the precursor to the mid-November follow-up that included the straw poll in Figure 3.1). One of the items on this pre-election survey asked candidates to think back to when they first ran for office and to recall whether they were encouraged to run by any of a long list of different civic leaders.

Even in this highly qualified, heavily recruited group, there were clear social class gaps in elite encouragement. (And even with a small sample of workers—just 52—two of the five gaps documented in Figure 3.12 were statistically significant at the $p < .10$ level.) Among the people running for state legislature, working-class candidates were less likely to report being recruited by local politicians, community leaders, interest groups, candidate training programs, and journalists. And this was true in a survey of people who actually chose to run—the gaps documented in Figure 3.12 would probably be even larger if we had data not just on the people who

FIGURE 3.12. Working-Class Candidates Report Less Encouragement

When you first ran, did any of the following people encourage you?

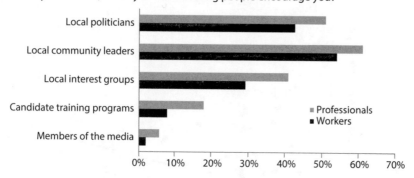

Source: Broockman et al. 2012.

Note: Respondents were candidates for state legislature; 1,736 respondents completed questions about candidate recruitment (52 workers and 1,684 professionals).

ran but also on the qualified workers who *didn't* run. Party leaders say they give less encouragement to working-class citizens, and candidates from the working class say they get less encouragement from political and civic leaders—and that's probably only the tip of the iceberg.

Indeed, aggregate-level data on state legislatures tell a similar story. Figure 3.13 uses data on the percentages of state lawmakers from the working class in 1979, 1993, 1995, and 2007 (the same data used in Figures 3.5 and 3.8), this time plotting how those data relate to rough estimates of the percentage of working-class people in each state who were *politically active and connected*. Every election cycle, the National Election Study asks representative samples of Americans whether they engaged in a large number of activities, like attending political rallies or talking to their friends and neighbors about politics. One question asks respondents whether they worked for a candidate or party during the election. Using these data, I estimated the percentage of working-class people in each state who were working on campaigns—and, presumably, connecting with the kinds of political elites who might one day recruit them to run for office.[45]

The same caveats that applied to Figure 3.8 apply here, of course: these estimates are only an indirect way to measure the concept in question

FIGURE 3.13. When Workers Are Connected to Potential Recruiters, They Hold More Offices

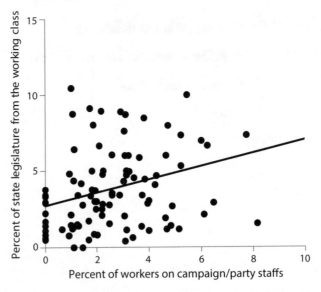

Source: Insurance Information Institute 1979; National Conference of State Legislatures 2015; American National Election Studies 2014.

Note: Dots represent state averages collected in 1979, 1993, 1995, and 2007. The best-fit line is statistically significant at $p < 0.05$.

(contact with candidate recruiters), and pooling multiple waves of NES surveys still yields small sample sizes in each state (just 203 respondents, on average). Even so, the results were squarely in line with the NSPL and the 2012 survey of state legislative candidates. In times and places where working-class people are better integrated into the community of political elites, more working-class people hold office. (And this result holds in more rigorous statistical analyses, too.)[46]

Why do so few working-class Americans run for political office? Evidence from a variety of sources points to the same conclusion. It isn't just that workers don't have the resources—another important reason so few workers run is that so few workers are asked. These outcomes are natural by-products of the basic logic of American elections (as chapter 4 will discuss in more detail); they are the individual-level manifestations of our country's cash ceiling. Working-class Americans rarely hold office in the United States because they rarely run, and they rarely run because often they can't and nobody asks them.

RESOURCES AND RECRUITMENT

In April 2016, long before I ever publicly shared the analysis in this chapter, I received an email from a legislative aide for a city council in the state of Washington. In it, the aide mentioned a qualified worker who had *almost* run for elected office in his city:

> A working-class candidate was initially courted to run for a city council seat in what is perhaps the poorest district in our city. Despite some initial enthusiasm, he ended up receiving little support from the party outside of the obligatory party fundraising email. Movers and shakers in Democratic politics in the city consistently said he was "too unpolished." This may have been true, although what constitutes a sufficiently polished candidate is inherently subjective, but I was struck by how they failed to see the systemic forces keeping him from being able to become more polished: He was trying to raise three children on a little less than $30,000 a year and was working full-time while campaigning. Even reciting a stump speech a few times in a day requires . . . resources that seem hard to come by in that situation, to say nothing of the social connections and money required to run for local office.[47]

What kept this qualified working-class American from running for public office? According to one firsthand account, it was exactly the forces documented in this chapter: resources and recruitment.

Elections are by their very nature burdensome for everyone involved. When people choose not to participate in routine ways like voting or attending campaign rallies, it's often because they can't, they don't want to, or they don't get enough encouragement from others. The same seems to be true for the decision to run for political office: the only people who take on such a significant personal burden are those who can shoulder the practical costs associated with campaigning, those who really want to hold office, and those who are encouraged by important political and civic leaders.

In this deeply personal decision-making process, working-class Americans seem to be uniquely discouraged in two important ways. They are understandably more likely to worry about the practical burdens associated with campaigning; qualified workers are less able to put their jobs and their lives on hold to campaign. And workers are less likely to be encouraged by party leaders and others who recruit new candidates, who often don't believe in workers, especially when it comes to fundraising and winning elections. These differences in resources and recruitment seem to be the main reasons that qualified workers are less likely to run than qualified professionals; there doesn't seem to be an analogous gap in political ambition. The practical burdens associated with elections—not some difference in socialization or attitudes about politics—seem to be what keep working-class Americans from running for office.

These findings are somewhat different from what many political observers think about the shortage of working-class candidates. Many point to the huge sums that candidates raise and spend in modern elections, but there is more to the role of money than just campaign costs. It is actually the *personal* costs—the prospect of taking time off work and losing needed income—that pose unique obstacles for the working class. Many observers think that working-class Americans are less interested in politics, less politically confident, or less ambitious, but workers actually seem just as interested, confident, and ambitious as professionals. And many observers don't think about candidate recruitment as a potential barrier for workers, but candidate recruiters appear to have significant misgivings about working-class Americans. The individual-level manifestations of America's cash ceiling aren't always what people think.

Of course, there are many limitations to the preceding analyses that are worth reiterating here. The research in this chapter is rooted in prior work on political participation and descriptive representation, and the analysis draws on every available source of relevant, systematic data that I know of. Even so, there's still a lot more that could be done. In a 2014 national survey, working-class respondents said that they worry more about practical resources like income and free time, and in state-level data, workers tend to hold more offices in places where they take home a larger share of the economic pie. But, of course, more evidence would always be better; in particular, it would be nice to see what happens when politically qualified working-class people unexpectedly get a boost in resources (for instance, because of a sudden shock to the economy or to their personal finances).

Likewise for recruitment: survey data on party leaders and candidates point clearly to the conclusion that so few workers run because so few workers are asked. But more research would still be better. Randomized studies of real-world recruitment would be helpful; so, too, would surveys with large enough samples to determine whether qualified working-class people report that they aren't recruited as often as their white-collar counterparts.

Ambition—one of the most important factors in the shortage of women in public office—did not appear to be a significant factor in the shortage of workers. In the same national survey and state-level data in which I found consequential resource gaps, I could not find any concrete evidence that ambition gaps are part of the reason why so few working-class people run. Again, though, more research would be better, and future studies could always find evidence of a link between ambition and white-collar government.

Another important gap in the evidence in this chapter is that it is difficult to directly compare the relative importance of resources and recruitment. Chapter 1 noted that working-class people make up 50 percent of the country but 3 to 10 percent of elected officials in most levels and branches of government (and 0 percent in a few offices). How much of that gap can we attribute to differences in resources and in recruitment? This chapter aimed to test the *feasibility* of different hypotheses about why so few workers run, but my analysis cannot put the associations reported here on some common scale. The statistical relationships between working-class candidacy on the one hand and resources or recruitment on the other were large in some absolute sense and seemed generally comparable (Figure 3.9

suggested that party leaders recruit at most 28 percent working-class people, or about 20 percentage points less than their share of the politically qualified population; Figure 3.2 suggested that qualified working-class people are 13 percentage points more likely to say that they would worry about losing income while campaigning and 7 percentage points more likely to worry about losing free time). But we will need more research if we wish to directly compare the relative importance of resources and recruitment—or if we wish to check that resources and recruitment do, in fact, explain the *entire* social class gap in who runs.

We will also need new research to help us understand how resource and recruitment gaps reinforce one another. Research on routine forms of political participation has long recognized that the people who encourage others to get involved in politics engage in *rational prospecting*: they recruit the people who are already the most predisposed to participate.[48] This chapter finds some evidence of analogous behavior on the part of candidate recruiters: party leaders say they worry that workers will be hard to recruit, perhaps because they know that workers don't have the time or money to run. However, the available data don't allow us to go further, to really see how resource gaps drive recruitment gaps, and vice versa.

There is still a great deal more work to do in this area, but as it stands, resources and recruitment seem to be realistic answers to the question of why so few workers run for office. They square with prior theory and with the available empirical data.

Of course, as the legislative aide from Washington noted, these individual-level outcomes are no accident—they are the natural products of "systemic forces," powerful and enduring features of the American political process. If we want to understand why so few workers run for and hold office, we need to understand not just the individual-level effects of America's cash ceiling, but their structural foundations, too.

CHAPTER 3 SUMMARY

Working-class Americans almost never hold office because they almost never run. So why don't they run?

- *When I did an unusual straw poll—of state legislative candidates—they said that the main factors were social class gaps in resources and ambition.*

In general, people tend to run for public office when *they can, they want to,* and *someone asks them.* (People also tend to participate in politics in more routine ways for the same three reasons, as the Civic Voluntarism Model explains.) If we want to understand why so few workers run, these are our prime suspects.

- *Running for office is like building a DIY in-ground swimming pool: people only do it when everything is working in their favor, that is, when they'll be able to pull it off, they want to do the work, and important actors give them the green light.*

One reason workers so seldom run for office is that they can't. Running takes *resources* like time and money. Many qualified working-class Americans simply can't put their jobs and lives on hold to campaign.

- *How likely is it that you could quit your day job and devote all your time to campaigning? How likely would it be if you were working two jobs and barely making ends meet?*

Although it's tempting to think that workers are less likely to want to run for office, I did not find any evidence of social class gaps in *ambition.*

- *Lawless and Fox's groundbreaking research on gender gaps in political ambition loomed large at the start of this study, but I never found evidence of analogous social class gaps in ambition.*

Workers aren't less ambitious, but they're less likely to be *recruited* by political and civic leaders.

- *In 2013, Rick Santorum complained that the GOP wasn't doing enough to recruit working-class leaders. He was right—about both parties.*

The bottom line: Working-class Americans seldom run for office for some of the same reasons that they're less likely to participate in politics in other ways, namely, that often they can't, and no one asks them. These are the individual-level manifestations of America's cash ceiling.

4

WHAT'S STOPPING THEM?

In 2011, a twenty-something bartender named Ruth Ellen Brosseau ran for the Canadian Parliament. Brosseau had never run for office before; after becoming a mother in her teens, she had dropped out of community college and had worked in bars and restaurants ever since. But her party, the New Democratic Party, or NDP, needed *someone* to list as a nominee for what they thought was an unwinnable seat in Quebec. A few party activists happened to drink at the bar where Brosseau worked, and on a whim, one night they asked if she would help. Brosseau agreed, and a few days later she was on the ballot. She didn't bother raising money or campaigning—in fact, she didn't even cancel a planned birthday trip to Las Vegas just before election day. She didn't have the time or resources to run even a minimal campaign, and she didn't have any reason to: she was happy just to serve as a "paper candidate" so that her party could avoid the embarrassment of not fielding anyone in a major race.[1]

But to her surprise—and to the dismay of many in the Canadian political establishment—in 2011, Ruth Ellen Brosseau was elected a Member of Parliament.

In the years leading up to the 2011 election, voters in Quebec had become more and more dissatisfied with their traditional majority party, Bloc Québécois. At the same time, the New Democrats had been steadily attracting support nationwide under the direction of a charismatic new leader named Jack Layton. In 2011, the NDP made stunning gains across the country, most notably in Quebec: the party had previously held just one seat in the province, but in 2011, they won in fifty-eight new districts. Ruth Ellen Brosseau's race happened to be one of them.

Within hours of the polls closing, Brosseau was the center of a firestorm of controversy. Establishment critics sneered at her prior work as a bartender, her lack of a college education, and her teen pregnancy. Members of the opposing party demanded her resignation. The press branded her "Vegas Girl" and "the accidental MP." A *Toronto Sun* headlined declared that her win "debase[d] politicians." Internet message boards were even more vicious. NDP leaders began distancing themselves from their paper candidate. "She was so much of a distraction," the *Globe and Mail* reported, "that some people in the party [simply] wanted to cut her loose."[2]

Of course, the revolt against Brosseau in the days after the election should hardly come as a surprise. People from working-class jobs rarely go on to hold high-level elected offices in Canada. Workers in Canada usually can't afford to shoulder the practical burdens associated with campaigning, and they usually aren't encouraged to run by political and civic leaders.

But in Ruth Ellen Brosseau's rare case, the usual obstacles to public office were removed from her path. She didn't have to take time off work or change her life in significant ways in order to run. She wasn't ignored or discouraged by political elites; in fact, she was actively recruited. For a moment, the gates that normally keep workers out of office in Canada were left unlocked, and a twenty-something bartender walked right through them.

The goal of this chapter is to shed light on the gates that keep workers out of office here in the United States. In the United States, like Canada, working-class citizens almost never go on to hold public office, as chapter 1 noted. In the United States, like Canada, political observers often scoff at the idea of workers going on to govern, and workers seldom run, as chapter 2 illustrated.

But why, exactly, do so few workers try? Chapter 3 showed that individual working-class Americans worry more about making ends meet while campaigning, and that party leaders and other elites tend not to see workers as viable candidates. This chapter takes a step backward in the larger theory and explores the *structural* or *macro-level forces* behind these micro-level outcomes, the enduring features of our political process that make gaps in resources and recruitment such a burden for politically qualified working-class Americans. If we want to know why so few workers go on to hold public office, we need to understand not just the personal considerations that keep workers from running, but also the larger system-level forces behind them. We need to study the gates, not just the people they keep out.

My analysis in this chapter focuses on the two features of elections that seem to be behind the micro-level inequalities documented in chapter 3, namely, the high and rising burdens associated with campaigning and the insular world of candidate recruitment. The practical anxieties that keep individual workers from running appear to stem from the very nature of elections in a representative democracy like ours. And the encouragement gaps that workers experience seem to arise from the basic logic of the candidate recruitment process, the fundamental challenges that lead many recruiters to simply look for new recruits within their own mostly white-collar personal networks.

Of course, there are other structural phenomena that give each of these aspects of our political environment their bite, such as economic inequality, the decline of labor unions, and the inertia of historical path dependence. The practical burdens associated with elections wouldn't matter if workers weren't significantly less well-off than white-collar professionals; insular candidate recruitment practices wouldn't matter if political elites weren't mostly white-collar professionals themselves. My focus here, however, is on the *political institutions* that make these phenomena relevant to the candidate entry process. Costly and uncertain elections and the insular candidate recruitment practices they inspire are the structural foundations of America's cash ceiling—they are the first links in the causal chains that eventually lead qualified workers to stay out of elections.

Studying these macro-level forces doesn't just add to what we know about the shortage of working-class candidates; it also sheds new light on the consequences of some of the most dramatic changes that are occurring in contemporary American politics. Elections are becoming even more demanding. Unions and other organizations that encourage working-class political engagement are declining. These sea changes in the American political landscape could have far-reaching consequences, and scholars and political observers are just beginning to understand their effects. One outcome that needs to be a part of the conversation is how these kinds of changes affect who runs for public office. Studying the gates that keep workers out is all the more important during a historical era when those gates are getting higher and higher.

Once we understand the structural barriers that discourage working-class Americans from running, it is relatively straightforward to devise ways to help workers break through them. Chapter 5 will pick up there.

But before we can discuss reform, we need to focus carefully on structure—because many smart observers don't believe that there *are* structural obstacles discouraging working-class citizens from getting into politics.

IS THE POLITICAL PROCESS REALLY BIASED AGAINST WORKERS?

In 2012, an anonymous reviewer at a top political science journal nicely summarized an argument I sometimes hear privately from other political scientists (but which none of my colleagues has ever publicly written about, as far as I know). The argument says, in a nutshell, that there aren't really any structural barriers keeping working-class Americans out of office:

> Although the author speaks briefly (too briefly, I think) about the reasons it is important to have less economic inequality separating elected officials and their constituents, he/she tends to rely on the rationale underpinning the study of women and people of color's underrepresentation in legislatures as conferring normative importance to the study at hand. Yet the author is really comparing apples to oranges.[3] Part of the reason that women and racial minorities have been the focus of studies pertaining to ambition and candidate emergence is not only because they might bring a different voice to the political process, *but also because overt structural and institutional biases precluded these groups from acquiring power for so long. The "working class" has not suffered in the same way—i.e., an*

ascriptive characteristic did not preclude them from acquiring the backgrounds and credentials that people expect of candidates; race and/or sex did not keep them from entering "pipeline professions"; and public attitudes grounded in centuries of gender and racial stereotypes did not erect a series of barriers that made traversing the campaign trail more difficult and complex. (emphasis added)

According to this view, the things that keep workers out of office simply aren't the kind of structural, societal, institutional barriers that have kept other historically underrepresented social groups out of office. And if there isn't evidence that working-class people have been kept out of office by structural forces, the argument goes, then scholars and activists don't have as much of a normative or moral case for paying attention to the underrepresentation of the working class.

Intellectually, this argument is quite different from the John Parker-style line of reasoning outlined in chapter 2. Whereas Parker-style arguments discourage us from studying the underrepresentation of workers on the grounds that workers aren't qualified and voters rightly prefer affluent politicians, this *antistructural argument* discourages research in this area on the simple grounds that there *is nothing structural or institutional in our political process that stops workers from holding office.* Parker-style arguments make the bold claim that workers are unfit to lead; antistructural arguments simply question whether there really are structural obstacles keeping workers out of office.

Like the Parker-style theory, this antistructural theory deserves careful consideration. Of course, some of the particular claims in the quotation above are at odds with evidence that has already been presented in this book. Chapter 2 showed, for instance, that the average worker isn't much less qualified to hold office than the average white-collar professional, and that voters don't consider professional credentials a prerequisite for holding office. The evidence in chapter 3, moreover, *hints at* structural forces that could be keeping workers out—workers seldom run because they say they lack the resources and they aren't encouraged.

But that isn't the same as direct evidence linking enduring aspects of how our society and government are organized to the low numbers of politicians from the working class—and we shouldn't dismiss the antistructural perspective without that kind of evidence. If there really are structural or institutional biases keeping workers out of office, we should be able to see those biases in action.

Scholars who study other historically underrepresented groups have long sought to do exactly that. After Lawless and Fox discovered gender gaps in nascent ambition, for instance, they went on to study the structural origins of those gaps, the features of our society that lead women to be treated differently throughout their lives, to have fewer encouraging socializing experiences, less political encouragement from their parents, fewer political discussions with friends, and so on.[4]

These kinds of early life experiences probably aren't behind the shortage of workers in public office—as chapter 3 showed, qualified workers don't seem to be less ambitious than qualified professionals—but the general research strategy seems to be exactly what we need here. After scholars identify the attitudes and behaviors that keep qualified members of a given social group from running for public office, the next logical step is to test hypotheses about where those individual-level attitudes and behaviors come from.

If there is a single structural feature of our political process that might explain why resources and recruitment are such important barriers for qualified working-class Americans, it is that *elections in the United States are—by their very nature—costly, uncertain, and consequential for everyone involved.* As chapter 3 noted, running for office takes a lot from candidates—it takes time and resources—and the outcome is never a sure thing. But candidates aren't alone: elections are costly and uncertain for everyone. It takes voters time and resources to follow campaigns, research candidates, and show up at the polls. It takes volunteers and campaign workers time and resources to strategize, advertise, survey, and canvass. It takes political elites time and resources to identify, recruit, train, and support new candidates. And everyone involved faces tremendous uncertainty: voters, volunteers, and elites can never be sure which candidates will win or whether the winners will keep their promises.

Against this backdrop, it would actually be more surprising if there *weren't* "a series of barriers that made traversing the campaign trail more difficult and complex" for potential candidates from the working class. In costly and uncertain elections, practical resources like time and money are essentially de facto prerequisites to candidate entry. There is no law that says that working-class people can't be politicians, but selecting leaders via competitive elections creates practical obstacles that could easily discourage people with fewer resources from running. In democratic elections, any social group that has less money, less flexible schedules, fewer well-resourced friends, and less of an appetite for risky endeavors should naturally be disadvantaged in the candidate entry process.[5]

Selecting politicians via elections also creates significant burdens for party leaders and other elite actors, burdens that could easily encourage them to recruit in an insular fashion that excludes working-class people. Finding and enlisting a new bench of candidates takes time and energy. Candidate recruiters can never know in advance how likely a potential candidate is to run, how much effort it will take to get her to throw her hat into the ring, how much support she will require on the campaign trail, whether she will win, and what she will do in office once elected. Working-class candidates, moreover, face real personal obstacles that other candidates do not. And most people who recruit new candidates are themselves white-collar professionals. In this kind of environment, why wouldn't we expect elite recruiters to routinely pass over qualified workers?

The very logic of how elections work would seem to raise serious doubts about the antistructural theory that working-class Americans have not faced "structural and institutional biases [that] precluded [them] from acquiring power." Actual data on how elections work raise even more.

OUR COSTLY ELECTIONS

If there were a poster child for working-class politicians, it would probably be Representative Edward P. Beard. Beard was a house painter in

Providence with only a high school diploma when he ran for the Rhode Island state legislature in 1972. He won the race, then served for two years while continuing to work as a painter, occasionally missing last-minute floor votes because he couldn't leave his job site fast enough to get to the statehouse. In 1974, Beard ran for Congress with only $12,000 in campaign funds and stunned the Rhode Island political establishment by winning the race (after spending months personally canvassing in downtown Providence for hours every night after work). He went on to serve in Congress for three terms, during which he chaired the House Subcommittee on Labor Standards, founded the first congressional caucus for members from working-class occupations (which enlisted thirteen legislators in its heyday), and routinely gave out commemorative paintbrushes to other politicians to remind them to consider the needs of working-class Americans. Even Beard's departure from Congress was emblematic of his working-class roots: he lost his 1980 bid for re-election to a Chamber of Commerce–backed rival, and when Beard left Congress, his Blue-Collar Caucus was disbanded.

For Edward Beard, getting to Congress was extremely challenging: he reportedly wore out six pairs of shoes walking door-to-door during his first bid for the House of Representatives. And according to Beard, his story would be impossible today. In an interview in 2010, Beard put it bluntly: "I won for $12,000. That simply can't be done now."[6] Running for state or federal office was almost impossible for a house painter in the 1970s. Since then, the barriers to entry have only become harder to surmount: spending on campaigns has soared in the last four decades, and the time and energy needed to field a modern campaign have followed suit. According to the poster child for working-class politicians—the only person in history to quit a house-painting job in order to serve in the U.S. Congress—the personal burdens that naturally accompany democratic elections are the single most powerful obstacles keeping working-class Americans out of office—and they're only getting worse.

As chapter 3 showed, qualified working-class Americans are uniquely deterred from running for public office by the basic practical burdens associated with campaigning. Compared to qualified professionals, qualified workers are more likely to say that the free time they would lose and the work time and income they would have to give up would keep them from running for public office. And they seem to be telling the truth: in states where the income gap between workers and professionals is smaller, more workers really do go on to hold office. (See the section "Workers Can't Run" in chapter 3.)

But why, exactly, do elections screen out people without resources? What specifically about running for office creates the practical anxieties that pull working-class people out of the candidate pipeline at higher rates?

The answer matters here. For one, reformers can't know how to address America's cash ceiling unless they understand exactly how it operates. (More on that in the next chapter.) Moreover, some political observers question whether there are any structural barriers preventing working-class people from running. If we want to know whether this perspective has any merit, we need to be clear about exactly what makes running for office so burdensome, *because only then can we know where to look for empirical evidence one way or another.* And studying structural barriers is difficult; by definition, they don't vary much. When it comes to an alleged structural barrier like the inherent burdens associated with democratic elections, we can only really see the barrier's effects by studying *marginal* differences. That is, we can't see what happens when democratic elections are easy (they almost never are); we can only study differences between elections that are personally burdensome and elections that are *extremely* personally burdensome. In order to do even that, however, we need to know exactly what makes an election practically burdensome in the first place.

As I see it, the most likely suspects are the *size of the electorate* and the *scope of the campaign activities* candidates engage in. Elections are personally burdensome to candidates because they require them to appeal to huge numbers of people, far more than they would ever normally interact with in their everyday lives. The average American personally knows about six hundred people[7]—the average city council member, in contrast, represents more than five times that many. And the more potential voters there are to turn out, the more time and energy candidates have to expend. (If Edward

Beard had been campaigning for a city council seat in 1974 instead of a U.S. House seat, he would have had to appeal to a few thousand people rather than a few hundred thousand.)

The things candidates do to turn out those voters on election day are in turn what take time and energy in the first place. And as the scope of those activities grows—as campaigns require more and more volunteers, staff, advertisements, fundraising, and so on—the personal burdens that candidates face grow, too. (If Edward Beard had been running for the same U.S. House seat in today's more time- and money-intensive campaign environment, he wouldn't have been able to shoulder the practical burdens.)

If the practical burdens associated with running for office really are the structural origins of the personal concerns that keep workers from running for public office, we should be able to see some evidence that more workers run and hold office in political jurisdictions where the electorate is smaller and where campaigns are smaller in scope. Of course, the differences we observe will only be differences *on the margin*; virtually all elections require some time and energy, and that's probably enough to discourage many resource-strapped people from getting involved.[8] That is, we rarely observe cases like Ruth Ellen Brosseau's in which a candidate can campaign for a public office without making *any* personal sacrifices. But if it's really the case that the practical burdens associated with campaigning keep qualified workers from running, there should be differences in working-class representation between places where electorates are larger and smaller or where campaigns are more and less involved—differences that give us at least a partial view of the structural barriers keeping working-class people out of office.

This book has actually already presented some evidence that supports this line of reasoning. Chapter 1 showed that workers are more likely to hold office in lower levels of government (e.g., Figure 1.1), where electorates are smaller, campaigns are less involved, and the burdens associated with running are therefore lower. In the rare public offices for which we have over-time data on politicians' occupations (Congress and, to a lesser extent, state legislatures), moreover, workers have tended to hold *slightly* fewer seats as the scope of congressional and state legislative campaigns has steadily risen over the last few decades (e.g., Figure 1.2).

But even within a single level of government or a given point in time, workers appear to be less likely to hold office in places where elections are more burdensome.

There are a few data sets on U.S. politics that are suitable for studying the relationship between the size of electorates and the scopes of campaigns in a given area and the share of workers who run or go on to hold office. At the city level, Trounstine has compiled data on government and finances that combine information from four waves of Municipal Form of Government surveys (the only available source of systematic data on the occupational backgrounds of city officials) with city finance data from the U.S. Census Bureau's Census of Governments and data on other city characteristics from the decennial Census (see also Figure 2.6).[9] At the state level, the Insurance Information Institute compiled aggregate-level occupational data on state legislatures in 1979, and the National Conference of State Legislatures followed up in 1993, 1995, and 2007 (see also Figures 3.5, 3.8, and 3.13). At the federal level, we have data on legislators' occupational backgrounds from the Roster of U.S. Congressional Officeholders (1789–1997) and the Congressional Leadership and Social Status data set (1999–2008). And the 2012 Cooperative Congressional Election Study, or CCES—a large-scale nationally representative survey—includes information about the occupational backgrounds of ordinary citizens and whether they have ever run for public office at any level of government.

All of these data sets—data on city councils, state legislatures, and even the U.S. Congress—point clearly to the same conclusion, namely, that marginal differences in the burdens associated with elections are indeed associated with marginal differences in the share of working-class people who run or hold office.

Figure 4.1 analyzes Trounstine's data on government and finances in American cities. I focus here on data from 1996 and 2001, the two years

FIGURE 4.1. Workers Hold Fewer Offices in Cities with More Burden-some Elections

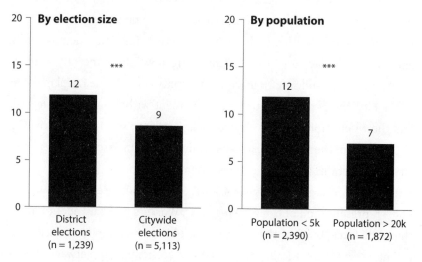

Source: Trounstine and Valdini 2008.

Note: Bars represent the average percentage of working-class people in city councils in 1996 and 2001. Statistical significance is denoted as follows: ***$p < 0.001$.

when the Form of Government survey asked respondents (city clerks) to record the number of city council members who fell into each of eleven occupational categories.[10] These data don't directly tap *the scope of city council campaigns*, unfortunately, but they include two good measures of *the size of city electorates*.

The first panel in Figure 4.1 plots the average percentage of city council members from the working class, dividing the sample of cities by one marker of the size of the electorate, namely, whether city council members represent specific districts or the entire city (since campaigning tends to be more burdensome in places where a candidate must attract the votes of the entire city, not just a slice of it).[11] The second panel divides the cities by the population of the city, an even more direct measure of the size of the electorate (and therefore how burdensome campaigning is).

Both measures predict significant differences in the share of workers on the city council. Workers were five percentage points more likely to hold office in small towns (populations under 5,000) than in bigger ones (populations over 20,000) and three percentage points more likely to hold office in cities with smaller district-wide elections relative to those with bigger citywide elections. Both associations were negative but smaller in regression models with a wide range of controls for cities' demographic and institutional characteristics (including how often the city council meets, the racial and gender makeup of the city council, the racial makeup of the city, the percent in poverty, the percent without a college degree, and the re-election rate for city council members; see Table A4.1 in the appendix), but there was still a statistically significant association between citywide elections and working-class representation.

Of course, the gaps in Figure 4.1 were small compared to the overall underrepresentation of the working class. Workers make up about half of the labor force, but less than 10 percent of the average city council. The estimates in Figure 4.1 suggested that the economic gap between politicians and citizens was smaller in cities where campaigning is easier, but only by a few percentage points. It is important to keep in mind, however, that what we are seeing in Figure 4.1 is not the *total effect* of elections on working-class representation, but only the marginal difference between somewhat more and less burdensome electoral environments.[12]

The same marginal differences appear in data on the fifty states. Figure 4.2 plots aggregate-level data from the National Conference of State Legislatures on the percentage of members in each state's legislature in 2007 who worked primarily in working-class jobs, this time dividing states by the population size in a typical state legislative seat and the amount of money candidates spend in a typical race, a measure of the scope of campaigns that was not available at the city level (and that was only available at the state level for one of the years for which we have legislator occupation data, 2007). Of course, as chapter 3 noted, the high cost of elections is just as much of a general deterrent to qualified professionals as it is to qualified workers. When comparing elections across different jurisdictions, however, higher costs provide a useful signal of places where campaigns require more of the kinds of personal sacrifices that *do* keep workers from running. That is, if campaigns that cost more are also campaigns that are

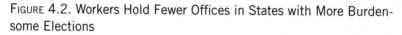

FIGURE 4.2. Workers Hold Fewer Offices in States with More Burdensome Elections

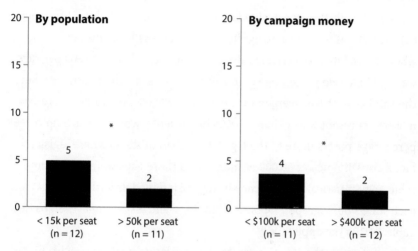

Source: Insurance Information Institute 1979; National Conference of State Legislatures 2015; Carnes and Hansen 2016.

Note: Bars represent the average percentage of working-class people in state legislatures in 2007. Statistical significance is denoted as follows: *$p < 0.05$.

more time-consuming, the amount that candidates raise and spend in a given election can still be a useful indicator of how burdensome the race is.

Indeed, whether measured as campaign costs or population size, the burdens associated with campaigning for a given state's legislature were associated with significant differences in the shares of workers who went on to hold office. The personal costs that come with state-level races are of course far greater than the costs associated with city races. As a result, fewer workers hold state office overall (all of the bars in Figure 4.2 are smaller than the bars in Figure 4.1), and there is less variation in the percentage of workers in state legislatures. That is, the gaps in Figure 4.2 would probably be even larger if we could single out states where legislative elections were even cheaper ($100,000 per seat is a high cutoff) and where districts were even smaller, but there simply aren't many American states like that in our recent history. When it comes to the links between the high cost of entry in American elections and the number of workers who hold office, what we see in Figure 4.2 is probably only the tip of the iceberg.

And even in this constrained setting, there are still clear differences between states where campaigning is more or less burdensome. In states where candidates collectively raise and spend less than $100,000 per race, workers hold two percentage points more of the seats than in states where the total cost of the average race exceeds $400,000. In states where lawmakers represent fewer than 15,000 constituents, workers make up three percentage points more of the legislature than in states where legislators face a constituency of 50,000 or more. (And these gaps were again comparable and statistically significant in regression models with controls[13] for each state's demographics, political leanings, and institutional designs; see Table A4.2 in the appendix.)[14]

Even data on the U.S. Congress—the legislative institution with by far the highest resource-related barriers to entry—tell a similar story. Figure 4.3 plots data from the Roster of U.S. Congressional Officeholders database (which includes all members who served before 1996; left panel) and the Congressional Leadership and Social Status data set (which covers the members who held office from 1999 to 2008; right panel). Although it is essentially impossible to know how many workers would hold office if congressional campaigns were small in scope (they never are), even comparing *huge* campaigns—those where candidates spend a total of up to $600,000—to *extremely huge* campaigns—those where candidates spend more than $2.5 million—reveals statistically significant differences in the (already miniscule) odds that a working-class person will hold office.

Perhaps most importantly, these patterns in who *wins* are exactly mirrored in data on who *runs*. Figure 4.4 plots data from the 2012 Cooperative Congressional Election Study, the only large-scale national survey that has recently asked representative samples of Americans both their occupations and whether they have ever run for office. (Unfortunately, my own 2014 national survey did not have enough cases in each state to conduct the kind of analysis reported here.) Using these data, I computed the average percentage of working-class respondents in each state who reported

Figure 4.3. Workers Hold Fewer Seats in More Expensive Congressional Districts

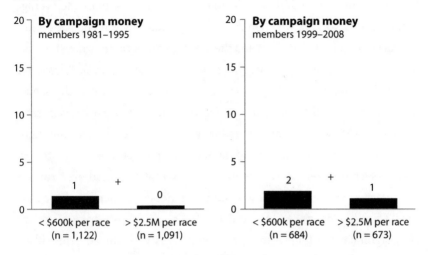

Source: Bonica 2013; Carnes 2011; ICPSR and McKibbin 1997.

Note: Bars report the average percentage of legislators employed in working-class jobs when they entered politics (left panel) and the average percentage of legislators' pre-congressional careers spent in working-class jobs (right panel). Statistical significance is denoted as follows: ⁺p < 0.10.

Figure 4.4. Workers Run Less Often in States with More Expensive Politics

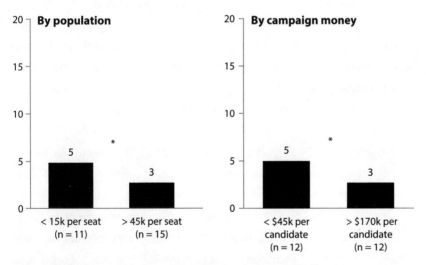

Source: Ansolabehere and Schaffner 2013; Bonica 2013; author's data collection.

Note: Bars represent the average percentage of working-class respondents in the CCES who reported that they had ever run for elected office. Statistical significance is denoted as follows: *p < 0.05.

that they had ever run for any elected office. Figure 4.4 plots the average percentage of workers who had run, dividing states by the population in a typical state legislative district and the average cost of campaigning for state legislature (from Adam Bonica's *Database on Ideology, Money in Politics, and Elections*), again, reasonable proxies for the sizes of electorates, the scopes of campaigns, and therefore how burdensome elections are in a given state.

Again, in states with more personally costly electoral environments—more campaign money per candidate, bigger populations per state legislative seat—workers were less likely to say that they had ever run for public office at any level. These results were less statistically robust than the findings in Figures 4.1, 4.2, and 4.3—the associations were not statistically significant in follow-up regression models with the controls (likely because with data from just a single year, I had only fifty state-level observations; and unfortunately other waves of the publicly available portion of the CCES do not include occupational data). Overall, however, the findings were squarely in line with what workers report in other surveys and with what we see in data on who actually holds city, state, and national offices. In places where campaigning is more of a burden, working-class Americans are less likely to run for and hold office. The gaps are never large—we aren't observing elections that are *easy* in some practical sense, just elections that are a little less hard. But this marginal variation illustrates the larger structural barrier keeping workers out of office. Elections are inherently personally costly—the very way that we select leaders seems to be behind the shortage of candidates from the working class.

Congressman Beard's conjecture appears to be right: it seems to be extremely hard for working-class Americans to hold office, even when elections are relatively cheap. And when they are more expensive, even fewer workers run and win, consistent with what workers say in surveys. In sharp contrast to the antistructural theory—the idea that workers don't face any systematic barriers to inclusion in our political institutions—it seems that many qualified working-class Americans are essentially kept out of the political institutions that are supposed to represent them.

Beyond the question of why so few workers run for public office, this aspect of our electoral process also has important implications for people who care about the soaring cost of elections in the United States. In the 1970s and 1980s, the price tags associated with campaigns began rising: in 1974, the typical candidate for the U.S. House spent around $250,000 (adjusted to present-day values), but by 1984 that figure had more than doubled to around $635,000, and by 1996 the average House campaign was a million-dollar affair.[15] As campaign spending (and therefore campaign donations) climbed higher and higher, institutional critics increasingly sounded alarms. A first wave of research in the 1980s looked for evidence that wealthy donors and political action committees (PACs) were buying the loyalty of elected officials; thankfully, this early work didn't find evidence of quid pro quo deals.[16] Unfortunately, a second wave of research on more subtle forms of influence has found copious evidence that money talks in American politics: Hall and Wayman found that PAC contributions couldn't buy votes, but they could buy time and attention from sympathetic legislators, especially during the early stages of the legislative process, when bills were being crafted and shepherded through committees. Hacker and Pierson showed that wealthy Americans could sway elite opinion by funding organized groups and think tanks like the Chamber of Commerce, the National Federation of Independent Businesses, the Club for Growth, and the Heritage Foundation. Broockman and Kalla showed that campaign donors could get meetings with politicians far more easily than nondonors could. Powell and Grimmer showed that business PACs stop funding legislators who are removed from important committees. Skocpol and Hertel-Fernandez showed that wealthy donors organized full-blown consortia to amplify their influence on elections, candidates, and even entire political parties.[17] Today, many political scientists still reflexively recite the first-wave mantra about how there isn't strong evidence that money matters in politics, but at this point, that mantra is badly out of date: the second wave of money and politics research has clearly illustrated that the high cost of elections gives people and groups with money oversized influence in the American political process, albeit in ways that are more complex than the simple act of buying law-makers' votes.

One potential consequence of the soaring costs of campaigns hasn't received much attention yet, however, namely, how rising campaign costs affect *the practical burdens associated with running for public office* and, consequently, the economic makeup of candidates and politicians themselves.[18] Second-wave research on money and political influence has overwhelmingly focused on how the high cost of elections empowers the rich to influence government from the outside through lobbyists, interests groups, and donations. But expensive elections also change the basic experience of campaigning in ways that seem to empower the rich to influence government from the *inside*. As Congressman Beard noted about his own unlikely path from house painter to the U.S. House: "That simply can't be done now." Expensive elections are burdensome elections, and as this section has shown, burdensome elections are elections that produce white-collar candidates and white-collar governments.

And the practical burdens associated with costly and uncertain elections aren't the only structural barriers that qualified workers face.

THE CANDIDATE RECRUITMENT INDUSTRY

In April 2015, I organized a program at Duke University for people in the area who were interested in running for political office. (It was the precursor to the November 2015 candidate training described in chapter 2.) The April program attracted fifty brave souls willing to spend 8:00 a.m. to 3:00 p.m. on a Saturday learning how to launch a career in elected political office.

But those fifty people weren't a random cross-section of the politically qualified citizens in the Durham area. To the contrary, like most potential candidates, they were handpicked by local political elites.

A few weeks before the April training, I emailed forty-two local organizations. The organizations included the state-level branches of the Republican, Democratic, and Libertarian parties; the county-level branches of those three parties in four adjacent counties (Durham, Chatham, Orange, and Wake); and twenty-seven local nonprofit or advocacy organizations (twelve right-leaning organizations, like the North Carolina Chamber of Commerce, and fifteen left-leaning organizations, like the North Carolina Sierra Club). The subject of my email read, "free 'Ready to Run' campaign workshop at Duke on April 11th," and the email briefly described the program, then asked the recipient if he or she could recommend anyone:

> Would you like to nominate someone you know? We'll be accepting recommendations until next Wednesday, March 25th. To nominate up to five people, please just reply to this email with the nominee's name, email address (if you have it), phone number (if you have it), and what they do for a living (if you know).

In half of the emails, chosen at random, I then added another line, embellished with asterisks:

> ***We're especially interested in identifying people in manual labor and service industry jobs who might be interested in this opportunity.***

The email was, in part, an experiment to see if a small nudge could be enough to get political and civic leaders to recruit more working-class people to political office.

It wasn't—not by a long shot. Not only did the recipients of the worker-focused treatment email *not* suggest more workers, but *neither version of the email elicited a single working-class suggestion* for the free candidate training program. My forty-two recipients collectively provided twelve names, seven from the control group, five from the treatment group, all of them white-collar professionals.

I eventually received several working-class recommendations from one of the directors of the North Carolina AFL-CIO (who had helped me design the candidate training program), and I recruited several more workers through my own personal network. But my simple experiment underscored an important fact of life about the *candidate recruitment industry*. The important elites who regularly identify, recruit, and support new candidates for public office almost never reach out to working-class people when they need to find someone to run for public office. And that bias isn't something that can be overcome with a simple nudge—it's the result of the basic logic of how candidate recruitment works.

As chapter 3 showed, workers are less likely to be encouraged to run for office. Party leaders say they seldom recruit working-class Americans to run for office, and the rare workers who run report receiving far less encouragement from elite actors. (See the section "Workers Aren't Asked to Run" in chapter 3.)

But why? What is it exactly about the candidate recruitment process that keeps politicians, party leaders, interest groups, and journalists from encouraging qualified working-class Americans to run for office?

As in the previous section, the answer matters here. Antistructural theories claim that workers don't face any institutional or societal barriers to full inclusion in American political institutions—if those barriers are really out there, scholars need to present concrete evidence. From a reform standpoint, moreover, the reasons *why* elites are less likely to recruit workers are just as important as the basic fact that they seldom recruit workers. Activists can't solve a problem unless they understand what causes it.

From a scholarly standpoint, moreover, the question represents an important scientific opportunity. Political scientists know that most candidates decide to run only after being strongly encouraged by political leaders,[19] that candidate recruitment is a powerful tool for party leaders and other actors to influence who runs,[20] and that candidate recruitment often plays a role in the shortage of historically underrepresented groups in our political institutions.[21] However, we still have a lot to learn about the basic operation of the candidate recruitment process: scholars don't know much, for instance, about where elites look for new candidates, what kinds of institutional resources influence how they search, how electoral uncertainty factors into their decisions, how personal connections matter, or what kinds of qualities elite recruiters look for in a potential candidate. Broadly speaking, studying the factors that keep political and civic leaders from encouraging working-class candidates can not only help us understand why so few workers run, but also enrich our understanding of the consequential and understudied world of candidate recruitment.

So why exactly don't candidate recruiters encourage more workers to run for public office? The answer, in short, is that competitive elections aren't just costly and uncertain for candidates—they're also costly and uncertain for the people who *recruit* candidates. And this defining feature of democratic elections creates strategic challenges for those who recruit new candidates, challenges that ultimately discourage them from supporting workers.

Understanding this point requires a brief digression about *the logic of candidate recruitment*. Whereas the logic of how resources matter in candidate entry is relatively straightforward—elections are burdensome because they require reaching lots of people and doing lots of campaigning—candidate recruitment is more complex.

Recruiting candidates usually isn't a full-time job. The elites who recruit and support new candidates are people who work in politics in other capacities: party leaders, politicians, journalists, activists, interest group leaders, and others. They have a special stake in the outcomes of elections; they care deeply about politics and policy and therefore about who holds office.[22] Like everyone, however, their time and resources are limited—they have day jobs and families and other practical constraints. And that affects how they recruit new candidates.

There are at least three challenges associated with recruiting people to run for office. The first is that candidate recruitment is *personally costly*. Finding and evaluating promising newcomers takes time and energy. Recruiting the individuals who seem to have the most potential takes time and energy. And even after someone decides to run, new candidates often require support throughout their campaigns (in the form of training, advice, campaign funds, volunteers, and other resources).[23] For recruiters, these kinds of costs can add up quickly: recruiting and supporting new candidates is difficult work.

Moreover, the process is *highly uncertain*. A recruiter can never be sure how likely it is that a candidate will really run, how much support the candidate will require throughout the campaign, whether the candidate will win, or what the candidate will actually do once elected.

And, third, candidate recruitment is a *highly social* activity; it requires getting to know the potential candidate on a personal level, spending time with the candidate and his or her family, and interacting with the candidate in social situations. This imposes another kind of burden on candidate recruiters, namely, that they have to find candidates with whom they are personally compatible. Candidate recruitment is costly and uncertain (just as all forms of political participation are costly and uncertain), but candidate recruitment is also a uniquely social activity. Voters don't have to personally interact with the candidates they support on election day; in contrast, party officials and other civic leaders have to work closely with candidates, and that creates powerful incentives for them to recruit candidates who have similar tastes, senses of humor, interests, friends, and so on. The ideal candidate isn't just the candidate who's easiest to find or most likely to succeed—the ideal candidate is also the easiest to get along with.

Against this backdrop, candidate recruiters have powerful strategic incentives to recruit candidates with talents and resources that will help them navigate the campaign process (thereby reducing the resources required from the recruiter) and that will make the candidate's odds of winning greater (thereby reducing the recruiter's uncertainty about the election outcome). Recruiters also have strategic incentives to seek out candidates whose policy views are well-known and who have established track records in politics (thereby reducing the recruiter's uncertainty about how the candidate will behave once in office).

But candidate recruitment is about more than mechanically searching for ideal-type candidates. It is a fundamentally social process. Candidate recruiters don't exhaustively survey every co-partisan in the relevant geographic area, estimate the costs and benefits, then recruit the optimal candidate. Like everyone, they use social shortcuts. They recruit through their *personal networks* of friends and acquaintances (in an effort to reduce the time and energy needed to find the candidate, the uncertainty about the candidate's abilities and political views, and the chances that the candidate will be unpleasant to work with). They seek out candidates who are *similar to themselves*; a party leader who works as an attorney likely has an easier time finding attorneys who might be good candidates, convincing them to run, correctly judging their chances of success and their future behaviors, and getting along with them one-on-one. And they look for potential candidates who are *similar to successful candidates in the past*, a strategy that reduces the costs and uncertainty associated with a candidate (although it may not guard against unlikable people). These social shortcuts are driven by the fundamental strategic challenges that elections naturally impose on candidate recruiters, of course. But the solutions recruiters devise in response to those strategic challenges are not themselves purely strategic. Candidate recruitment is a social activity.[24]

The social nature of recruitment can in turn be a powerful force for exclusion. If elites recruit friends and acquaintances, people outside of their personal networks will be significantly disadvantaged. If they look for candidates who resemble themselves or other officeholders, they will naturally reproduce any inequalities in who holds office in the first place. Social shortcuts can easily devolve into *in-group favoritism*.

Candidate recruiters aren't alone in this respect, of course. In the business world, one important reason so few women and racial minorities hold high-level management positions is that hiring managers often prefer personal acquaintances, friends of friends, people like themselves, or people like other successful CEOs.[25] When who gets hired depends on more than just who has the best skills—when it also depends on who you know and what you have in common with the boss—historically underrepresented social groups naturally lose out.

The same is often true in the world of candidate recruitment. Most elite recruiters tend to be affluent white-collar professionals themselves;[26] in the 2013 National Survey of Party Leaders discussed in chapter 3, for instance, only about 4 percent of party chairs reported having working-class jobs. If recruiters seeking to minimize the costs, uncertainty, and unpleasantness associated with finding new candidates look to their acquaintances, to people like themselves, or to people like other successful candidates, they will tend to overwhelmingly recruit white-collar professionals—and pass over qualified working-class Americans.

Of course, the purely strategic aspects of candidate recruitment undoubtedly work against working-class candidates, too, at least some of the time. As chapter 2 showed, workers are slightly less likely to have some of the raw characteristics voters and party leaders say they look for in a candidate. And, of course, workers have fewer resources, and they hold fewer offices, which makes them costlier and more uncertain in a way that transcends social affinities and connections. There are plenty of nonsocial reasons why political and civic leaders might prefer white-collar professionals.

However, the data suggest that the social consequences of the structure of candidate recruitment—and not just pure strategic necessity—are what stop elites from recruiting workers or even seeing them as viable candidates. Selecting leaders via competitive elections creates tremendous pressure for elites to recruit candidates who seem like safe bets. And because most political elites are white-collar professionals themselves, when they look for low-hanging fruit, they wind up recruiting mostly white-collar professionals.

The best source of systematic evidence on how candidate recruiters treat potential working-class candidates is probably the 2013 National Survey of Party Leaders, or NSPL, the survey of county-level political party leaders that I organized with my long-time collaborators David Broockman, Chris Skovron, and Melody Crowder-Meyer. As chapter 3 explained, the NSPL was sent to over 6,000 leaders of the county-level branches of the Republican and Democratic parties, and of those, 1,118 (about 18 percent) completed the survey, a response rate comparable to that of other elite surveys (and more than double the response rate of election surveys administered to the general public by telephone; for more information, see the "Survey Details" section of the appendix).

The NSPL's snapshot of the practices and attitudes of county party leaders gives us a rare opportunity to ask whether workers are more likely to be recruited in places where the challenges associated with candidate recruitment are more severe. We can also investigate the role of social processes, that is, we can see whether workers are more likely to be recruited in places where party leaders are more socially connected to workers.

If strategic necessity is the only thing responsible for the fact that workers are seldom recruited—if the challenges associated with candidate recruitment and the practical obstacles workers face drive *all* elites to recruit white-collar professionals—then where those challenges are less severe, elites should be more favorable to working-class candidates. That is, it should be that elites are more likely to recruit workers either in places where candidate recruiters have more resources (to help them overcome the challenges of candidate recruitment) or in places where the electoral environment is easier (where the challenges of candidate recruitment are less severe).

For the most part, however, candidate recruitment doesn't seem to work that way. Figure 4.5 plots the NSPL's measures of party leaders' attitudes about workers (from Figure 3.10 in chapter 3; whether they felt that relative to white-collar professionals, workers were more or less qualified, easy to recruit, good at fundraising, good at campaigning, or able to win support from voters) along with the average percentage of workers that party leaders said they had recruited in the previous few years (from Figure 3.9). In Figure 4.5, I have simply divided the pool of party leaders based on other items on the survey that asked about the institutional resources available to leaders. Does their party have a year-round physical office? A separate campaign headquarters? A website? A constitution? Does it meet at least once a month? Does it have a formal candidate recruitment program? (For complete question wording, see the "Question Wording" section of the appendix.)

None of these institutional resources predicted significant improvements in how party leaders felt about working-class candidates. In fact, most of them were associated with significantly *worse* attitudes about candidates from the working class. Leaders of parties with offices, websites, and regular meetings were significantly less likely to view workers as qualified candidates or to say that they had recruited large numbers of workers in the past. The one exception in Figure 4.5 was that party leaders with a candidate recruitment program were two to five percentage points more likely to say they felt that workers were qualified, good fundraisers, good campaigners, and able to win. This result may have been a fluke, however—none of the gaps was statistically significant, and party leaders with a candidate recruitment program were no more likely to see workers as easy to recruit (the one measure a candidate recruitment program should be most likely to impact) and no more likely to say they had recruited workers in the past (the one measure that matters most).

Of course, it could be that party leaders who have more institutional resources also face tougher electoral environments—maybe their party's resources are a response to the larger political fight the party faces. Figure 4.6 plots party leaders' answers to the same questions about working-class recruitment, this time dividing party leaders by several measures of how burdensome local elections are.

The first set of estimates in Figure 4.6 compares party leaders who reported that 51–75 percent of the seats in their area were "safe" to party leaders who reported that 75–100 percent of the seats in their area were safe for their party. The second set of estimates compares marginally unsafe party leaders (26–50 percent safe seats) to extremely unsafe party leaders (0–25 percent). If party leaders pass over workers because of a neutral, strategic concern about their chances of winning, then party leaders in extremely safe and extremely unsafe locations should be more likely to view workers favorably. If the party always wins—or if the party always loses—then concerns about the occupational backgrounds of candidates shouldn't matter as much.

That doesn't seem to be the case, however—just the opposite, in fact. Party leaders in extremely safe counties were slightly less likely to rate workers recruitable and good fundraisers relative to party leaders in only marginally safe counties. Likewise, party leaders in extremely unsafe counties were slightly less favorable to workers on most measures than party leaders in only marginally unsafe counties. And none of the gaps was large

FIGURE 4.5. Parties with Institutional Resources Don't Recruit More Workers

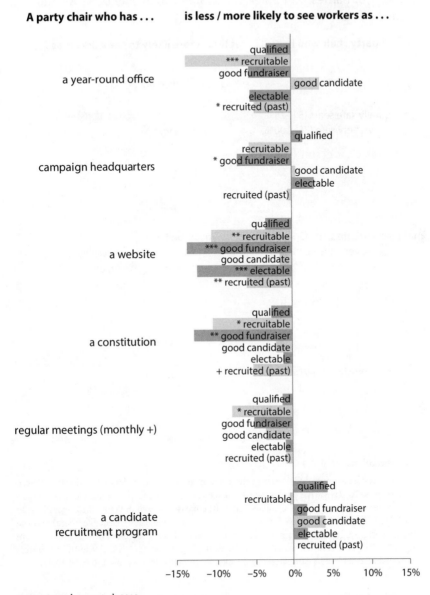

A party chair who has . . .   **is less / more likely to see workers as . . .**

Source: Broockman et al. 2013.

Note: Bars report average differences in the percentages of party leaders who said they viewed workers as worse (negative percentages), the same (0), or better than (positive percentages) white-collar candidates on five campaign skills (the measures used in Figure 3.10, again labeled "qualified," "recruitable," "good fundraiser," "good campaigner," and "electable" here) and the average percentages of workers party leaders remembered being recruited (the measure used in Figure 3.9, labeled "recruited (past)" here). Results for regression models with additional controls are available in Table A3.4. Statistical significance is denoted as follows: *$p < 0.05$, **$p < 0.01$, ***$p < 0.001$.

FIGURE 4.6. Parties with Safer Electoral Environments Don't Recruit More Workers

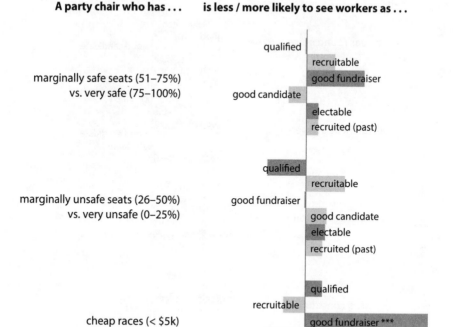

A party chair who has . . .   **is less / more likely to see workers as . . .**

Source: Broockman et al. 2013.

Note: Bars report average differences in the percentages of party leaders who said they viewed workers as worse (negative percentages), the same (0), or better than (positive percentages) white-collar candidates on five campaign skills (the measures used in Figure 3.10, again labeled "qualified," "recruitable," "good fundraiser," "good campaigner," and "electable" here) and the average percentages of workers party leaders remembered being recruited (the measure used in Figure 3.9, labeled "recruited (past)" here). Results for regression models with additional controls are available in Table A3.4. Statistical significance is denoted as follows: ⋅$p < 0.10$, ***$p < 0.001$.

or statistically significant. For the most part, the strategic environment seemed to be a wash.

The notable exception was a measure that asked party leaders how much a typical race for county offices cost in their area. In places where campaigns and elections are relatively inexpensive (under $5,000 on average), party leaders were fifteen percentage points more likely to report that working-class people were capable of raising money and seven percentage points more likely to report that workers stood a good chance of winning the election. (And this remained statistically significant in follow-up regression models with dozens of control variables; see Table A3.4 in the appendix, under "Workers less fundable? [ind].") To some extent, party leaders' dim view of working-class candidates appears to be a response to the high cost of running a modern campaign, an unavoidable strategic feature of American elections.

But there also appears to be an important social component to how party leaders view and recruit potential candidates from the working class. The top set of bars in Figure 4.7 plots the same data on how party leaders view workers, this time dividing leaders by their own incomes (there weren't enough party leaders who were blue-collar workers in the sample to draw meaningful inferences, so I simply divided the sample by income). The bottom set of bars divides party leaders by whether they reported that there was at least one working-class person on their executive board. These measures captured—albeit crudely—the extent to which social shortcuts would lead a given party leader to or away from working-class candidates. If busy party leaders cope with the burdens associated with recruiting candidates by seeking them out the way hiring managers at businesses do—seeking out people they know, people like themselves, or people similar to past officeholders—then affluent party leaders whose executive boards don't have any workers on them should be the least likely to view workers favorably.

And, indeed, they are. These social measures in the National Survey of Party Leaders were by far the best predictors of how party leaders felt about recruiting candidates from the working class. Party leaders with lower incomes (under $50,000) were 3 to 12 percentage points more likely to rate workers favorably on every measure in Figure 4.7 (relative to party leaders with incomes over $100,000). Party leaders with at least one worker on their executive boards were 7 to 10 percentage points more likely to rate workers qualified, recruitable, and electable and said that workers

FIGURE 4.7. Party Leaders with Personal Connections to Workers Recruit More Workers

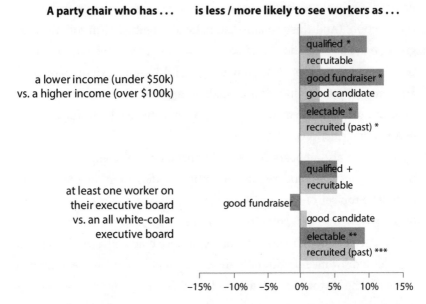

A party chair who has . . .   **is less / more likely to see workers as . . .**

a lower income (under $50k) vs. a higher income (over $100k)

- qualified *
- recruitable
- good fundraiser *
- good candidate
- electable *
- recruited (past) *

at least one worker on their executive board vs. an all white-collar executive board

- qualified +
- recruitable
- good fundraiser
- good candidate
- electable **
- recruited (past) ***

-15%   -10%   -5%   0%   5%   10%   15%

Source: Broockman et al. 2013.

Note: Bars report average differences in the percentages of party leaders who said they viewed workers as worse (negative percentages), the same (0), or better than (positive percentages) white-collar candidates on five campaign skills (the measures used in Figure 3.10, again labeled "qualified," "recruitable," "good fundraiser," "good campaigner," and "electable" here) and the average percentages of workers party leaders remembered being recruited (the measure used in Figure 3.9, labeled "recruited (past)" here). Results for regression models with additional controls are available in Table A3.4. Statistical significance is denoted as follows: $p < 0.10$, *$p < 0.05$, **$p < 0.01$, ***$p < 0.001$.

made up 8 percentage points more of the people they recruited on average. (And on this item about past recruitment practices, the gaps in Figure 4.7 remained statistically significant in regression models with controls; see Table A3.4 in the appendix.)

Gaps this size are nothing to sneeze at. If workers held 8 percentage points more of the seats in our state legislatures, for instance, that would increase their representation by almost 400 percent and would close the social class gap in officeholding by one-sixth. And, of course, the differences documented here probably understate the true gaps in recruitment; party leaders completing this survey almost certainly exaggerated how many workers they had recruited, which could dilute the estimates in Figure 4.7.

Even so, the size and consistency of the differences documented here illustrate vividly how social the candidate recruitment industry is—and how that can affect historically underrepresented groups. Identifying, recruiting, and training new candidates is extremely challenging. To cope with these practical obstacles, candidate recruiters often use social shortcuts: they recruit people like themselves, they look to their profession and personal networks, and so on. The result, however, can often be in-group favoritism. White-collar candidate recruiters often reach out to white-collar professionals. Even party leaders with good organizational resources and safe seats don't seem to recruit more workers. In a world where candidate recruitment is a taxing process done mostly by busy people with other responsibilities, what really seems to matter is who you know.

Of course, it would be useful to test this hunch with aggregate-level data on who runs and wins. Unfortunately, there isn't an analogous source of aggregate-level data on how well-integrated candidate recruiters are with working-class people. The NSPL has its limits; with just one or two cases per county—and only 1,118 cases overall (under 30 per state on average)—it isn't well suited to generating reliable state- or county-level averages. As it stands, there isn't a good way to directly study place-to-place variation in how well-integrated workers are into elites' social networks.

We can, however, study variation across states in whether the interest group landscape includes one kind of organization that explicitly promotes the political participation of working-class Americans, namely, *labor unions*. Labor scholars have long argued that unions serve as "schools of democracy"[27] that teach working-class Americans civic values and political skills. As important players in electoral politics, moreover, unions often serve as a bridge between workers and political elites, getting talented blue-collar Americans involved in the kind of activism that connects them to party leaders, politicians, interest groups, and other elite actors. In some states, unions actively partner with candidate recruitment and training organizations (like Emerge, a national organization that promotes female candidates); in a handful of states, labor unions even run their own candidate recruitment and training programs (for more on those programs, see chapter 5). Unions, in other words, often work—sometimes aggressively—to close the social gaps that normally keep workers out of sight and out of mind to candidate recruiters.

And workers are substantially (and statistically significantly) more likely to run and hold office in states where unions are stronger. Figure 4.8 plots the unionization rate in each of the fifty states against the rate at which working-class people hold state legislative seats (left panel) and run for them (right panel). Clearly there is a positive association: in the most heavily unionized states, workers have historically held about two percentage points more seats and have run for three percentage points more seats.

Importantly, the relationship in Figure 4.8 holds—and is actually stronger—in follow-up regression models that control for other ways that unions might promote working-class officeholding. In addition to measuring the associations between unionization rates and working-class officeholding, these models (reported in their entirety in a paper published in 2016)[28] also

FIGURE 4.8. More Workers Run and Win in States Where Unions Are Stronger

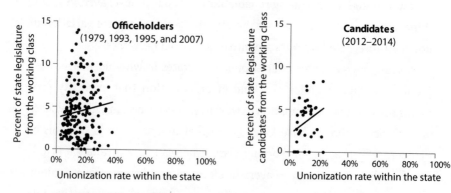

Source: Broockman et al. 2012, 2014b; Hirsch and Macpherson 2003; Insurance Information Institute 1979; National Conference of State Legislatures 2015.

Note: Dots represent state averages collected in 1979, 1993, 1995, and 2007 (left panel) and estimated using combined data from the 2012 and 2014 National Candidate Studies (right panel). The best-fit lines are statistically significant at $p < 0.10$.

control for indirect ways that unions might promote working-class office-holding; they include measures of how politically knowledgeable working-class people are, how often workers volunteer for political campaigns and causes, how much money the average worker earns, how expensive the average campaign is, and how far to the political right or left the voters in each state lean. Even when controlling for the many other ways that unions might help working-class candidates—and many other factors that might affect working-class representation—there is still a significant association between unions and the number of workers who hold office.

Of course, this isn't the same as direct evidence that unions connect workers to elite recruiters and ultimately promote working-class office-holding. And unions can only do so much—even in the most union-dense times and places, workers still make up small percentages of candidates and officeholders. But it represents an important diagnostic check, a way to determine whether what individual party leaders report squares with data on larger patterns of candidate entry. If candidate recruitment is challenging, and if elites respond by looking for low-hanging fruit—people in their social network and people like themselves or other elites—then it should be the case that more workers run and win in places where there are more interest groups that promote workers. The analysis here cannot close the case on the question of why unions are associated with working-class officeholding, but the evidence is consistent with what we learn from surveys of party leaders. When busy elites need to find new candidates, they can't afford to look far. When their personal network doesn't include many workers—and when the interest group community doesn't have as many pro-worker organizations—qualified working-class citizens are less likely to be asked.

In hindsight, it was naïve to think back in April 2015 that a simple nudge would be enough to change how leaders in North Carolina identify and recruit potential candidates. Candidate recruitment is costly, time-consuming, and fundamentally social. Political and civic leaders get the job done, often by using social shortcuts, but it isn't easy. The challenges associated with candidate recruitment—and the strategies that elites use in response—aren't things that can be significantly altered by a simple nudge.

Unfortunately, in this process, outsider groups are often left behind. When candidate recruiters go out in search of new talent, they often look to their friends, to their personal and professional networks, and to people already working in politics. And in those crowds, there usually aren't many working-class Americans to be found. The result is another powerful structural obstacle keeping workers out of office: they aren't asked, because the people doing the asking usually don't know many workers.

WHAT THE CASH CEILING IS MADE OF

These days, Ruth Ellen Brosseau isn't called "Vegas Girl" anymore. During her first year in office, she spent time getting to know her district and meeting with local politicians, businesses, and constituents. She improved her rusty French, opened a local constituency service office, took on leadership roles in her party (including deputy agriculture critic and eventually party vice-chair), championed legislation to offset the high cost of repairing a faulty type of home foundation that was common in her district, and became a nationally visible proponent of the less fortunate. When she won re-election easily—and in a more traditional race—in 2015, the political establishment could only marvel at her transformation. "Since her surprise election," the Canadian women's magazine *Chatelaine* wrote, "the 31-year-old has quietly evolved into an effective and highly regarded politician."[29]

Brosseau adapted so well, in fact, that most media coverage of "Elbowgate"—an incident in which Canadian prime minister Justin Trudeau elbowed Brosseau in the chest during a physical altercation on the floor of Parliament in May 2016—didn't say a word about bartending, single motherhood, or Las Vegas. By then, Brosseau was just another MP.

Ruth Ellen Brosseau's story was only possible, however, because she was able to sidestep two structural obstacles that the Canadian electoral process has in common with elections in the United States, namely, the high cost of campaigning and a candidate recruitment industry that usually fills its benches of new candidates with white-collar professionals. Brosseau ran only because her race didn't take any time or money. She was recruited only because party activists happened to drink at the bar where she worked. Brosseau's political career was possible only because for a brief moment in political time, the structural gates that normally discourage working-class citizens from running for office were left wide open.

Those moments are incredibly rare in U.S. politics (so rare, in fact, that the only anecdote I could find to illustrate this point was a story about a candidate in another country). The structural obstacles that keep working-class Americans out of office seldom waver. And many of them are only getting stronger. Elections have always been burdensome: the classic quip "There are two things that are important in politics. The first is money, and I can't remember the second" was first uttered by Mark Hannah, the Ohio political boss who raised the equivalent of $3 billion for William McKinley's presidential election in 1896. Elections have only become more costly since then: parties, candidates, and outside groups are estimated to have spent almost $7 billion during the 2016 presidential race.[30] And with soaring campaign costs at all levels of government come untold personal burdens for candidates—burdens that disproportionately screen out working-class people.

Likewise, finding and recruiting new candidates has always been as difficult, uncertain, and social as it is today. Although there are no historical data on candidate recruitment in the past, there was probably never a time in our country's history when recruiters weren't overwhelmingly drawn from white-collar occupations, or when they didn't look to their own overwhelmingly white-collar social circles for new candidates. Today, however, the one kind of institutional actor that might have disrupted this process—the labor union—is rapidly disappearing from the American political landscape. Fifty years ago, one in three American workers belonged to a union; today, that figure is only about one in ten. The cash ceiling is made of tough stuff—and it only seems to be getting tougher.

Of course, the barriers that keep workers out of office *are* fundamentally different from the legal prohibitions and voter prejudices and social customs that have kept other historically underrepresented groups like women and racial or ethnic minorities out. But they are structural barriers all the same, significant and enduring features of the way our society and our political process are organized.

Moreover, they are a troubling kind of structural barrier—they are rooted in the very fabric of how we select candidates in our representative democracy. Competitive elections lie at the very heart of American political thought, but they naturally entail a great deal of cost and uncertainty. That in turn disadvantages resource-poor groups while giving recruiters incentives to look for candidates within their own social circles. This isn't to say that other common modes of leadership selection would produce different outcomes, of course. But it is important—and normatively concerning—to acknowledge that our country has a cash ceiling, that the way we select leaders can itself discourage working-class Americans from holding office. Representative democracy seems to have built-in biases against working-class candidates.

If there is any hope of overcoming those biases, it will require finding ways to help workers get around powerful structural obstacles. But—somewhat remarkably—a few trailblazing reformers seem to have figured out how.

There seem to be major structural barriers keeping qualified workers out of office. What are they?

- *In 2011, a twenty-seven-year-old bartender in Canada named Ruth Ellen Brosseau won a seat in Parliament. It was only possible, however, because the usual obstacles weren't there: Brosseau was a "paper candidate," someone who was actively recruited by a party and who didn't have to run a campaign.*

The most obvious possibility is that elections are costly, uncertain, and important to everyone involved—not just candidates, but also those who recruit them. Expensive and uncertain elections may deter workers and discourage elites from recruiting them.

- *Political observers sometimes question whether there are really any structural barriers keeping working-class people out of office. But the basic logic of how American elections work suggests that there are.*

Indeed, in cities and states (and even congressional seats) with larger electorates and more involved campaigns, fewer workers run and hold office.

- *Representative Edward Beard—a house painter who spent a mere $12,000 on his successful campaign for Congress in the 1970s—says his story would be impossible today because of how complicated elections have become.*

The candidate recruitment industry is another important barrier: finding new candidates is difficult, uncertain, and highly social, and many elite recruiters simply look to their own friends and acquaintances. They don't find many workers there.

- *I naïvely thought that a simple nudge in an email would be enough to get local elites to recruit workers for a candidate training program at Duke. I didn't realize then how fundamentally challenging it is to find new candidates, or how elites look to their social networks for new talent.*

The bottom line: There are two important structural barriers keeping working-class Americans out of office, each built into democracy itself. Campaigning is complex and personally burdensome, which makes it hard for economically disadvantaged people to run. And candidate recruitment is difficult, which gives political and civic leaders incentives to look for new candidates within their own white-collar social circles. These barriers keep individual workers from running—they are the structural backbone of America's cash ceiling.

5

WHAT CAN WE DO ABOUT IT?

A little over a decade ago, Harvard University launched a financial aid program that started a small revolution in higher education. Historically, Harvard's student body had been drawn overwhelmingly from the richest families in the country, but university leaders wanted to make the Ivy League school more accessible to the less affluent. Back in the 1990s, the university had introduced *need-blind admissions*; Harvard stopped using an applicant's parents' income as a consideration when deciding whom to admit. However, like many other colleges that had gone need blind, Harvard hadn't experienced the hoped-for surge in applications from lower-income students.

So in 2005, Harvard took an unprecedented step: the university guaranteed full-ride scholarships to all admitted students from low-income families. Successful applicants from families with household incomes below $40,000—just under the national median at the time—would be given free tuition, room, and board. (Families with incomes under $120,000 would also receive generous scholarships on a sliding scale.) Two years later, the university raised the income cap on its full-ride policy from $40,000 to $60,000; four years later they raised the cap again to $65,000 (more than $10,000 above than the national median).

The practice—which came to be known as *demonstrated need financial aid*—spread quickly. Within a few years of Harvard's 2005 announcement, competitors like Yale and Princeton announced similar programs. Other elite colleges quickly followed suit. By 2009, a student from a family in the bottom fifth of the income distribution could expect to pay just $6,700 on average to attend *any* of the 78 schools ranked "most selective" by *Barron's Profiles of American Colleges.*[1] Today, more than 40 major colleges and universities have both need-blind admissions and demonstrated need financial aid policies. Ivy League schools; national universities like Notre Dame, Stanford, Georgetown, Northwestern, Vanderbilt, Cal Tech, and Duke; elite liberal arts colleges like Pomona, Rice, Grinnell, Bowdoin, and Boston College; and even public flagship universities like Michigan and North Carolina—they all bear the imprint of Harvard's trailblazing effort to increase the economic diversity of its student body by guaranteeing scholarships to low-income students.

Unfortunately, Harvard's program and many of the follow-up efforts it inspired didn't actually work.

Designing programs that change major social phenomena can be difficult, even for smart, well-meaning people. It requires intimately understanding the root causes of the undesirable outcome in question. It requires imagining effective and sometimes highly creative ways to change that outcome. It requires being mindful of a wide range of practical considerations, from program costs to negative side effects to political roadblocks. And it requires drawing the right lessons from setbacks and failures. Silver bullets are rare. As most serious reformers know, it takes more than good intentions to change the world.

The history of efforts to increase the number of students from low-income families at elite universities is a case in point. Reformers were intelligent and well-intentioned—in fact, they were working at institutions jam-packed with smart, compassionate people. But their interventions still followed the "shoot first, ask questions later" logic that so often characterizes enthusiastic reform efforts. Early adopters invested in interventions before anyone really understood the problem they were trying to solve. (It wasn't until almost a decade after Harvard's bold financial aid effort that researchers began carefully studying the factors that keep talented low-income students out of elite colleges.) Their theories were based on an incomplete understanding of the root causes of the problem. (As it turns out, financial aid is only one of *several* significant barriers that must be addressed in order to substantially increase the number of high achievers from poor families who apply to a school like Harvard.)[2] And competitors copied one other's programs before anyone really knew whether they worked.

The proliferation of need-blind admissions and demonstrated need financial aid has done a lot of good, of course. (Just ask the thousands of students from low-income families who have graduated from elite colleges debt free.) But those programs still haven't delivered on the original promise of significantly increasing the economic diversity of elite colleges and universities. The year after Harvard began offering full rides to students from low-income families, a study (coauthored by a Harvard economist) found just 15 additional students from those backgrounds were a part of the next incoming class (of 1,600 total students).[3] The story has been largely the same at other universities that adopted Harvard's approach: national surveys of selective colleges have "found virtually no change from the 1990s . . . in enrollment of students who are less well off."[4]

Worse still, the gap between expectations and reality has dampened some universities' enthusiasm for reform. When demonstrated need financial aid programs failed to deliver expected surges in applications from lower-income families, administrators at many elite schools began privately admitting that they "had reluctantly come to the conclusion that the pool of low-income students with top academic credentials was just limited, and there wasn't much they could do to change that."[5] That conclusion was deeply mistaken: actual research on low-income students suggests that there are more than enough with top academic credentials to diversify America's elite colleges (and that other factors beyond financial aid keep them away, like bad advice from guidance counselors, a desire to stay close to family, and the stubborn perception that elite schools don't want them). Even so, when a major reform effort fails to live up to advocates' promises, well-meaning people often get discouraged.

Reform doesn't have to be a "shoot first" exercise, of course. Researchers and activists can do their homework beforehand—they can learn about the causes of an outcome and design reforms that get to the heart of the problem long before they get a window of opportunity to try an intervention. They can also take the time to study pilot efforts carefully before copying and expanding them. (And studying reforms can in turn help scholars continue testing their theories.)

The goal of this chapter is to do exactly that. Chapters 2, 3, and 4 explored the causes of government by the privileged in the United States. One of my goals in doing so was simply to understand the factors that keep working-class Americans out of office (knowledge for the sake of knowledge—or *Veritas*, the motto of Harvard University). But part of my aim was also to develop a body of evidence that could inform real-world interventions ("Knowledge in the service of society," one of our mottos here at Duke).

Indeed, the last few chapters provide important guidance for reformers. Workers seldom hold office because they can't shoulder the practical burdens associated with democratic elections and because recruiters often pass them over in favor of white-collar candidates. If reformers want more workers to hold office, any proposal will have to be *responsive* to these realities; a program to increase political ambition probably won't do much good (see chapter 3). Reform, moreover, will have to be carefully *targeted* at qualified working-class Americans. The barriers that keep workers from running are natural by-products of democracy itself. Against this backdrop, the most effective way to level the playing field will probably be to simply offset the unique costs that workers shoulder. Rather than redesign the entire golf course, we can simply take a few strokes off of workers' scores. That might involve somehow lightening the load, that is, somehow offsetting the practical burdens that prove too much for workers (e.g., with political scholarships or seed money targeted at workers). Or reformers might try to close the recruitment gap, either by recruiting talented workers themselves or by somehow changing the incentives of elites so that they recruit more candidates from the working class. The key will be designing reforms that single out workers and address the unique obstacles that they face.

Unfortunately, many of the ideas circulating in the reform community right now aren't targeted or responsive—or even feasible. The most popular proposals are universal interventions—like pay raises for politicians or publicly financing elections—that don't single workers out or directly address the most pressing obstacles that they face. These kinds of reforms might make running for office slightly easier or more attractive to working-class candidates, but they would also make running more appealing to white-collar candidates, and in the end, they would probably leave the playing field about as uneven as it is today. Other popular reform proposals wouldn't even make it that far: many of the ideas reformers commonly discuss don't stand any real chance of being implemented in the first place (because they involve bulldozing the entire golf course and rebuilding it from scratch).

This chapter discusses every major reform proposal that has claimed to address the shortage of politicians from lower-income and working-class backgrounds. My aim here is to be comprehensive; that is, I try to explain not just what could work, but also what exactly is wrong with the bad ideas, in the hopes of helping reformers fast-forward through the usual trial-and-error process. (Readers who just want to learn about the most promising proposals may wish to skip ahead to the section titled "Ideas with Potential.")

In the next section, I begin with the least promising ideas, proposals that would require massive social changes far beyond the scope of what any single reform program could accomplish (ideas like reinvigorating labor unions, redistributing income and wealth, or massively expanding higher education). These *long shot* ideas are common refrains in the reform community, and they deserve some attention here. (I do not devote any space to two ideas that reformers sometimes discuss but that seem truly hopeless, namely government by lottery and quotas for working-class politicians. These kinds of pipe dreams might work in principle—both could be designed in ways that would increase the representation of the less fortunate—but they stand no chance of being implemented in the United States any time soon.)

After discussing the long shots, I then focus on two popular proposals that are more feasible, namely, publicly financing elections and raising the salaries paid to politicians. Both ideas are often touted as easy ways to increase the representation of the less fortunate. However, what we've learned in the last few chapters suggests that neither intervention will do much to increase working-class representation: public financing makes running easier for everyone (untargeted) and ultimately doesn't seem to do much to reduce the practical burdens associated with running for office or the biases in the candidate recruitment process (unresponsive). Likewise, pay raises for politicians apply to everyone (untargeted), and although they might help offset the practical burdens associated with *holding* office, they don't do anything to offset the burdens associated with *running* for office, and those are the burdens that seem to keep workers out (unresponsive). Using data on the fifty states, I show that there isn't much reason to expect either of these interventions to increase the number of working-class Americans who run or hold office. I refer to policies like these as *empty promises*, at least as they pertain to the numerical representation of the working class.

This chapter then discusses the interventions that seem to have more potential, programs that try to encourage more workers to hold office by addressing gaps in the resources needed to campaign and the encouragement that comes from being actively recruited. Those interventions (candidate training programs, seed money programs, and political scholarships) are squarely in line with what the last few chapters have shown. And when they've been attempted, they've demonstrated tremendous promise. Although more research is still needed, it seems as though the activists who understand how America's cash ceiling works may have developed effective ways to help workers get around it.

Before we examine these *ideas with potential*, however, it is important to give the other popular reform proposals that are out there a fair hearing.

LONG SHOTS

When people discuss reforms that might address the shortage of politicians from the working class, they often float what I call *long shots*, interventions that—although technically feasible—would require massively changing how society is organized.

From a research standpoint, these kinds of proposals have obvious limitations. Real-world interventions can inform social science research and vice versa; they are especially useful as critical tests of theories about the origins of social problems. But if an intervention won't happen any time soon, then obviously scholars can't learn from it.

What we *can* learn from discussing long shots is where the limits of reform are. To know how to solve a social problem, activists need to know which options are on the table and which options aren't. Studying long shots can't teach scholars much about the causes of government by the rich, but identifying which proposals *are* long shots can at least help guide the conversation about reform.

Reformers and scholars interested in the shortage of working-class politicians sometimes contemplate three policies that seem to be long shots: *revitalizing the labor movement, redistributing resources*, and *expanding access to higher education*. If our goal is to think comprehensively about policy solutions, each proposal deserves some consideration, even if only to illustrate its practical limitations. The sections that follow briefly make the case for why scholars and reformers should classify each of these proposals as a long shot—so we can quickly move on to more promising ideas.

Revitalizing the Labor Movement

One suggestion I often hear is that revitalizing the American labor movement would in turn give rise to greater equality in the economic and social class makeup of government. Scholars note that "as unions decline, no other institution seems poised to . . . [invest] in the political development of middle class, working Americans, in organizing around their economic interests."[6] Reformers suggest that "in a country where few politicians come from a blue collar background, unions have often been a conduit for workers to enter politics. . . . But unions have always faced deep opposition, especially in the South, where many of the first right-to-work laws were passed."[7] If we could just revive the declining American labor movement, the argument goes, more working-class Americans would go on to hold public office.

The basic theoretical logic underlying this proposal seems squarely in line with the findings in chapters 3 and 4. Working-class people seldom run for office because they usually can't afford to participate in personally costly campaigns and because they aren't recruited by established political leaders, who focus instead on easier white-collar recruits. If practical resources and recruitment are what keep people out, then organizations like unions—which fight to secure more resources for workers and which have both political training programs and relationships with other elite actors—*should* encourage more working-class people to run and hold office. That is, revitalizing the labor movement should be responsive to the factors that keep workers out of office, and it should target working-class Americans. The idea seems especially compelling given the evidence in chapter 4 that working-class people are more likely to run and win in states with higher rates of union membership (see Figure 4.8). In light of these findings, it's understandable that people who want to do something about America's white-collar government would conclude that strengthening labor unions is the way to do it.

This proposal has some important practical limitations, however. First, revitalizing the American labor movement would be a long and slow process—it took generations for unions to organize at the national level in the United States and generations more for them to decline to their present low point, and it would most likely take generations for them to rebuild. Second, it is unclear whether the labor movement will ever return to its former glory. Unions represented more than a third of Americans in the 1950s, but union membership has declined steadily ever since as a result of a host of factors, including deindustrialization, globalization, demographic changes, political and organizational missteps by labor unions, anti-union laws at the state and federal levels, and attacks by employer-led organizations.[8] Despite creative and wide-ranging efforts on the part of pro-union reformers, unionization rates have continued to slide for the last seventy years; some scholars of labor politics now argue that social and legal conditions doomed unions from the start to "perpetual struggle rather than . . . a long-term accord."[9] When people answer the question of how to address the shortage of working-class politicians by proposing to revitalize organized labor, they raise another significant question, namely, how to revitalize organized labor.

Moreover, even if reformers somehow manage to restore American unions to their high-water mark, there are reasons to wonder *how much* it would affect the shortage of workers in public office. In the 1950s when unions were booming, workers made up less than 2 percent of Congress— about what they make up today (see Figure 1.2). Unions sometimes support working-class candidates, but in most elections, unions don't attempt to identify, recruit, and train homegrown candidates; they simply back the pro-union candidates who are nominated through the traditional pipeline (although there are instructive exceptions, as I discuss below). Unions have many jobs to do—negotiating with management, training workers, responding to complaints, organizing get-out-the-vote drives—and recruiting working-class candidates can't always be a priority.

Indeed, most of the evidence in this book suggests that places with more labor unions have more working-class politicians, but not *many* more (see Figure 4.8). Revitalizing the labor movement might help address some of the barriers to working-class representation, but doing so would take generations, it might prove impossible, and even if reformers succeed, it might not close very much of the economic gap between politicians and the people they represent.

This isn't to say that revitalizing the labor movement is a bad idea in itself—proponents of unions point to a host of benefits. But as a proposal to address America's cash ceiling, revitalizing the labor movement is a long-shot strategy. Saving the American labor movement shouldn't be regarded as a substitute for interventions with more immediate potential.

Redistributing Income and Expanding Educational Opportunities

In a similar vein, proponents of economic diversity in government sometimes suggest large-scale social policies, like redistributing income and wealth or expanding higher education. Both proposals seem like they could have many benefits. But both would require massive social and political changes (on the scale of revitalizing the labor movement). That is, both proposals would be slow, their success would be uncertain, and even if they succeeded they still might not be enough to close the social class gap between politicians and the people they represent.

Expanding access to higher education is probably the less promising of the two. The proposal itself isn't really responsive to the factors that keep workers out of office; to the contrary, it is premised on the idea that workers are less qualified, an idea that doesn't find much support in hard data, as chapter 2 showed. In practice, moreover, expanding access to higher education has never increased the representation of working-class people. Educational attainment soared during the twentieth century: in the 1940s, just 5 percent of Americans over age twenty-five had a college degree; today, that number is close to 30 percent. However, working-class representation was stagnant during that time period. It's doubtful, then, that expanding college attainment to 40 or 50 percent would do much to increase the political representation of the less fortunate—to say nothing of the considerable practical and political challenges reformers would have to overcome to get there.

Redistributing economic resources like income or wealth seems more promising, at least in terms of how it might affect working-class representation. If qualified working-class people can't shoulder the practical burdens associated with running for office, wouldn't simply giving American workers more economic resources make up the difference?

Like the proposal to revitalize the labor movement, the proposal to redistribute income has a significant missing link, namely, the question of how exactly we would massively expand income or wealth redistribution in the United States. Since World War II, economic inequality has grown steadily in the United States. Progressive reformers have pushed for wave after wave of redistributive policies, but those policies have always been controversial. Although it's at least feasible that the United States might someday implement more substantial redistributive programs, it is difficult to envision how that would come about. Economic redistribution on a massive scale might help encourage more working-class Americans to run for public office, but the prospects for redistribution of that magnitude seem dim.

Long-shot proposals often come up in conversations about reform, and it is important to acknowledge them—but also to recognize them for what they are. They provide useful guidance for reformers who have long-term visions for social change. But they are not substitutes for interventions with more immediate promise. When we dwell on long shots for too long, we risk simply procrastinating on important social problems. "In a few years, I'll build a garage so that the car won't get so dirty" is never a satisfying response to the question, "Will you please wash the car?"

Neither is washing the car with muddy water. Some reforms that might be effective aren't really feasible, but there are also proposals out there that are feasible but don't align with what we know about the shortage of working-class candidates in principle—and don't seem to live up to proponents' expectations in practice. Those kinds of interventions, which I call *empty promises*, also have important lessons for reformers and researchers interested in America's cash ceiling.

EMPTY PROMISES

Unemployment. Child malnutrition. Domestic abuse. Criminal assault. Public indecency. What if the United States could make significant progress on all of these social ills with a single policy intervention? That was exactly the promise of a reform proposal that would eventually be enshrined in the U.S. Constitution: outlawing the sale of alcohol.

After decades of work by dedicated prohibitionists, in 1919 the United States ratified the Eighteenth Amendment to the Constitution, which banned the production, transportation, and sale of alcohol in the United States. And the United States wasn't alone. Between 1913 and 1920, eleven countries enacted national prohibition laws in an unprecedented global wave of temperance legislation.

Of course, this cross-national policy experiment would go down in history as an unqualified failure. No country that adopted prohibition laws saw improvements in important social outcomes. To the contrary, all eleven experienced the same painful unintended side effects—black markets, organized crime, political corruption, and so on—without any of the promised quality-of-life boosts. By the time the United States annulled the Eighteenth Amendment with the passage of the Twenty-First Amendment in 1933, prohibition had already been repealed in all ten of the other nations that had implemented the doomed policy. The case for prohibition, the world had learned, was built on empty promises.[10]

Policies that seem sensible on paper don't always live up to proponents' expectations. Temperance supporters promised that banning the sale and production of alcohol would cure myriad social ills. Harvard administrators hoped that demonstrated need financial aid would significantly increase the economic diversity of the student body.

Of course, these kinds of interventions—which I refer to collectively as *empty promises*—still have both practical and scientific value. From a practical standpoint, empty-promise policies are often important steps in the larger trial-and-error process by which reformers ultimately discover the interventions that really work. From a scientific standpoint, moreover, interventions that don't succeed can still teach researchers important lessons about the root causes of a given social outcome—even if just by helping to rule out potential suspects. When Harvard's demonstrated need financial aid program failed to deliver droves of lower-income applicants, it sparked a new wave of research and university programming aimed at understanding and addressing the complex forces that keep talented students from less affluent families out of elite universities. A reform that turns out to be an empty promise can still be an important step in the right direction.

For that to happen, however, people have to see an empty promise for what it is. Without concrete evidence that a program doesn't work, proponents will often continue praising its virtues, reciting the promises that made the intervention sound so attractive in the first place.

And that's exactly the case with two of the major reforms that have been held up as solutions to the shortage of politicians from the working class, namely *pay raises for politicians* and *publicly financing elections*. Both interventions seem to strike people in and around government as plausible ways to increase the economic diversity of our political institutions. However, neither program targets workers—both make running for office more attractive to white-collar and working-class candidates alike. Neither program is responsive to the many barriers that keep workers out—neither addresses the habits of candidate recruiters or the myriad practical burdens that stop qualified workers from running. And neither delivers results: states with publicly financed elections and higher salaries for politicians haven't experienced promised surges in working-class candidates or officeholders.

For a reform to work, it has to target workers and the barriers that keep them out of office. Interventions that don't seem to be empty promises.

Pay Raises for Politicians

In January 2017, NPR ran a story that nicely summarized one common strain of advice about how to increase the political representation of the working class. The piece—titled "Low Pay in State Legislatures Means Some Can't Afford the Job"—noted that in many state legislatures, "salaries are often low and many would-be politicians can't afford to be lawmakers." It summarized data from the National Conference of State Legislatures showing that "30 states pay $30,000 a year or less to legislators." And it concluded by noting that the "low level of pay . . . keeps many people from entering politics" and may be responsible for the fact that we see "very few working class people in legislatures."[11] According to this line of reasoning, if the pay for politicians is too low, people who have to work for a living won't be able to keep paying the bills while holding office, so they won't run, and only the extremely rich will go on to hold office.

This argument has long had considerable sway in American politics, especially among proponents of pay raises for politicians. Activists argue that "as long as state legislatures are part-time and poorly funded, it is an uphill battle for an ordinary person to serve and pay the bills at the same time," that "it's still kind of a situation where you've got lawyers, teachers, real-estate agents . . . people that can afford to be there, where John Q. Public really can't," and that "it is past time for an honest debate about [raising] legislative pay . . . to make it possible for a broad cross section of people to serve."[12]

The basic theory behind claims like these seems sensible enough on its face. Everyone needs some fixed amount of income to maintain their current standard of living, and if the pay for politicians is set too low, people who don't have savings or flexible high-paying jobs or other independent sources of wealth won't be able to hold office and still make ends meet, so they won't run in the first place.[13] If we increase the pay for politicians, especially at the state and local levels, holding public office will be more financially feasible for lower-income and working-class Americans.

Although this argument has a certain intuitive appeal, proponents have never presented any empirical evidence to support it. Just as Harvard administrators were confident that demonstrated need financial aid would boost the number of lower-income students who applied to Harvard (but didn't initially have any systematic evidence to back their hunch), supporters of pay raises for politicians often argue low pay prevents qualified working-class people from running for public office, but to my knowledge, there has never been any systematic research to back this claim.

There is a rival school of thought, moreover, that has received less attention from journalists and activists. This alternative line of reasoning—which is more popular among labor economists than political reformers—argues that paying politicians more should actually increase the number of *professionals* who run and win. According to this view, higher pay reduces the opportunity cost associated with holding office, which is especially important to people who already earn high salaries and who might therefore be more sensitive to the pay cut they would take if they entered politics.[14] Paying politicians more could make holding office more attractive to workers, but it could just as easily make holding office less of a sacrifice for white-collar professionals. For those who wish to increase the number of working-class Americans who go on to hold public office, pay raises for politicians may be a textbook example of an empty promise.

The evidence presented so far in this book would predict exactly that. As chapters 3 and 4 showed, there are many other factors besides legislative salaries that prevent workers from considering a career in politics. The practical burdens associated with *campaigning* seem to be far more important to workers than the practical burdens associated with *holding office*: qualified workers are just as confident about their ability to hold office (see Figures 3.6 and 3.7), and in cities where *holding office* is less burdensome, workers don't hold more seats (see notes 12 and 14 in chapter 4). And then there's recruitment: workers seldom run because they're seldom encouraged by political elites. It is difficult to imagine how pay raises for politicians would address that problem—and, therefore, how they would deliver promised increases in working-class representation. If a qualified worker never hears about an open seat or can't afford to take time off work to campaign for it, it doesn't really matter what the seat pays. America's cash ceiling seems to be rooted in the burdens associated with *running* for office, not the rewards associated with *holding* it. And if that's the case—if this book's central argument is correct—then reforms like pay raises that don't target workers and that aren't responsive to the practical burdens associated with elections or the natural biases in the candidate recruitment process don't really have much potential.

And that's exactly the picture that emerges from the available data on who actually runs and wins in places that pay politicians higher salaries.

In 2015, my coauthor Eric Hansen and I conducted the first-ever study of the relationship between the salaries offered to politicians in the United States and the political representation of working-class people.[15] We focused on state legislatures, which vary a great deal in terms of the salaries they pay to politicians, and which provided a useful middle ground between national leaders (whose salaries don't tend to vary much—they all make vastly more than the national median household income, and they always have) and local politicians (for whom it can be difficult to obtain reliable salary data that match the available data on social class). Our analysis relied on the best available data on the aggregate social class makeup of state legislatures—the data from 1979, 1993, 1995, and 2007 compiled by the Insurance Information Institute and the National Conference of State Legislatures (see, for instance, Figure 3.5)—and the most comparable data we could find on the social class makeup of the candidate pool, the 2012 National Candidate Study (for complete details about the survey, see the "Survey Details" section of the appendix).

Using these data, we first asked whether the salaries offered to state legislators in a given time and place were associated with the number of candidates or officeholders in each state legislature who worked primarily in working-class jobs. Figure 5.1 begins to answer that question by plotting data from the 2012 National Candidate Study and the 2014 National Candidate Study (which was released shortly after my research with Hansen was published; in this updated figure, I have simply pooled the responses to the two surveys). The first panel in the figure plots the percentage of working-class people among candidates, and the second plots the percentage among winners. In each panel, I have divided the candidates who responded to the 2012 or 2014 National Candidate Study by how much a typical state lawmaker would earn in their home state. That is, the figure asks, when holding office pays more, are workers actually more likely to run and win?

The answer seems to be no. In both panels, there were virtually no differences between the share of workers in states that paid the least ($0 to $9,999), the states that paid more ($10,000 to $39,999), and the states that paid the most ($40,000 and up). In the lowest-paying states, workers made up 3.4 percent of state legislative candidates; in the highest-paying states, workers made up 4 percent of state legislative candidates (left panel). In the lowest-paying states, workers made up 3 percent of successful candidates; in the highest-paying, they made up 2.9 percent (right panel). In short, the percentage of working-class citizens who run and win doesn't seem to budge—let alone soar—when public office comes with a higher salary.

But why? The 2012 National Candidate Study's questions about the concerns candidates had when they first ran for public office suggested one possible answer: pay raises may address candidates' concerns about making ends meet while *holding* office, but they don't address concerns about

FIGURE 5.1. Even When the Office Pays More, Workers Still Don't Run or Win

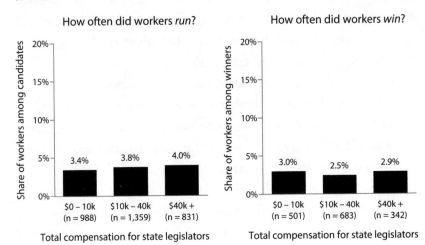

How often did workers *run*?

How often did workers *win*?

Source: Broockman et al. 2012, 2014b; Carnes and Hansen 2016.

making ends meet while *running for* office. The left panel of Figure 5.2 plots the percentage of white-collar and working-class candidates who said that when they first ran for public office[16] they were worried about "losing out on income while serving in office." (For complete question wording, see the "Question Wording" section of the appendix.) The pattern in responses to this item was unmistakable: in states where holding office pays more, both workers and professionals worry less about losing income while holding office.

However, professionals—not workers—actually seem to worry more about losing income while holding office, as the labor economics perspective argues. Consistent with the idea that professionals often take painful pay cuts when they make the move to public office, across the board, professionals were more worried than working-class citizens about losing income while governing. The money woes that pay raises for politicians are supposed to address seem to be more common among white-collar candidates than working-class candidates.

And they aren't the only personal financial concerns that stop people from running. The right panel of Figure 5.2 plots data on the percentages

FIGURE 5.2. Even When Holding Office Pays, Unpaid Campaigning Is Still a Burden

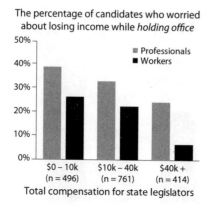

The percentage of candidates who worried about losing income while *holding office*

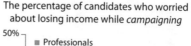

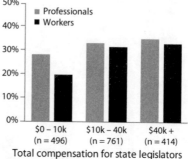

The percentage of candidates who worried about losing income while *campaigning*

Source: Broockman et al. 2012; Carnes and Hansen 2016.

of professionals and workers who reported worrying about losing income while *running for* office. In states that pay more, workers worry less about their incomes while holding office, but they worry significantly more about losing income while on the campaign trail. The same is true for white-collar professionals; offering higher salaries to politicians seems to help address one concern (although it is a concern that is more common among professionals), but it doesn't address *every* practical consideration that keeps people out of office, including the reality that many Americans simply can't afford to take months off work to field a political campaign. If anything, the practical burdens that keep workers from campaigning seem to be higher in states that pay higher salaries (consistent with the idea that states that pay more have more hotly contested elections, which in turn demand more time and resources from candidates). Salary hikes simply don't appear to improve the representation of lower-income or working-class Americans. If someone can't afford to campaign for a given seat without giving up his or her basic standard of living, it doesn't really matter what the winner's salary would be.

Of course, the respondents who completed the National Candidate Study were declared candidates for state legislature; they were people

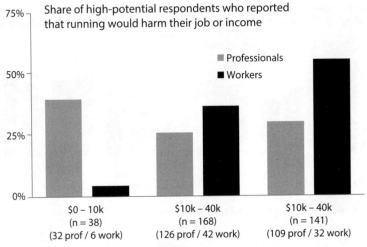

FIGURE 5.3. When Holding Office Pays, Qualified Workers Still Face Obstacles

Source: Broockman et al. 2014a; Carnes and Hansen 2016.

for whom the barriers to public office ultimately weren't enough to stop them from running. What about qualified workers and professionals in the general public? Figure 5.3 uses the data from my 2014 survey of the general public (see, for instance, Figure 3.2), which included an item that asked respondents to imagine that they were considering running for public office and that then prompted them to think about what their main concerns would be. In the figure, I've plotted the percentage of people who were "high-potential"—that is, who reported that they had four or more of the qualities that party leaders and voters say they look for in a candidate—who said that giving up their job or income would be a major impediment that could prevent them from running for public office (the income anxiety measure that most clearly distinguished workers and professionals in Figure 3.2).

Like actual candidates for state legislature, qualified working-class citizens were more likely to worry about giving up time to run for public office in states that offered higher salaries. Because there were so few highly qualified survey respondents in states that pay low salaries (38 in all; 32

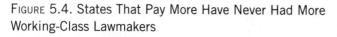

FIGURE 5.4. States That Pay More Have Never Had More
Working-Class Lawmakers

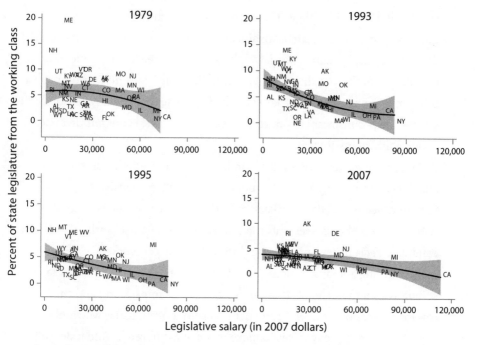

Source: Carnes and Hansen 2016.

Note: Each panel plots the relationship between total compensation (adjusted to 2007 dollars)
for the average state legislator in a given state against the share of state lawmakers who were
primarily employed in working-class jobs.

professionals and 6 blue-collar workers), the differences in Figure 5.3
should be interpreted cautiously. But they are squarely in line with what
Figure 5.2 documented. Higher pay is not a silver bullet, and it doesn't
address—and may indirectly exacerbate—the practical concerns about
campaigning that keep working-class people from running.

And this doesn't appear to be a recent phenomenon. Figure 5.4 plots
data on the share of workers in each state's legislature against the average compensation lawmakers were paid in 1979, 1993, 1995, and 2007 (the
four years for which we have reliable data on the social class makeup of
officeholders). In all four years, states that paid more seemed to have significantly *fewer* working-class politicians.

Of course, there are many other factors that could influence where and when working-class people run for public office. But even when Hansen and I controlled for a wide range of characteristics of each state—demographics, governing institutions, partisanship, and so on—we couldn't find any evidence that raising salaries for lawmakers would increase the political representation of the working class. Pay raises for politicians may accomplish other important goals, but there simply doesn't seem to be any reason to believe the promises about politicians' salaries and the economic diversity of our political institutions.

And that conclusion is squarely in line with the evidence presented in chapters 3 and 4. Pay raises for politicians aren't responsive to the factors that seem to keep workers out—the practical burdens associated with elections themselves and the natural biases against workers in the candidate recruitment process. And they don't target workers; pay raises make running for office more attractive to everyone. If America's cash ceiling is rooted in the burdens associated with campaigning and the tilt toward professionals in the candidate recruitment industry, we wouldn't expect a policy like pay raises to make much of a difference. And it doesn't seem to.

But what about a reform that claims to make campaign fundraising easier for regular Americans? Could that be the answer?

Public Financing

Public financing—the practice of giving government money to candidates to cover their campaign expenses, usually in exchange for a promise that they will not take donations—is one of the most popular ideas about how to address government by the rich in the United States. Proponents of public financing routinely highlight how the practice would allow "qualified people to run for office without needing deep pockets or high-powered connections."[17] People who care about the social class makeup of government often seem to agree: online articles about the shortage of politicians from the working class routinely elicit comments like, "This country needs campaign finance reform more than ever if we're ever to stop the proliferation of government of the wealthy, for the wealthy, and by the wealthy,"[18] "It would be a big help if we went back to publicly funding elections using the tax form checkbox and giving candidates no other financial resources,"[19] and "The only thing that would change anything would be a new set of campaign finance reforms."[20] In this view, publicly financing elections would help address the shortage of politicians from lower-income and working-class backgrounds—and might even be our *only* hope of addressing America's white-collar government.

Like the theory that pay raises for politicians would encourage more workers to run, this line of reasoning about public financing has an understandable intuitive appeal. Even at the state and local levels, political campaigns can cost tens or even hundreds of thousands of dollars. In that environment, wealthier people naturally have advantages: they have more money themselves and more affluent friends to call on for support. In contrast, many of the public financing systems in use today simply require candidates to solicit a fixed number of small donations (under Maine's "clean elections" system, candidates for the state legislature only need to receive 60 to 75 donations of $5 each in order to qualify) and promise not to raise or spend any outside money. After that, candidates receive enough money from the government to bankroll a viable campaign, and off they go. Shouldn't elections that offer candidates a public financing option encourage more working-class Americans to run?

Although the idea seems encouraging on its face, there are a few (seldom discussed) reasons to be skeptical about whether reformers' claims will pan out in practice. The first is that many public financing systems that promise boosts in working-class representation still impose considerable burdens on candidates. Under Hawaii's *matching-funds* system, a candidate must raise $100,000 in contributions before the primary election in order to be eligible for a matching contribution of $100,000 from the state. Although this system makes fundraising less of a burden, the prospect of raising the first $100,000 probably still discourages many qualified working-class people from considering a bid for office. Not all public financing systems are as generous as the name suggests.

Moreover, raising money is just one of many practical burdens that might screen out working-class Americans. It is undoubtedly an important consideration: 71 percent of the state legislative candidates who responded to the 2012 National Candidate Study, or NCS, reported that they were concerned about the need to raise lots of money the first time they ran for political office. But fundraising isn't the *only* concern that might keep someone out—or that might disproportionately impact qualified working-class citizens. In the 2012 NCS, 41 percent of candidates also said that they were concerned about giving up work time when they first ran for public office, 37 percent said that they were worried about giving up personal income while campaigning, and 57 percent said they were concerned about the general difficulty associated with running a political campaign. Publicly financing elections may lower some of the barriers to running for office, but fundraising is by no means the only practical obstacle keeping workers off the ballot.

It also isn't a practical obstacle that is *unique* to workers. Like pay raises for politicians, public financing systems don't just change the incentives for working-class people who are considering running—they also change white-collar professionals' strategic calculations. And professionals seem to worry just as much about fundraising as workers do. In the 2012 NCS, the two groups were indistinguishable: 69 percent of workers and 72 percent of professionals said that fundraising was a major obstacle the first time they ran for office. If public financing makes fundraising less of a burden, it may make it less of a burden *for everyone*, which may not do much to level the playing field for the working class. Although proponents of public financing routinely promise that it will increase the economic diversity of American political institutions, the reform is only responsive to one of the many barriers that keep workers from running, and it doesn't target workers specifically.

Perhaps the most concerning consideration is the checkered history of empirical research on campaign finance reform. Public financing systems have been adopted in more than a dozen U.S. states, most often in elections for state legislatures.[21] There have been some signs that public financing alters the electoral landscape in these states: candidates tend to spend less time fundraising and more time contacting and mobilizing voters,[22] they tend to raise more money from small donors and have more diverse pools of contributors,[23] they tend to run uncontested less often,[24] and voters tend to cast more ballots for down-ticket races.[25] However, many other outcomes don't seem to live up to reformers' hopes: publicly funded candidates seem to face significant disadvantages relative to privately funded candidates,[26] campaign spending and interest group influence don't seem to shrink in public financing states,[27] citizens don't seem more confident in democratic institutions,[28] and voter turnout and electoral competition ultimately seem to return to their prior levels (if they change at all) just a few years after public financing laws go into effect.[29]

Perhaps most telling is what happens (or, rather, *doesn't* happen) to the demographic makeup of candidates and politicians. Reformers often promise that public financing will make campaigning more accessible not just to working-class people, but also to other historically underrepresented groups, like women and racial or ethnic minorities. In reality, however, under public financing systems, the racial and gender backgrounds of politicians tend to be more or less the same. Some studies have found evidence of modest differences in who *accepts* public funds (there is some evidence that women are more likely to take public funding when they have the option). But in general, scholars have not detected significant differences in the makeup of candidates or officeholders in public financing states (although women are more likely to accept public funding, they are *not* more likely to run in the first place). In a recent review of the available research, Mayer noted that "even generously funded programs, such as Connecticut's, have had at best a marginal impact on . . . candidate demographics."[30]

In short, the promise that public financing will help improve working-class representation seems shakier than reformers often make it out to be. Empirical data from the nation's fifty state legislatures cast even more serious doubt.

Figure 5.5 plots data on the percentage of working-class candidates (left panel) and winners (right panel) in the 2012 and 2014 waves of the NCS

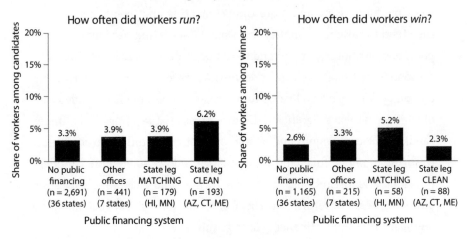

FIGURE 5.5. Public Financing May Help, but Not Much

Source: Broockman et al. 2012, 2014b.

(like Figure 5.1), this time dividing states by whether they had no public financing whatsoever, public financing for offices other than the state legislature, a Hawaii-style matching-funds public financing system for state legislative elections, or a Maine-style clean elections public financing system for state legislative races.

The differences in working-class representation in Figure 5.5 are a far cry from reformers' promises. As the left panel of the figure illustrates, working-class candidates were slightly more likely to run in states with clean elections laws, but the gap was just two percentage points, a small gain compared to the roughly forty-five-percentage-point gap between the share of workers in office and the share in the general public. And that modest improvement disappeared in data on winners; working-class candidates were no more likely to actually hold office in clean elections states. In matching-funds states, the reverse was true: workers were no more likely to run but were marginally more likely to win. Regression models with controls for institutional characteristics (compensation, staff size, session length, term limit laws, and the share of Democrats in the legislature) and state characteristics (poverty rate, unionization rate, racial makeup, republic two-party vote share, top 1 percent income share, and per capita personal income) reached nearly identical conclusions (see Table A5.1 in the appendix). Consistent with what Mayer and others have observed in data on candidates' and officeholders' racial and gender backgrounds, data on state legislative candidates in 2012 and 2014 suggest that even generously funded public financing programs have at best a marginal impact on the social class makeup of government.

And that seems to have always been the case in the United States. Figure 5.6 plots the limited available historical data on the overall percentages of working-class lawmakers in state legislatures (compiled by the Insurance Information Institute in 1979 and the National Conference of State Legislatures in 1993, 1995, and 2007). For the sake of completeness, the figure focuses on the five states that have implemented major matching-funds or clean elections programs for state legislative races.

None of them has experienced increases in working-class representation. The first states to launch public financing programs for state legislative races—Minnesota and Hawaii—implemented matching-funds programs in the mid- to late 1970s, just before researchers first collected nationwide data on the occupational backgrounds of state lawmakers. Although we cannot compare pre- and post-reform levels, we can see whether there was a subsequent long-term boost in working-class representation. There was not: by the mid-1990s, the numbers of workers had declined in both states' legislatures, and by the late 2000s, they had declined even further. Arizona and Maine launched their clean elections programs in 2000. In both states, the share of workers fell between 1995 and 2007. The National Conference of State Legislatures has not released data on the occupational makeup of state legislatures since Connecticut's clean elections law went into effect in 2008, but the outlook isn't sunny. In every public financing state, the share of workers in the legislature has fallen steadily since the late 1970s— regardless of when public financing laws took effect. There simply isn't any concrete evidence that public financing systems increase the social class diversity of candidates or officeholders.

But why not? The 2012 and 2014 NCS suggest one potential explanation. If we take seriously the findings in chapters 2, 3, and 4, any intervention

FIGURE 5.6. Public Financing Has Never Led to Increases in Working-Class Representation

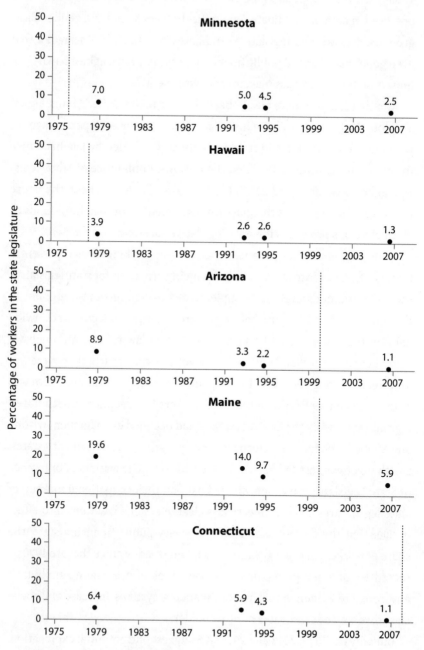

Source: Carnes and Hansen 2016; Wyatt 2002.

Note: Vertical lines represent the year a major public financing program went into effect.

that hopes to increase the representation of working-class people must be responsive to the practical burdens that keep working-class people from running and/or the natural biases against workers in the candidate recruitment process. Surveys of candidates suggest that public financing may not do either. The first panel in Figure 5.7 plots data on the percentage of state legislative candidates in the NCS who reported that they worried about fundraising the first time they ran for office (because of the small number of cases in public financing states, in this figure I have collapsed matching-funds and clean elections states). The pattern is exactly what the proponents of public financing would expect: working-class candidates were far less likely to say that they worried about fundraising in states with public financing systems. However, campaigning was still a burden for workers in other ways. The second panel in Figure 5.7 plots data on the percentage of candidates who said they worried about the overall difficulty associated with running a campaign. In public financing states, workers still found the larger prospect of running a campaign to be just as daunting.

Even when fundraising is less of a burden, candidates must still devote huge amounts of time and energy to their campaigns. The bottom panels of Figure 5.7 plot data from a series of questions on the 2012 NCS that asked candidates how many hours they spend in a typical week on a variety of campaign activities. In states with public financing systems, candidates—and workers in particular—report spending one to two fewer hours each week raising money. However, they report spending roughly the same amount of time overall on their campaigns. As the right panel illustrates, there is essentially no difference between public financing states and others. Running for political office is a daunting burden and a time-consuming process—and public financing doesn't seem to do much to change that.

Nor does public financing seem to change the habits of the people who recruit new candidates. Figure 5.8 plots data from the National Survey of Party Leaders on the share of working-class people (and, for reference, the share of women) that county party leaders reported actively recruiting to run for public office in the previous few years (see Figure 3.9). By this measure, workers don't seem to fare any better in states that publicly finance

FIGURE 5.7. Public Financing Doesn't Address Non-Financial Obstacles to Running

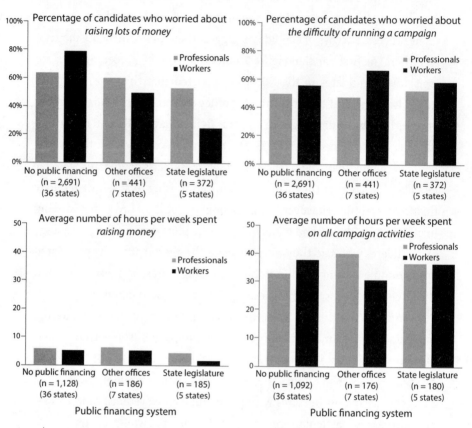

Source: Broockman et al. 2012, 2014a.

Note: The top panels are based on data from 2012 and 2014. The bottom panels are based on data from 2012 only.

elections. Interestingly, party leaders report recruiting more women in states with public financing (which is consistent with activist claims about the benefits of public financing for some underrepresented groups). But when it comes to the working class, public financing by itself doesn't seem to change the self-reported habits of candidate recruiters.

Of course, it's possible that public financing systems—especially more generous interventions like Maine's clean elections program—might do more to help workers if they were used in conjunction with other reforms.

Figure 5.8. Public Financing Doesn't Address Recruitment Biases

In the last few elections, what percentage of the candidates your party tried to recruit were workers? Women?

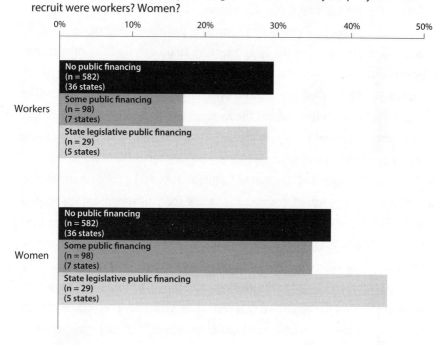

Source: Broockman et al. 2013.

But the available evidence suggests that public financing alone isn't enough, that public financing is not a sufficient condition for promoting working-class representation. Demonstrated need financial aid programs increase the economic diversity of universities only when they are paired with aggressive outreach programs to encourage lower-income students to apply. Public financing programs might boost working-class represen-tation when combined with interventions that address the other practical burdens associated with running or that aggressively recruit new candi-dates. But by itself, public financing seems to be an empty promise.

If a reform doesn't target workers and address the practical burdens as-sociated with elections and the natural biases in the candidate recruit-ment process—the factors that keep working-class people from running for public office, as we saw in chapters 3 and 4—it doesn't have much hope of increasing the representation of working-class people. You can't get around the cash ceiling if you don't know where it is.

Unfortunately, two promising-sounding proposals, pay raises for politicians and public financing systems, seem to do exactly that, missing the underlying causes of social class gaps in who runs for public office in the United States. Neither is premised on a theory that has much grounding in the available evidence about the factors that keep workers out of office. Neither targets workers—both are universal programs that make running for office more appealing to everyone. And neither of them works.

This isn't to say that pay raises for politicians and public financing are bad ideas in general, of course. Pay raises for politicians are associated with many good outcomes: when politicians in the United States are paid more, they are less likely to pursue outside employment while serving in office, they introduce more legislation and miss fewer votes, they are more in-step with their constituents ideologically, they are more likely to run for re-election, they favor citizen interests over business interests, and they face more competition from qualified challengers.[31] Public financing has a more mixed empirical record, but it hasn't been attempted in many places, and the specific form it takes is still evolving (in 2016, for instance, the city of Seattle implemented a program that gives every registered voter $100 in "democracy vouchers," coupons that can be donated to candidates to cover the cost of their races). In time, public financing may prove to be a tremendous boon to our democratic process and maybe even to working-class representation.

To date, however, neither public financing nor pay raises for politicians have lived up to reformers' promises about the political representation of lower-income and working-class Americans. Neither intervention is premised on a complete understanding of the factors that keep working-class people out of office, and neither seems to help more workers run or win. In that sense, both are textbook examples of empty promises.

Given what we know about America's cash ceiling, what *would* we expect to change the social class makeup of government? When those kinds of interventions have been attempted, have they produced the results we would expect?

IDEAS WITH POTENTIAL

The Working Families Party, or WFP, is probably best known for helping elect New York City mayor Bill de Blasio in 2013. Founded in New York in the late 1990s, the progressive independent party emerged from a coalition of pro-worker groups, labor unions, and community organizations. At first, Working Families focused on endorsing high-profile candidates and developing a following among progressive voters. (Under New York's "fusion" election laws, candidates can run under multiple party affiliations, which can give third parties considerable clout.) By the early 2000s, WFP was screening and backing scores of candidates for city and state offices; in 2003, incumbent New York City councilwoman Letitia James became the first person ever to win as an exclusively Working Families candidate. WFP continued building steam, and when long-time ally Bill de Blasio emerged as the Democratic nominee for New York City mayor in 2013, the party enthusiastically supported his campaign. In the days after the election, many observers marveled at the Working Families Party's political muscle: a *New York Times* headline proclaimed, "De Blasio's Win Is Sign of Working Families Party's Advance." Although "the mainstream media had not been paying extensive attention" to WFP, the article noted, if not for the party and its leadership, "we might now be approaching the era of Mayor Someone Else."[32]

But a few years before the party's headline-grabbing victory in the 2013 mayoral race, its leadership quietly launched a far-less-publicized program that may ultimately prove just as influential to the future of Working Families: its Candidate Pipeline Project.

The program—often just called "Pipeline" by WFP leaders—was designed to solve a simple problem. In many races, neither of the two major parties would field a candidate that shared the Working Families Party's core values. Ari Kamen, WFP's New York State political director, put it bluntly: Republican and Democratic leaders "would come to us . . . with candidates that they wanted us to support, and we would interview them . . . and we would go back" without an endorsement. The party leaders, in turn, "would come back and say, 'well who else you got?'" So Working Families started recruiting its own candidates. "The goal was to create a farm team across the state," Kamen said, "so that when there was an opportunity, we had our people there and we were ready to go."[33] If the party wants to elect more candidates who share its policy goals, the reasoning went, why wait and hope that the two major parties will supply those candidates? Why not just recruit the candidates ourselves?

The strategy was an immediate hit, especially in down-ballot local races, which are often less burdensome for new candidates, and which often serve as stepping-stones to state and national offices. In 2015, the Working Families Party recruited and supported 111 candidates in local elections in New York. Of those, 71 (or 64 percent) won their races.[34] In 2018, the party hopes to field over 200 homegrown candidates. If Bill de Blasio is the poster child for the Working Families Party, its Pipeline program may be its secret weapon.

When political and civic leaders want to change the makeup of candidates and officeholders, they seldom spend time debating long-shot social projects or attempt to tinker with institutional rules like salaries and election laws. Instead, they go directly to the population they want, recruit qualified people, help them overcome practical hurdles, train them, support their campaigns, and send them on their way. Their interventions are targeted, not universal, and carefully tailored to the specific needs of the group in question.

This approach is used broadly in the world of political advocacy: there are organizations that work to increase the political representation of conservatives, liberals, racial and ethnic minorities, LGBTQ Americans, religious people, atheists, veterans, and even scientists.[35] For one historically underrepresented social group alone—women—there are over 140 organizations nationwide devoted to increasing the group's representation in public office through recruitment, training, and campaign support.[36]

The strategy seems to have tremendous potential: EMILY's List (the oldest women's representation group), for instance, has helped elect 12 female governors, 23 female senators, 116 female House members, and over 800 female state and local officials.[37]

These kinds of programs are rooted in theories about candidate emergence that are squarely in line with this book's arguments about the obstacles that keep working-class Americans out of office. Workers seldom run because of the practical burdens associated with campaigning and the natural biases in the candidate recruitment process. Groups like EMILY's List combat exactly those barriers: as their website notes, "We travel all across the country to find, recruit, and train the women who are already leaders in their communities and we give them the tools they need to take the next step and run for office."[38] Whereas the false promise reforms described in the last section are universal interventions premised on narrow theories about one-off factors that might encourage more workers to run (e.g., the theory that workers seldom run because holding office doesn't pay enough), programs like EMILY's List are targeted and premised on clear-eyed ideas about the numerous practical barriers facing first-time candidates and the importance of recruitment—exactly the factors that seem to be at the heart of America's cash ceiling.

When pro-worker groups have set up similar interventions targeting working-class candidates, the results have been far more promising than any of the other leading proposals for increasing the economic diversity of candidates and officeholders. If practical burdens and recruitment differences really are what keep workers out of office—as this book has argued—we would expect candidate recruitment programs and other reforms that address those barriers through targeted interventions to deliver measureable results. So far, they seem to.

The next section discusses the most promising reform proposals out there right now, namely, pro-worker *candidate recruitment programs*. I then describe two previously untested reforms that align with the basic theory outlined in this book, *seed money programs* and *political scholarships* targeting working-class people. These kinds of interventions receive far less attention than the empty promises discussed in the last section, but they are more closely aligned with what we know about America's cash ceiling. And they seem to have far more potential.

Candidate Recruitment Programs

In the mid-1990s—a few years before the Working Families Party began its forays into candidate recruitment—the New Jersey AFL-CIO launched the country's first and largest candidate recruitment program that specifically targeted working-class Americans. The program was spearheaded by the union's president, Charles Wowkanech, who was frustrated by the slow pace of pro-worker legislation in the state. Inspired by the apprenticeship model in the building trades, Wowkanech founded a program that matched politically qualified workers with experienced politicians. The effort eventually grew into an annual two-week school with a half-million-dollar budget, an impressive 76 percent win rate, and a total of 915 electoral victories in offices ranging from school board to the U.S. House of Representatives.

The basic model the program uses is relatively straightforward. Each year, the state office puts out a call to its partner organizations and local affiliates for recommendations. Local leaders suggest politically qualified workers, then the state office reaches out to them. They recruit aggressively, stressing the importance of politics to everything "from the quality of the air that we're breathing in this room to the quality of the water that you're drinking . . . to your taxes to your education to your religion to your health insurance to your environment . . . everything goes through the state legislature . . . why wouldn't you want to be involved?"[39] Those who say yes are invited to a two-week Labor Candidates School, where they are trained in how to run a campaign. And those who complete the school are given support throughout their races with volunteers, endorsements, strategic advice, and other resources.

The model seems to work well in New Jersey. And since the mid-1990s, the approach has been quietly spreading to other states. Some have been one-time interventions: in 2011, the union coalition UNITE-HERE recruited seventeen candidates to run for the New Haven, Connecticut, board of aldermen in the hopes of thwarting a newly re-elected mayor who promised to gut the city's collective bargaining protections. (Sixteen of them won, giving the organization an overnight majority on the thirty-person board and halting the mayor's union-busting proposals.) Other organizations have established more permanent training programs. In 2012, the Maine AFL-CIO launched an annual statewide Labor Candidates School, and in 2013, the Nevada AFL-CIO and a coalition of Oregon labor unions followed suit. Even the Working Families Party—which has sometimes been at odds with the New Jersey AFL-CIO—may have been at least partly inspired by the New Jersey Labor Candidates School model.

Do programs like these actually increase the representation of workers? Could they be a viable way to help workers break through America's cash ceiling? The available evidence suggests that the answer is yes.

In general, candidate recruitment seems to be a powerful way to influence who runs for public office. In an exhaustive review of the research on this topic,[40] Broockman recently analyzed twenty-four surveys of candidates or candidate recruiters. The importance of recruitment is difficult to overstate: in virtually every existing study, most candidates cite recruitment as the most important factor in their decision to run. And they seem to be telling the truth: Broockman checked their claims by running the first-ever randomized experiment on candidate recruitment. Working with a progressive advocacy organization, the study sent appeals to run for office to the group's 100,000 most active members. Compared to a generic email referring activists to a website for potential candidates, an email that recruited members with personal appeals (by stressing that the leaders of the interest group were specifically interested in the recipient, not just anyone) more than doubled the likelihood that an activist would commit to running for public office in the next major election. Recruitment programs—even relatively low-cost email-based interventions—seem to work.

But do recruitment programs *that target working-class Americans* work as well as these more general efforts? The evidence presented so far in this book suggests that they should. As chapter 2 showed, there are many working-class Americans with the skills and abilities that voters and party leaders look for in a candidate. And the basic theory behind candidate training programs is squarely in line with what we know about the factors keeping working-class Americans out of office. In an interview after the 2011 New Haven elections, a UNITE-HERE representative explained that their candidate program's basic premise was that qualified workers simply need to be recruited and supported in overcoming the practical barriers to holding office: "We started essentially by going through union membership lists," he noted. "We looked first to those districts to find members we knew were active in politics . . . maybe they want to run, maybe they know someone else who can run." Then they interviewed potential candidates. "People got a little freaked out by the time commitment," but "we very much emphasized the community and the team they would have supporting them throughout the process. We [stressed that we] were able to centralize training—how to be a candidate—and the purchasing of campaign materials—that we were able to provide a lot of services for them."[41] If workers seldom run because of the practical burdens and candidate recruitment biases that naturally occur in competitive elections, programs that recruit qualified workers and help them overcome practical hurdles should work like a charm.

Indeed, the anecdotal evidence on worker training programs is overwhelmingly positive. The half dozen organizations that have set up worker candidate schools have, to my knowledge, never conducted systematic evaluations of their efforts, but their leaders uniformly report positive results. Most, moreover, say that the model is easy to set up in new places, *even places where labor unions are weak or uninterested in running candidate training programs.* Unlike pipe-dream and long-shot reforms, candidate recruitment efforts don't require passing controversial legislation or massively changing society. They simply require organizations that have regular contact with working-class people—unionized or not—to partner with political organizations in order to identify qualified workers, recruit them to run, and support them in doing so. There are scores of candidate training organizations out there that could easily provide the political half of the equation: in the last five years, close to five hundred organizations nationwide have sponsored or run candidate training programs.[42] And groups that have regular contact with working-class people are numerous and varied: labor unions, churches, activist organizations, government agencies, and community organizations would all fit the bill.

Candidate training programs are easy to adapt to fit different local contexts, too; Ari Kamen of Working Families put it bluntly: "I've got [new candidate recruitment programs] scheduled with . . . folks in Pennsylvania, New Jersey, Rhode Island, Wisconsin, Maryland . . . the list goes on. They're all at different levels with it, they're still figuring out how to do it in their own states, but they're definitely getting it right."[43] Indeed, even organizations that don't regularly conduct candidate training programs have found it easy to contract with national candidate training groups like EMILY's List, Wellstone Action, and Emerge. In Nevada, the AFL-CIO leader in charge of the worker candidate school, Yvanna Cancela, created her organization's program in less than six weeks.

Empirical research on these interventions is still in its infancy, and hard data on worker candidate recruitment programs (or even simply on how workers function in general candidate recruitment programs) are extremely limited. There are still only a few worker candidate programs nationwide, and most groups that train candidates—workers or otherwise— tend to be understandably guarded about data on the people they recruit. One group interviewed for this book flatly refused to disclose the names of its trainees, citing strict privacy policies that promise participants that their identities and personal information will never be shared.

What we can observe from the outside, however, seems promising. There are at least two sources of data suitable for preliminary quantitative analyses. The first is the data on working-class representation in state legislatures that the last section analyzed to study pay raises and public financing. Figure 5.9, for instance, analyzes changes in working-class representation in state legislatures between 1995 and 2007 (the last two years for which we have comprehensive national data), comparing the change in Maine and Arizona—two states that implemented robust public financing

FIGURE 5.9. Worker Representation Grew after New Jersey's Candidate School Opened

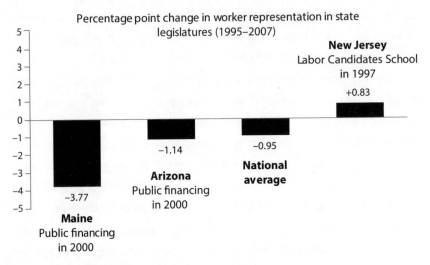

Percentage point change in worker representation in state legislatures (1995–2007)

New Jersey
Labor Candidates School
in 1997
+0.83

−1.14

−0.95

National
average

Arizona
Public financing
in 2000

−3.77

Maine
Public financing
in 2000

Source: Carnes and Hansen 2016; Wyatt 2002.

Note: The estimates for Maine and New Jersey are statistically significantly distinct from the national average at $p < 0.05$; the estimate for Arizona is not.

programs in the year 2000—to the average change in all fifty states during that period, and to the change in New Jersey—the state where the nation's first working-class candidate recruitment program went online in 1997. In Maine and Arizona, working-class representation declined from the mid-1990s to the mid-2000s. In New Jersey, in contrast, working-class representation in the state legislature actually grew, even during a period of national decline. And New Jersey's standout growth in working-class representation during this period was statistically significant (and substantively larger—about four percentage points) in follow-up regression models that controlled for changes in the ideological makeup of the state, the partisan makeup, the unionization rate, the state's legislative professionalization score, and the share of votes earned by Republican presidential candidates (see Table A5.2 in the appendix).

Of course, there are still many other factors that could explain New Jersey's unusual upturn in working-class representation during this period. But unlike with the false-promise programs documented in the last section, the available data on working-class representation in state legislatures are at least *consistent* with the idea that candidate training programs can increase the number of politicians from the working class.

The only other source of relevant data that I know of—data from inside a candidate training program itself—paints an encouraging picture, too. Because many organizations that recruit working-class candidates are reluctant to share their internal data, in April and November 2015, I ran two small candidate training programs of my own at Duke University. With each, the goal was to re-create as closely as possible the kinds of conditions that exist in standard candidate recruitment and training initiatives: the nonpartisan trainings were conducted by Lillian's List, an organization that regularly runs candidate recruitment and training efforts in North Carolina, and I recruited candidates based on the recommendations of political party leaders and activists, with a special emphasis on finding working-class trainees. (In April, most of the trainees were identified by Lillian's List and a few of their partner organizations. In November, I recruited trainees by emailing the leaders of forty-two local organizations, including the state-level branches of the Republican, Democratic, and Libertarian parties; the county-level branches of those three parties in Durham, Chatham, Orange, and Wake counties; twelve right-leaning advocacy organizations, like the North Carolina Chamber of Commerce; and fifteen left-leaning organizations, like the North Carolina Sierra Club.)

One of my aims in running these programs was simply to study the differences between the workers who showed up and the professionals. The basic premise of training programs targeting workers is that there are qualified workers out there to recruit in the first place, workers who can learn to be candidates just as easily as professionals can. If that claim is true, then the workers who are referred to candidate training programs should tend to be comparable to the professionals, at least on average.

To test this argument, I asked each of the 100 participants at the April and November trainings (who included 94 professionals and 6 workers) to complete a brief survey beforehand. Although my sample size was small—and the sample itself came from one pair of candidate training programs in one state during one year—these data constitute the only systematic research to my knowledge on whether the workers who attend candidate training programs really have as much potential as the professionals.

At least in this small sample, they did. The top panel of Figure 5.10 plots professionals' and workers' responses to a series of questions on the pre-survey that asked about past levels of political engagement, a cardinal marker of political experience and ability. The bottom panel plots trainees' responses to questions that asked whether they were above average, average, or below average on five skills that Lillian's List regarded as highly important to a candidate's future success. Because these data are based on a small and geographically constrained sample—and because only 46 of the 100 attendees completed the survey—these findings can only be interpreted as suggestive, of course.

What they suggest, however, is squarely in line with what proponents of working-class candidate training programs often argue, namely, that the programs should work just as well for working-class Americans as they do for the professionals who more often come through the candidate pipeline. As the top panel of Figure 5.10 illustrates, there were not meaningful social class gaps in trainees' prior levels of political engagement. Workers were about as likely to say that they voted, donated to political causes, and worked for campaigns or parties; they were less likely to say that they regularly contacted politicians, volunteered for community organizations, or worked for a business that was connected to government; but they were more likely to say that they had volunteered for a campaign or party or for a civic organization. Likewise, there were no obvious social class differences in self-reported skills; workers were less likely to report being "above average" at public speaking, describing their own values, or making quick decisions, but they were more likely than professionals to report being above average at working hard and asking for help. The workers who showed up at my candidate training programs may have had different strengths and weaknesses than the professionals, but on balance they did not seem to be worse potential candidates.

FIGURE 5.10. Do Workers Bring Comparable Skills to Candidate Schools?

Percent self-reporting political engagement

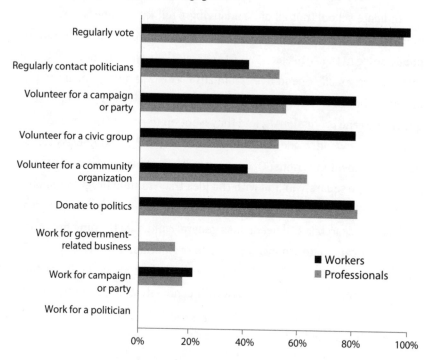

Percent self-reporting "above-average" skills

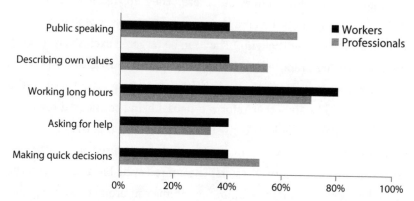

Source: Author's data collection.

Perhaps most importantly, the workers who attended these candidate training programs were just as likely to actually run for office afterward. Of the 65 professionals who disclosed their full names during the course of candidate school (not all did, and giving a full legal name was not a requirement for attending), 11 of them—about one in six—actually ran for public office in the 2016 elections. Of the 5 workers who attended and gave their names, *exactly* one in five ran in 2016. This was a very small sample, of course, but in this exercise, the workers who showed up seemed just as qualified as the professionals, and they went on to run at the same rate.

Does this evidence add up to an airtight case for working-class candidate recruitment programs? Of course not. The 2015 Duke candidate training data were squarely in line with the idea that training programs should work as well for workers as they do for professionals, but obviously a great deal more research is still needed. As general candidate training programs and worker candidate schools continue to proliferate, research opportunities will proliferate, too. But for now, we can only draw preliminary conclusions about how workers function in candidate training programs or how worker-focused candidate training programs affect the numbers of workers who run and win.

What we *can* say on the basis of these preliminary data is that programs to identify, recruit, and train working-class people have more potential than any other reform effort out there. They are feasible, unlike pipe dreams and long shots. (Even a busy assistant professor who is relatively new to a state can set them up.) They can be targeted exclusively at workers, and they are premised on theories that are responsive to the practical and recruitment-related obstacles that keep working-class people out of office. And unlike any other reform proposal being considered today, the available evidence is at least consistent with the idea that they work.

The activists who have set up candidate schools focused on workers have uniformly reported positive results. The limited available data suggest that candidate recruitment and training programs can promote working-class candidacy, both when they are limited to workers (like in New Jersey) and when they include workers alongside professionals (like at Duke). More research is still needed, but reformers may have found a way to help workers get around the cash ceiling, and it's remarkably simple: recruit and train qualified working-class candidates.

Seed Money Programs and Political Scholarships

This approach may not be the only game in town, however. There are at least two other targeted, responsive proposals out there that seem to have a great deal of potential. Neither has been attempted yet, to my knowledge, but both are squarely in line with what we know about how America's cash ceiling works.

The first proposal is seed money programs targeting working-class Americans (and paired with recruitment and training efforts). The idea has never had much traction in the reform community, but it follows logically from both the history of other successful reform efforts and the basic logic of candidate entry. By far the most successful program for encouraging women to run for public office—what is widely regarded as the gold standard—is EMILY's List, an organization that raises money year-round, then identifies promising female candidates and provides them up-front donations to begin their campaign fundraising efforts. The approach works because, as the organization's name argues, early money is like yeast—it makes the dough rise. Candidates who raise more money early on tend to attract more donations, endorsements, and support from elite recruiters and gatekeepers later in the campaign.[44] This, in turn, makes campaigning itself less burdensome, and the process snowballs.

The basic logic of seed money programs bears some similarity to campaign finance reforms (in that campaign fundraising is presumed to be an important obstacle). But seed money programs can be targeted at specific populations, and they are rooted in a broader theory about candidate entry that acknowledges the important role of candidate recruitment. That is, public financing programs reduce the difficulty of raising money, but they do so for all candidates. Seed money programs, on the other hand, can target candidates from specific social groups, and they don't just make fundraising less burdensome; they also make the candidates they target more attractive to elite recruiters. Whereas public financing lowers one barrier to entry for everyone, seed money programs lower multiple barriers—fundraising and elite recruitment—*and* target a specific social group. And unlike campaign finance reforms, which don't seem to change candidate demographics, seed money programs have a stellar track record at increasing the number of women who run and win in the United States, at least when they have been combined with standard candidate recruitment efforts.

Although there has never been an analogous program to provide seed money for working-class Americans, there are no obvious reasons to think that it wouldn't have a similar effect on the supply of candidates and politicians from the working class. Public financing programs don't seem to change the burdens associated with running or the logic of elite recruitment enough to affect the number of workers who launch campaigns, but seed money programs embedded in recruitment efforts may have the potential to turn qualified workers into instantly viable candidates.

The second approach is perhaps the most novel proposal to date to increase the political representation of the less fortunate: *political scholarships*. The basic idea would be for an advocacy organizations to raise money year-round—like EMILY's List—but use the funds not to provide seed money for political campaigns, but to provide candidates from the working class with money for their own personal use, funds that would help with the additional practical burdens associated with running. The idea has some precedent; Ari Kamen of the Working Families Party notes, for instance, that in the past, progressive groups have given money to homemakers-turned-candidates to pay for childcare, housekeeping, and laundry services.[45]

Of course, seed money programs and political scholarships for workers would probably have to be combined with a sustained recruitment effort. The mere existence of a scholarship or a cash benefit often isn't enough to get the target population to change its behavior, as Harvard administrators learned from demonstrated need financial aid programs. But in conjunction with candidate recruitment efforts, political scholarships and seed money programs that target workers seem to have real potential.

To date, neither program has ever been used to encourage working-class candidates to run for public office in the United States, so we can only guess at how these kinds of interventions would affect the social class makeup of government. But both ideas seem to have promise. Both could be used to target workers, and both seem to be responsive to different pillars of America's cash ceiling. Campaigns are burdensome, but political scholarships could help lighten the load for workers. Candidate recruiters tend to favor affluent professionals, largely because of concerns about fundraising, but seed money programs for working-class candidates could help put concerns like those to rest.

Both ideas deserve a chance. Neither is impractical, like the long-shot proposals considered earlier—they both simply require an advocacy organization to raise money and spend it on workers, the way many groups already do for female candidates. And neither is at odds with the available empirical evidence, like the empty promises in the last section—both are in line with what we know about America's cash ceiling.

When the Working Families Party wanted to change the makeup of the people running for public office in New York, they didn't spend time debating pie-in-the-sky ideas like quotas for elected officials, nor did they attempt to make minor changes to the institutional environment like the salaries politicians are offered. Instead, they went directly to the population they wanted, recruited qualified people, helped them overcome practical obstacles, trained them, supported their campaigns, and sent them on their way.

Reformers who care about the political representation of the working class should probably follow their lead. Some are already beginning to chip away at America's cash ceiling with programs that identify, recruit, and train talented workers. Adding programs that help candidates from the working class with seed money and scholarships to cover personal expenses might make even larger cracks. America's cash ceiling makes it difficult for working-class Americans to run for public office, but it isn't invincible.

FAST-FORWARDING REFORM

Reform sometimes follows a "shoot first, ask questions later" logic. Programs are implemented before anyone really understands the root causes of the problem at hand. Stakeholders copy one another's interventions before anyone has carefully evaluated their effects. Prohibition laws swept through Western democracies but never delivered promised improvements in social vices; demonstrated need financial aid programs revolutionized how elite universities conduct financial aid but often failed to deliver promised increases in applications from talented lower-income students. Reformers eventually caught on that these interventions didn't deliver, and the trial-and-error process plodded forward.

People who care about the political representation of the working class will almost certainly have to learn as they go, too. But they might be able to considerably shorten the trial-and-error process, to skip at least some of the errors they might otherwise have made and fast-forward to ideas that work. Reforms rooted in a clear-eyed understanding of a problem have a better chance of succeeding. Interventions informed by real-world data are less likely to go astray.

Chapters 2, 3, and 4 of this book showed that working-class Americans seldom hold office not because of a deficit in qualifications, a bias on the part of voters, or a shortage of ambition, but because qualified workers seldom have the resources to shoulder the practical burdens associated with democratic elections and because political elites often have incentives to recruit white-collar candidates. Any reform has to address these obstacles head-on.

Proposals that don't address them seem to hold little promise. Activists sometimes point to pay raises for politicians as a way to increase the economic diversity of political institutions, but higher pay for leaders doesn't change the burdens associated with *campaigning*, nor does it target workers specifically, and the available data suggest that states that offer politicians higher salaries don't seem to have more working-class candidates or politicians. Likewise, public financing is often presented as a way to make campaigning more accessible to workers, but it only seems to reduce one of the *many* practical burdens associated with campaigning, and it too seems to make running more attractive to candidates of all social classes.

Of course, those reforms may have other benefits besides their effects on the social class makeup of government. Indeed, they both seem to have the potential to improve other aspects of American democracy. And from a scientific standpoint, studying them is a useful opportunity to test alternative theories about the factors responsible for America's white-collar government. However, the available data suggest that neither alternative theory has much merit—there is more to the cash ceiling than politician salaries and campaign finance practices. People who want to promote economic diversity in our political institutions could skip the trial-and-error process twice over by moving on from these proposals to other more promising alternatives.

Reforms that address the broader practical burdens associated with holding office and that change the candidate recruitment industry seem to hold more promise. The available evidence is thinner, however: politician salaries vary from place to place, and some states have public financing programs, so it is possible to study how the social class makeup of government varies across these different contexts. In contrast, programs that directly address the barriers that keep workers out of office are still relatively new, and hard data are scarce.

What little evidence there is, however, suggests that candidate training programs that identify, recruit, and coach working-class Americans to run for public office hold real promise. And programs that provide scholarships or seed money deserve their day in court, too. These ideas are not pipe dreams like government by lottery or long shots like revitalizing the labor movement—they only require that dedicated pro-worker organizations borrow from the playbooks of successful groups like EMILY's List. They are not yet *proven* ideas, but they are still *promising*.

From here, reformers will have to proceed in a trial-and-error fashion. They can save themselves a lot of trouble, however, by heeding what we know about America's cash ceiling. They can avoid devoting time and resources to false-promise interventions like pay raises and public financing, and they can keep their heads out of the clouds by not dwelling on long shots for too long. For those who care about the shortage of politicians from the working class, the history of reform efforts is still being written, and it doesn't have to follow the fraught path that many well-meaning reforms have gone down. We understand the factors that keep working Americans out of office, we know which popular proposals don't work, and we know which reforms have potential.

And those reforms may ultimately be the key to making headway on the larger problem of political inequality in the United States.

When major social interventions aren't informed by good research and theory, they often fall flat. This chapter tries to help reformers skip some of the trial and error and get to the ideas with the most potential.

- *Harvard tried to increase the economic diversity of its student body by offering need-based full-ride scholarships, but it didn't work because (as researchers figured out a decade later) financial aid is only one of several barriers keeping lower-income kids away from elite schools.*

Some proposals don't have much immediate potential, either because they aren't feasible (these *pipe dreams* include policies like social class quotas or choosing politicians at random) or because they would require massively changing society (these *long shots* include reforms like reversing the decades-long decline of organized labor, further expanding access to higher education, and redistributing income and wealth).

- *The United States is one of the only advanced democracies that hasn't adopted quotas for women in office. There isn't much chance that we'll adopt quotas for workers any time soon, either—or implement the other pipe-dream and long-shot proposals that reformers sometimes suggest.*

Other proposals have the opposite problem: although feasible, *empty promises* like pay raises for politicians and public financing don't seem to have any impact on the social class makeup of government because they don't target workers specifically and because they aren't responsive to the actual barriers that workers face.

- *Prohibition was supposed to cure numerous social ills. It didn't. Pay raises for politicians and campaign finance reforms are supposed to increase working-class representation. They won't.*

The *ideas with potential* are things like candidate training programs for workers, scholarships for working-class candidates, and seed money programs targeting workers.

- *When the Working Families Party wanted more progressive candidates to run in New York, they didn't bother tinkering with institutional rules; they just went out and recruited new candidates.*

The bottom line: Workers seldom hold office because of the practical burdens associated with competitive elections and natural biases in the candidate recruitment process. The reforms that address these pillars of America's cash ceiling—candidate recruitment programs, political scholarships, and seed money programs—are the proposals with the most potential to increase the economic diversity of our political institutions.

6

MOVING THE NEEDLE

In 2011, Carmen Castillo became the first hotel housekeeper elected to a major political office in the United States. Castillo and her three young daughters had immigrated to Rhode Island from the Dominican Republic in 1994, and since then she had been working full-time as a room attendant at the Westin Hotel in Providence. In November 2011, a member of the Providence city council unexpectedly passed away, and leaders in the union that represented housekeepers in Castillo's hotel encouraged her to run for the seat. Like all first-time candidates, she had a lot to learn about the campaign process. But her biggest challenge was simply finding the time and energy to run while holding down a job and supporting three children: "I am still working in the hotel," she noted shortly after her election. "I didn't quit my job. When you are working 40 hours a week and working 40 hours on the campaign, it's too much. But I do it because I know that to win we need to work hard."[1]

Today, Castillo is generally regarded as a champion for poor and working-class residents of Providence. She has pioneered proposals to increase the city's minimum wage, pushed to distribute social services more evenly across rich and poor neighborhoods, and advocated measures that would renovate abandoned buildings. She was re-elected easily in 2014.

Castillo's experience is squarely in line with what we know about America's cash ceiling—the factors that keep working-class Americans out of office—and with what we know about what it takes to break through it. Elections are by their very nature difficult, time-consuming, and expensive. As a result, talented working-class Americans are often deterred by the practical burdens associated with running for office, and candidate recruiters often gravitate toward white-collar candidates. With encouragement and practical support, however, many qualified workers could make great candidates and successful politicians.

This simple theory about why so few working-class Americans go on to hold office is squarely at odds with many popular ideas about our white-collar government. But as the last few chapters have shown, many popular ideas don't find much support in data on U.S. politics. Workers are seldom elected because they seldom run, not because they aren't qualified or because voters prefer white-collar candidates. And they seldom run not because they lack ambition, but because many workers can't shoulder the practical burdens associated with running and many political power-brokers recruit more conventional white-collar candidates. The issue isn't ideological or partisan: Democratic and Republican voters seem equally supportive of working-class candidates, but workers seldom run on either party's ticket, and civic leaders on both sides of the aisle tend to have low opinions of working-class candidates. Although it might be tempting to hope that changing institutional rules like legislative salaries or campaign finance practices might encourage more workers to run, the barriers facing workers run far deeper—they are the natural by-products of how we select our leaders. If we want every class of Americans to have a seat at the table in our political institutions, reformers will have to find ways to offset the practical barriers and recruiting biases that keep qualified workers from running, either with worker-focused candidate recruitment efforts or perhaps even with seed money programs and political scholarships targeting the working class.

This book has attempted to test each part of this argument using every relevant source of systematic data that I know of, including several original surveys of candidates, party leaders, and the general public. To give readers a bird's-eye view of the evidence presented here, Table 6.1 reviews the many data sets used in this book and lists how each data set corresponds to each of the book's substantive claims. (The numbers in the table correspond to the figure numbers in the book; e.g., Figure 1.1.)[2]

Of course, as each chapter has noted, there is still room for a great deal more research on each of the empirical claims made in this book. I have done my best to make full use of every available source of relevant data, but that has often meant moving quickly between different samples and data from different levels of government. As Table 6.1 illustrates, moreover, most of the data I have examined are limited to a relatively narrow window of time. In most cases, I cannot compare the size of the associations I document across different data sets. And my research foregrounds questions about class but sets aside important questions about the intersections between class and other characteristics like gender and race. Scholars are constantly collecting new data on citizens, candidates, and civic leaders, and I hope that some will use the information they gather to continue improving our understanding of the factors that keep working-class Americans out of office. My aim here was not to have the last word, but to *start* a conversation about America's cash ceiling.

That conversation is long overdue. And it may be the key to making progress on the larger problem of political inequality in the United States.

WE KNOW WE HAVE A PROBLEM

In 2004, an American Political Science Association (APSA) task force released a twenty-two-page report on the links between economic inequality and American democracy. In many respects, the report's conclusions were long overdue. Scholars had known for decades about significant economic gaps in political voice and influence in the United States. However, their findings had often been scattered across different subfields and literatures. The APSA task force report, titled "American Democracy in an Age of Rising Inequality," wove together disparate threads of scholarship in a way that had never been done before—and that had alarming implications. Drawing on decades of research, the report noted that affluent people participate more actively in politics and are better represented in the organized

TABLE 6.1. An Overview of the Analysis in This Book

	Data set	Nat'l Candidate Study	Nat'l Survey of Party Leaders
	sample	candidates	party leaders
	level of office	state	county
	Time frame	2012, 2014	2013
	format	ind.-level survey	ind.-level surv
Ch. 1 **The shortage of politicians from the working class matters.**			
Working-class Americans rarely go on to hold office.			
Workers bring different perspectives to public office		1.3	
Ch. 2 **Workers seldom hold office because they seldom run.**			
(Aside: How voters and party leaders define "qualified.")			2.1, 2.2
Workers are about as qualified as professionals.			
Workers do about as well in elections as professionals.			
Workers seldom hold office because they seldom run.		2.9	
Ch. 3 **Workers seldom run because they can't and no one asks them.**			
Workers can't shoulder the practical burdens associated with running.			
Workers are *not* less interested in holding office.			
Workers are less likely to be encouraged by civic leaders.		3.12	3.9–3.11
Ch. 4 **Elections by their very nature discourage workers.**			
In places with burdensome elections, workers run and govern less often.			
Civic leaders tend to prefer candidates who are friends and acquaintances.			4.5–4.7
Ch. 5 **Reforms should focus on practical burdens and recruitment gaps.**			
Increasing politician salaries won't help.		5.1–5.3	
Publicly financing elections won't help.		5.5, 5.7	5.8
Candidate recruitment and training programs seem to hold promise.			

Note: The numbers listed here correspond to the figure numbers in the book (e.g., Figure 1.1).

ьblic Opinion llow-up	Nat'l Conf. of State Leg.	ICMA/Census of Gov'ts	CLASS Data set	Roster Data set	Other Data sets
пeral public	elected officials	elected officials	elected officials	elected officials	various
а	state	City	federal	federal	various
)14	79, 93, 95, 07	1996, 2001	1999–2008	1789–1996	various
d.-level survey	agg.-level data	agg.-level data	ind.-level data	ind.-level data	various
	1.1, 1.2	1.1	1.1, 1.2	1.1, 1.2	1.1, 1.2
2.1, 2.2					
2.3, 2.4		2.6			2.5
2.8			2.7	2.7	2.7
					2.9
3.2, 3.3	3.5				3.4
3.6, 3.7	3.8				
	3.13				
	4.2	4.1	4.3	4.3	4.4
	4.8				
	5.4				
	5.6				
	5.9				5.10

pressure system. As a result, "public officials . . . are much more responsive to the privileged than to average citizens and the least affluent. Citizens with lower or moderate incomes speak with a whisper that is lost on the ears of inattentive government officials, while the advantaged roar with a clarity and consistency that policy-makers readily hear and routinely follow."[3] For the first time, the field of political science had collectively and forcefully acknowledged that Americans who are disadvantaged economically are also profoundly disadvantaged politically.

The task force report was a watershed moment for research on the politics of economic inequality. In the years that followed, the report inspired a number of lengthy extensions, debates, and even some emotional criticisms.[4] The report and the edited volume and journal symposium that grew out of it[5] have since been cited more than 650 times, and the APSA now has a standing Organized Section on Economic and Social Class Inequality. When the APSA held a retrospective panel on the task force report at its 2016 annual meeting, more than 100 scholars packed the room.

In the span of just over a decade, the relationship between economic inequality and political inequality has become a front-and-center topic among scholars of American politics. And scholars have in turn vastly expanded what we know about the mechanisms by which economic power translates into political power. Political scientists know more than ever about biases in routine forms of political participation (e.g., how the less fortunate are less likely follow the news and turn out to vote, or whether the public is concerned about rising economic inequality).[6] They know more about inequalities in the organized pressure system (e.g., how unions are declining, the wealthy are spending more and more on campaigns, and business-backed interest groups are becoming more numerous and more sophisticated).[7] And about the rules and strategic incentives that discourage political institutions from supporting the less fortunate (e.g., how rules that encourage gridlock make it difficult for government to respond to rising economic inequality, or how parties have strategic incentives to direct resources to affluent constituents).[8]

But perhaps the most troubling finding that has emerged since the APSA task force report has to do not with *inputs* into the political process, but with *outcomes*. A few years after the report, two prominent political scientists (using very different research designs) confirmed what scholars of unequal political voice have long suspected, namely, that the views of the less fortunate have little influence on public policy in the United States. One study by Larry Bartels compared data on the political ideologies of the bottom, middle, and top thirds of income earners in each state to data on how senators cast their roll-call votes. Bartels found that voting in the Senate is strongly correlated with the ideologies of rich constituents but not poor constituents. Another scholar, Martin Gilens, investigated whether the average views of the rich and poor were associated with actual changes in public policy. Using data from 1,800 national surveys about particular policy proposals conducted between 1981 and 2002 and corresponding data on whether the proposals in question actually passed, Gilens found that when the views of the rich and the poor diverged, public policy almost always sided with the rich.[9]

Bartels and Gilens weren't the first to raise this possibility, of course,[10] but their work elevated the phenomenon of *unequal responsiveness* to national prominence, both in the field political science and beyond. (In 2014, Gilens even appeared alongside coauthor Ben Page on *The Daily Show with Jon Stewart*.) Subsequent studies have mostly reached the same dim conclusions.[11] The views of the poor, it would seem, are usually drowned out in American politics by the views of the well-off.

We know, in short, that the United States has a serious political inequality problem. What we don't know yet is how to solve it.

CASTING A WIDER NET

Reforms aimed at addressing the oversized political influence of the wealthy have historically tended to focus on inequalities in *political voice*, imbalances in the ways that citizens and groups pressure government from the outside. The ideas are familiar and well-worn in the reform community: when activists and reformers have tried to do something about inequalities in political power, most have focused either on closing gaps in *routine forms of political participation* like voting and contacting elected officials or on addressing *biases in the organized pressure system* like the decline of labor unions, the growing sophistication of pro-business lobbying, and the increasing importance of wealthy campaign donors. We've heard the same refrain for decades: if we could reform lobbying and campaign finance and get a handle on the flow of money in politics, the rich wouldn't have as much of a say in government. If we could promote broader political participation, enlighten the public, and revitalize the labor movement, the poor would have more of a say. The key to combating political inequality, in this view, is simply finding ways to make sure that everyone's voices can be heard.

This perspective has a wide reach in the reform community. Most private foundations that support research on political inequality, for instance, focus primarily on inequalities in political voice. The Ford Foundation's Civic Engagement and Government group funds work to "make the systems that govern political participation more fair and inclusive, particularly for historically excluded populations" and "to ensure that the rules of the game for political participation are inclusive of all, with a special focus on voting rights and democratizing money in politics in the US."[12] The Russell Sage Foundation's Program on Social Inequality funds research asking, "Has rising inequality affected legislative performance, political voice, political responsiveness, polarization, or government actions and reforms?" and "Has rising economic inequality allowed economic elites greater access to and influence on the policy process and policy outcomes at the national and subnational levels?"[13] In both cases, political inequality is framed as something that begins with inequalities in external pressure, that is, with gaps in participation, money, voice, and access.

Of course, correcting these kinds of inequalities would almost certainly help make American politics less beholden to the views of the wealthy and more responsive to the needs of ordinary Americans. But these familiar reform ideas have an important limitation: so far, they've been remarkably difficult to actually carry out. For at least the last half century, reformers have been trying to regulate lobbyists, combat soaring campaign spending, resuscitate the labor movement, enlighten the public, and increase political participation. But every major reform effort has proven more technically and politically challenging than its supporters had initially hoped. Regulating lobbying and campaign finance, for instance, has been fraught with technical hurdles: some compare it "to squeezing a balloon—if you squeeze in one place the balloon simply pops out in another."[14] Getting the money out of politics (or equalizing the money in politics), moreover, requires not just a loophole-free plan but also the political muscle to make it happen— something that is nearly impossible to marshal when most lawmakers depend on big money to finance tomorrow's campaigns. The same is true of efforts to equalize political participation. As Hacker and Pierson noted almost a decade ago, "We actually know how to increase voter turnout with relatively straightforward reforms" like same-day registration and early voting, but those reforms "have, not surprisingly, failed to gain traction within elite Washington."[15]

This isn't to say that reformers should give up on lobbying regulations, campaign finance reform, revitalizing organized labor, or expanding political participation. If dedicated activists hadn't been working on these issues the last few decades, political inequality in the United States would probably be even worse than it is today. But if reformers want to continue making headway on the problem of political inequality, they will need to cast an even wider net, to consider new and innovative approaches to the problem of political inequality.

In my view, one of the single most promising new proposals—one of the reforms best positioned to actually make progress on the problem of political inequality—is the simple idea of encouraging more qualified working-class Americans to run for and hold political office.

There is plenty of evidence that increasing the number of working-class people who hold office would make government more responsive to the needs of the less fortunate (as chapter 1 noted). When millionaires set the tax rate for millionaires, white-collar professionals set the minimum wage for blue-collar workers, and people who have always had health insurance get to decide whether to help people without it, the effects are predictable. As the old political proverb says, *If you're not at the table, you're on the menu.* If reformers want government to pay attention to the voices of the less fortunate, helping the less fortunate get a seat at the table would be a good way to do it.

Promoting this kind of economic diversity in our political institutions, moreover, seems more practically feasible than many of the ideas that are currently part of the mainstream political equality reform agenda. Unlike proposals to close participation gaps or regulate money in politics, programs that would increase the representation of the working class don't require passing major legislation or changing the civic habits of millions of Americans. To the contrary, helping workers break through America's cash ceiling seems to be as simple as setting up voluntary programs that identify, recruit, and train new candidates from the working class (as chapter 5 noted). There are scores of successful examples, both prominent national candidate recruitment organizations that target groups like women and a handful of pilot efforts to recruit and train working-class candidates in places like New Jersey, Maine, Oregon, and Nevada. Reformers have a great deal to show for these kinds of interventions. Since the 1960s, voter turnout has been stagnant or declining[16] and campaign spending has soared (between 2000 and 2016 alone, the amount of money spent on federal elections jumped from $4.3 billion to $6.4 billion).[17] In contrast, efforts to increase the gender diversity of American political institutions have delivered stunning results: in 1960, only 3 percent of members of Congress were women; today, that number is almost 20 percent.

The political equality reform community has always had a curious blind spot when it comes to the idea of helping working-class Americans get elected. Some reformers undoubtedly worry that workers aren't qualified, or that workers would bring regressive views on important social issues, or that increasing the number of workers in public office would mean sacrificing important gains in the numbers of women or racial and ethnic minorities. The available evidence, however, suggests that these kinds of reservations are utterly misplaced (as chapters 1 and 2 noted). There are lots of qualified workers out there. Many of them are also women, people of color, and members of other historically underrepresented groups.[18]

(Mike Michaud, the first working-class politician mentioned in this book, was also one of the first openly gay members of Congress.) And workers tend to do well in politics: when they run, they tend to win, and when they hold office, they tend to govern effectively.

In light of how hard it's been to close the gaps in who participates, organizes, donates, and votes, it may be time for reformers to consider ways to close the gap in *who governs*. It is of course important to try to make the voices of the poor louder and clearer by promoting broader political participation and to try to make the voices of the rich less of a roar by limiting lobbying and campaign donations. But the rich aren't just the ones doing the talking in American politics; they're also the ones *doing the listening*.

And that may be easier to change right now. Programs to increase the number of working-class people who go on to become politicians—programs to help qualified working-class Americans break through our country's cash ceiling—represent a new way of addressing the oversized political influence of the rich. And they seem straightforward to implement: if pro-equality foundations and donors partnered with organizations that recruit and train candidates (like political parties and interest groups) and organizations that have regular contact with working-class people (like labor unions, churches, government agencies, and community organizations), they could generate worker-focused candidate training programs, seed money programs, and political scholarships in the span of just a few years. In this case, reform isn't rocket science; the right political entrepreneur simply needs to come along. At a time when every other political equality reform strategy is struggling just to hold its ground, programs to encourage working-class people to hold office offer reformers a rare opportunity to actually move the needle toward greater political equality.

ADAM SMITH AND DONALD TRUMP

In 1776, the Scottish economist Adam Smith published *The Wealth of Nations*, a book widely credited as the first major work to outline the economic theory that when people pursue their own self-interest, they also promote the greater good of society. In a free-market economy, Smith argued, people have to compete to sell products, services, and their own labor. That competitive environment gives people who hope to get ahead natural incentives to work harder, produce more, innovate more, and sell their goods and services for lower prices. And that in turn is great for everyone else. In this view, free-market capitalism is essentially human society's ultimate win-win: the free market's influence—its invisible hand—guides even people who only care about themselves to do things that also make their neighbors' lives better.

Of course, Smith wasn't naïve about the many ways that purely self-interested people could still create problems for the rest of society. As long as the rules of the free-market game were in effect, Smith argued, self-interested people would have incentives to do socially valuable things like work hard and innovate. But if a self-interested person ever amassed enough power to *tinker with* the rules of the game, he reasoned, their self-interest could actually lead them to drown out free-market capitalism and the competition and social benefits that come with it. Monopolies were a case in point. If an industrialist could somehow ensure that no one else could sell a competing product, it would certainly be in his best interest to do so—but of course that would give him a stranglehold on the supply of that product, which could be disastrous for competition, quality, innovation, and prices.

Smith had an even graver concern than monopolies, however—a concern so significant that he made it the focus of the closing paragraphs of Book One of *The Wealth of Nations*. According to Smith, the most urgent danger that self-interested people posed to capitalism was not that they might take over a single industry, but that they might take over the institution that regulated *every* industry: government. Smith's parting words in Book One are worth quoting at length:

> The interest of the dealers . . . in any particular branch of trade or manufactures, is always in some respects different from, and even opposite to, that of the public. To widen the market and to narrow the competition, is always the interest of the dealers. To widen the market may

frequently be agreeable enough to the interest of the public; but to narrow the competition must always be against it, and can serve only to enable the dealers, by raising their profits above what they naturally would be, to levy, for their own benefit, an absurd tax upon the rest of their fellow-citizens.

For that reason, Smith warned, public policy should never be dictated by the people at the top of the economy:

The proposal of any new law or regulation of commerce which comes from this order ought always to be listened to with great precaution, and ought never to be adopted till after having been long and carefully examined, not only with the most scrupulous, but with the most suspicious attention. It comes from an order of men whose interest is never exactly the same with that of the public, who have generally an interest to deceive and even to oppress the public, and who accordingly have, upon many occasions, both deceived and oppressed it.[19]

Enter Donald Trump. If there were ever a critical test of Smith's arguments about putting the economic elite in charge of government, the present moment in American politics might just be it. The president is a billionaire with vast and complex ongoing business interests around the world. He has appointed the richest cabinet in U.S. history, drawing heavily on his personal connections within the business community. He has called for slashing taxes on the wealthy and cutting health care for the poor. He has used the office of the president to urge citizens to boycott a department store chain that dropped his daughter's clothing line, and his wife's attorney has described the office of First Lady as a "unique, once-in-a-lifetime opportunity . . . to launch a broad-based commercial brand in multiple product categories, each of which could [garner] multi-million dollar business relationships."[20]

All this, moreover, has played out against a political backdrop that has always been dominated by the wealthy. The outgoing president, after all, was a millionaire. Trump's opponent in the general election was a millionaire.

His opponents in the crowded Republican primary were mostly million-aires. Most members of Congress are millionaires. Most Supreme Court justices are millionaires. Adjusting for inflation, more than three-quarters of all U.S. presidents have been millionaires. The Trump administration is certainly a vivid example of government by the privileged—maybe the most vivid in American history—but Donald Trump didn't invent government by the rich in the United States. His administration simply set a new high score.

It's still too early to tell, of course, whether public policy under Trump will ultimately be as oppressive, deceptive, and harmful to the public inter-est as the policies Adam Smith envisioned in his warnings about the dan-gers of empowering economic elites. Trump has many supporters from the working class—like Mitt Romney before him, around one-third of Trump's voters came from the bottom half of the income distribution.[21] For his part, Trump's own view of government by the rich is far rosier than Adam Smith's: speaking about his decision to appoint Goldman Sachs president Wilbur Ross as secretary of commerce, Trump argued, for instance, "Why did [I] appoint a rich person to be in charge of the economy? . . . Because that's the kind of thinking we want. . . . These are people that are great brilliant business minds, and that's what we need, that's what we have to have. . . . And I love all people, rich or poor, but in those particular posi-tions, I just don't want a poor person."[22]

Rhetoric aside, the outlook for the working class isn't promising under a billionaire president. Research on the economic backgrounds of politi-cians in the United States has largely supported Smith's general intuition: the social classes that politicians come from seem to influence the policies they create. And the effect isn't just limited to the captains of industry that Smith warned about; politicians from all walks of life seem to bring their classes' perspectives with them to public office. If Donald Trump spends his time in office promoting the interests of his slice of the economy, he certainly won't be the first politician to do it.

Why, then, is the United States governed by affluent politicians? On this point, *The Wealth of Nations* offers far less guidance. Adam Smith may have been gravely concerned about the consequences of letting industrialists write a nation's laws, but he was silent about how that might come about or what concerned citizens could do to stop it.[23]

For the most part, modern research on U.S. politics has been silent, too. Only a handful of studies have ever asked what keeps lower-income and working-class Americans out of office or why a democracy where virtually anyone can stand for public office is governed almost exclusively by the rich.

This book has tried to begin changing that. To understand why so many billionaires and business owners write our country's laws, we need to understand what keeps people from the opposite end of the economic spectrum, working-class people, out of office. This book has tried to help answer that question, first by dispensing with political fictions that, although comforting to some, mischaracterize working-class Americans as unfit to govern or unelectable in the eyes of voters. What really keeps working-class people out isn't a deficit of qualifications, it's the practical burdens that elections inevitably impose on the people who campaign for public office and the people who recruit them. Our democratic process naturally creates a cash ceiling, a collection of structural barriers that powerfully discourage working-class people from becoming politicians.

Those barriers aren't invincible, however. To the contrary, strategies that are commonly used to increase the representation of women and other historically underrepresented groups seem to work just as well for the working class. There are lots of qualified workers out there, and when they run, they tend to do well. They seldom run because elections naturally create practical burdens that discourage the less fortunate and give candidate recruiters incentives to pass them over. But those are features of our political process that activist organizations know how to counteract—and that may be easier to change than many of the other barriers to political equality, like unequal political participation and soaring campaign spending. Programs that would increase the political representation of working-class Americans aren't risky bets; they're actually some of the most promising pro-equality reforms out there today.

This idea is certainly outside the mainstream, and that means that it will naturally face a great deal of skepticism and institutional inertia.

But if a foundation, political party, or large-scale advocacy organization ever launched a national program to recruit more working-class candidates, the results would likely be transformative. The opportunity to go down in history as the next EMILY's List is just waiting there for some forward-looking organization.

Until then, however, working-class Americans will continue to be just a trickle in the larger candidate pipeline. Most qualified workers will be discouraged from ever running by the painful realities of campaigns and elections in the United States. The few who do run will confront a cash ceiling that powerfully advantages the well-off. Only a handful will find ways to push through it, often out of a larger sense of economic and political desperation.

For Troy Jackson—the logger-turned-state-senator from Maine who almost became the first working-class person to succeed another worker in the same U.S. House seat—the final straw was what happened to his family every Sunday night:

> In order to do the best I could for my family, I was willing to take any logging job to keep a roof over our heads. Within a few years' time, that meant leaving Allagash every week for job sites far from home. . . . As most of us who live paycheck to paycheck do, I tried to accept it as just the way things were. But I knew that something wasn't right. Especially on Sunday nights. You see, Sunday nights, I packed my lunch box and packed some clothes for the week preparing for my long drive early in the morning to places down in the Golden Road. And Sunday nights, my son, who was three or four by then, would ask me not to go. He'd tell me that he was going to stay awake holding my hand all night so that when morning came I'd still be there for him. I used to watch him fight to stay awake with his little hand wrapped around my thumb, as if by strength of his will alone he could keep me at home. As if all the strength he had in that little hand could counter generations of corporate greed that was keeping other young children in the St. John Valley from their parents. It was on those long Sunday nights that turned into Monday mornings

that I stopped accepting things the way they were and started thinking about the way that they should be.[24]

It's time for those of us who care about the oversized political influence of the rich to do the same, to stop accepting that professionals and industrialists are the only people who can write our laws, to stop limiting the conversation about political inequality to familiar topics like voter turnout and campaign donors, and to start working to give every class of Americans a seat at the table in government.

CHAPTER 6 SUMMARY

We know we have a political inequality problem: political outcomes in the United States tend to be far more responsive to what the rich want than to what the poor want.

- *The problem has become so severe that political scientists have started sounding serious organizational alarms, like the 2004 American Political Science Association task force report "American Democracy in an Age of Rising Inequality."*

What reformers don't know is how to solve it: the mainstream reform conversation has largely centered on programs that would increase the political voice of the less fortunate or mute the political voice of the affluent, but those kinds of interventions are running into serious practical and political barriers.

- *Foundations that do work on political inequality focus primarily on inequalities in voter turnout and campaign donations, two phenomena that have proven remarkably resilient despite reformers' best efforts.*

Reformers should consider adding another strategy, namely, helping qualified working-class people get elected. Compared to other popular reform proposals, this approach may be the easiest and most effective way to make progress on the problem of political inequality.

- *If you're not at the table, you're on the menu.*

The bottom line: In an age of soaring campaign spending, record amounts of political lobbying, and declining labor unions, the best hope for combating the oversized political influence of the rich might simply be to help more working-class Americans become politicians.

Appendix

TABLE A1.1. Auxiliary Regression Models for Figure 1.3

Did the respondent agree with the statement . . . ?	Reduce bus. reg.	Gov. should reduce inequal.	Abolish welfare	Gov. not respons. for health care
Business owner (ind)	0.325**	−0.163	0.162	0.301**
	(0.103)	(0.092)	(0.092)	(0.098)
Business employee (ind)	0.280**	−0.133	0.193*	0.292**
	(0.105)	(0.094)	(0.094)	(0.100)
Technical professional (ind)	0.211	−0.066	0.183	0.304**
	(0.113)	(0.101)	(0.101)	(0.108)
Farm owner / manager (ind)	0.312*	0.011	0.166	0.274*
	(0.123)	(0.109)	(0.109)	(0.115)
Lawyer (ind)	0.312*	−0.135	0.132	0.427***
	(0.133)	(0.120)	(0.119)	(0.127)
Military/law enf (ind)	0.381**	−0.162	0.315**	0.313*
	(0.131)	(0.122)	(0.122)	(0.127)
Politician/staffer (ind)	0.172	−0.055	0.259*	0.284*
	(0.118)	(0.106)	(0.106)	(0.114)
Service Professional (ind)	0.208*	−0.120	0.183	0.325**
	(0.105)	(0.093)	(0.094)	(0.100)
Worker (omitted)	—	—	—	—
Other occ. (ind)	0.254*	−0.072	0.151	0.229*
	(0.114)	(0.102)	(0.101)	(0.108)
Democrat (ind)	−0.595***	0.650***	−0.229***	−0.639***
	(0.045)	(0.041)	(0.041)	(0.043)

continued

TABLE **A1.1.** *(Continued)*

Did the respondent agree with the statement . . . ?	Reduce bus. reg.	Gov. should reduce inequal.	Abolish welfare	Gov. not respons. for health care
Age 18–25 (omitted)	—	—	—	—
Age 26–34 (ind)	0.096	0.040	0.033	−0.070
	(0.187)	(0.171)	(0.172)	(0.180)
Age 35–44 (ind)	0.125	0.001	0.015	0.014
	(0.180)	(0.165)	(0.166)	(0.174)
Age 45–54 (ind)	0.174	−0.009	−0.079	−0.046
	(0.178)	(0.163)	(0.164)	(0.172)
Age 55–64 (ind)	0.115	−0.045	−0.050	−0.029
	(0.176)	(0.161)	(0.162)	(0.170)
Age 65+ (ind)	0.101	−0.060	−0.091	−0.078
	(0.177)	(0.162)	(0.163)	(0.171)
White (ind)	0.051	−0.115*	−0.153**	−0.066
	(0.055)	(0.051)	(0.051)	(0.053)
Education: High school (omitted)	—	—	—	—
Education: Vocational (ind)	0.214	−0.225	0.081	−0.020
	(0.173)	(0.154)	(0.152)	(0.167)
Education: Some college (ind)	0.067	−0.026	−0.049	0.110
	(0.111)	(0.106)	(0.102)	(0.107)
Education: College (ind)	0.028	−0.006	−0.068	0.087
	(0.105)	(0.100)	(0.096)	(0.101)
Education: Master's (ind)	0.015	−0.011	−0.108	0.052
	(0.107)	(0.102)	(0.099)	(0.104)
Education: Law degree (ind)	−0.024	0.036	−0.100	−0.018
	(0.131)	(0.124)	(0.120)	(0.126)
Education: Other prof degree (ind)	0.144	−0.037	0.067	0.147
	(0.127)	(0.119)	(0.116)	(0.123)
Education: Doctoral degree (ind)	0.041	−0.028	−0.138	0.033
	(0.119)	(0.112)	(0.108)	(0.114)

continued

AUXILIARY ANALYSES

TABLE **A1.1.** *(Continued)*

Did the respondent agree with the statement . . . ?	Reduce bus. reg.	Gov. should reduce inequal.	Abolish welfare	Gov. not respons. for health care
Education: Other (ind)	−0.068	−0.105	0.011	0.263
	(0.165)	(0.154)	(0.171)	(0.169)
Male (ind)	0.009	0.057	0.035	0.018
	(0.037)	(0.034)	(0.033)	(0.035)
State Squire Index (0 to 1)	0.154	−0.101	−0.214	−0.186
	(0.191)	(0.175)	(0.172)	(0.180)
District: Percent White	0.037	0.119	0.038	0.076
	(0.098)	(0.089)	(0.089)	(0.094)
District: Median Income	−0.000	0.000	0.000	0.000
	(0.000)	(0.000)	(0.000)	(0.000)
District: Total Population	0.000	0.000	0.000	−0.000
	(0.000)	(0.000)	(0.000)	(0.000)
District: Legislator's Estimate of Obama Vote Share	−0.002	0.005***	−0.001	−0.003*
	(0.001)	(0.001)	(0.001)	(0.001)
Intercept	0.481	0.001	0.336	0.578*
	(0.247)	(0.227)	(0.226)	(0.238)
N	519	513	515	521
R^2	0.536	0.631	0.220	0.581

Source: Broockman et al. 2012.

Note: Cells report coefficients (with clustered standard errors in parentheses). $*p < 0.05$, $**p < 0.01$, $***p < 0.001$, two-tailed.

TABLE **A2.1. Auxiliary Regression Models for Figure 2.3**

Did the respondent agree with the statement . . . ?	assertive	a hard worker	outgoing	honest	good pub. speaker	dedicated to party	five or six
Worker (ind)	−0.07	0.02	−0.05	−0.08*	−0.08+	−0.07*	−0.04
	(0.05)	(0.04)	(0.06)	(0.04)	(0.04)	(0.04)	(0.04)
Democrats (omitted)	—	—	—	—	—	—	—
Republicans (ind)	0.04	−0.08	−0.00	−0.06	−0.06	0.12*	−0.01
	(0.08)	(0.07)	(0.08)	(0.06)	(0.06)	(0.05)	(0.06)
Independents (ind)	0.01	−0.08	0.02	−0.01	−0.01	−0.08*	−0.06
	(0.06)	(0.05)	(0.06)	(0.05)	(0.05)	(0.03)	(0.05)
Other party (ind)	−0.01	−0.09	−0.22+	0.04	−0.23**	−0.16**	−0.18**
	(0.14)	(0.14)	(0.12)	(0.07)	(0.05)	(0.04)	(0.04)
Ext. liberal (omitted)	—	—	—	—	—	—	—
Liberal (ind)	−0.13	−0.11	0.04	0.02	0.11	−0.14	0.05
	(0.13)	(0.10)	(0.13)	(0.07)	(0.11)	(0.11)	(0.10)
Slightly liberal (ind)	−0.21	−0.01	−0.06	−0.09	0.00	−0.22*	0.01
	(0.14)	(0.09)	(0.14)	(0.08)	(0.11)	(0.10)	(0.10)
Moderate (ind)	−0.30*	0.04	−0.03	−0.02	−0.06	−0.21*	−0.09
	(0.13)	(0.08)	(0.12)	(0.07)	(0.09)	(0.10)	(0.08)
Slightly cons. (ind)	−0.32*	0.02	−0.08	0.11	0.05	−0.21*	0.01
	(0.14)	(0.10)	(0.14)	(0.07)	(0.11)	(0.10)	(0.10)
Conservative (ind)	−0.23	0.09	−0.04	0.10	0.04	−0.04	0.04
	(0.14)	(0.10)	(0.14)	(0.07)	(0.10)	(0.11)	(0.10)
Extremely cons. (ind)	−0.09	0.13	0.01	0.17*	0.16	0.02	0.10
	(0.18)	(0.09)	(0.18)	(0.08)	(0.16)	(0.18)	(0.16)
Male (omitted)	—	—	—	—	—	—	—
Female (ind)	−0.12*	−0.10*	−0.04	0.07*	−0.05	−0.06+	−0.07+
	(0.05)	(0.04)	(0.05)	(0.03)	(0.04)	(0.03)	(0.04)
Age (continuous)	−0.00*	−0.01**	0.00	0.00*	−0.00	0.00	−0.00
	(0.00)	(0.00)	(0.00)	(0.00)	(0.00)	(0.00)	(0.00)

continued

TABLE **A2.1.** *(Continued)*

Did the respondent agree with the statement . . . ?	assertive	a hard worker	outgoing	honest	good pub. speaker	dedicated to party	five or six
White (ind)	0.17+	0.12	0.07	−0.01	0.04	0.13+	0.11
	(0.09)	(0.08)	(0.10)	(0.07)	(0.10)	(0.07)	(0.09)
Black (ind)	0.32**	0.18*	0.26*	0.02	0.20+	0.28**	0.29**
	(0.10)	(0.07)	(0.10)	(0.07)	(0.11)	(0.08)	(0.10)
Hispanic (ind)	0.10	0.02	0.18*	−0.03	0.12	0.13*	0.14+
	(0.08)	(0.06)	(0.08)	(0.05)	(0.08)	(0.06)	(0.08)
Asian (ind)	0.12	0.13	0.14	−0.09	−0.10	0.06	0.00
	(0.11)	(0.09)	(0.12)	(0.08)	(0.10)	(0.07)	(0.09)
Native American (ind)	0.29*	0.20**	0.01	0.03	−0.21	0.13	0.21
	(0.12)	(0.08)	(0.14)	(0.07)	(0.13)	(0.14)	(0.17)
Pacific Islander (ind)	0.63**	0.33**	0.30	0.12	0.34	−0.05	0.45+
	(0.13)	(0.10)	(0.24)	(0.08)	(0.22)	(0.08)	(0.24)
Other race (ind)	0.23+	0.02	0.27*	0.11+	0.11	0.13	0.27*
	(0.13)	(0.11)	(0.13)	(0.06)	(0.14)	(0.10)	(0.14)
Married (omitted)	—	—	—	—	—	—	—
Not married (ind)	0.06	0.04	0.04	0.04	0.03	0.04	0.05
	(0.05)	(0.05)	(0.06)	(0.04)	(0.04)	(0.04)	(0.04)
Has children (omitted)	—	—	—	—	—	—	—
No children (ind)	−0.05	−0.10+	−0.07	0.07+	−0.00	0.04	0.02
	(0.06)	(0.06)	(0.06)	(0.04)	(0.04)	(0.04)	(0.04)
Intercept	0.67**	1.05**	0.35+	0.69**	0.21	0.18	0.12
	(0.18)	(0.13)	(0.18)	(0.10)	(0.14)	(0.14)	(0.13)
N	912	912	912	912	912	912	912
R^2	0.100	0.111	0.056	0.085	0.080	0.173	0.124

Source: Broockman et al. 2014a.

Note: Cells report coefficients (with clustered standard errors in parentheses). $+p < 0.10$, $*p < 0.05$, $**p < 0.01$, two-tailed.

Table A2.2. Auxiliary Regression Models for Figure 2.4

Did the respondent agree with the statement . . . ?	Vote	Contact elected officials	Volun. for camp. orgs.	Volun. for civic groups	Vol. for comm. orgs.	Donate money to polit. causes	Work for a gov.-related business	Work for a camp.	Work for a sitting pol.
Worker (ind)	-0.05 (0.04)	-0.08** (0.03)	-0.08** (0.03)	-0.01 (0.03)	-0.02 (0.04)	-0.11** (0.04)	0.02 (0.02)	0.02 (0.02)	-0.00 (0.00)
Democrats (omitted)	—	—	—	—	—	—	—	—	—
Republicans (ind)	0.06 (0.04)	-0.06 (0.06)	0.08+ (0.04)	0.03 (0.04)	-0.13* (0.06)	-0.09 (0.06)	-0.05 (0.03)	-0.00 (0.03)	-0.00 (0.00)
Independents (ind)	-0.05 (0.04)	0.00 (0.04)	-0.05 (0.03)	-0.01 (0.04)	-0.02 (0.05)	-0.10* (0.04)	-0.03 (0.02)	-0.03 (0.02)	-0.00 (0.00)
Other party (ind)	-0.04 (0.06)	0.05 (0.14)	0.04 (0.09)	-0.07* (0.03)	-0.09 (0.13)	-0.16* (0.07)	-0.00 (0.05)	0.02 (0.05)	-0.00 (0.00)
Ext lib. (omitted)	—	—	—	—	—	—	—	—	—
Liberal (ind)	0.17 (0.12)	-0.11 (0.07)	-0.11 (0.07)	-0.02 (0.07)	0.01 (0.09)	-0.13 (0.08)	-0.14 (0.11)	0.00 (0.02)	0.01+ (0.00)
Slightly liberal (ind)	0.05 (0.13)	-0.08 (0.09)	0.01 (0.09)	-0.01 (0.08)	0.10 (0.10)	-0.09 (0.09)	-0.13 (0.11)	0.00 (0.02)	-0.00 (0.00)
Moderate (ind)	0.13 (0.12)	-0.14+ (0.07)	-0.10 (0.07)	-0.06 (0.07)	0.05 (0.09)	-0.09 (0.08)	-0.13 (0.12)	0.01 (0.02)	0.00 (0.00)

Slightly cons. (ind)	0.08 (0.12)	-0.00 (0.09)	-0.02 (0.08)	0.06 (0.08)	0.19+ (0.10)	-0.07 (0.09)	-0.10 (0.13)	0.06 (0.04)	0.00 (0.00)
Conservative (ind)	0.06 (0.12)	0.02 (0.09)	-0.10 (0.08)	0.00 (0.07)	0.14 (0.10)	-0.09 (0.10)	-0.11 (0.12)	0.06 (0.05)	0.00 (0.00)
Ext cons. (ind)	-0.16 (0.17)	-0.03 (0.10)	-0.09 (0.09)	0.08 (0.13)	0.19 (0.16)	0.02 (0.16)	-0.13 (0.12)	-0.01 (0.03)	0.00 (0.00)
Male (omitted)	—	—	—	—	—	—	—	—	—
Female (ind)	-0.06+ (0.03)	-0.02 (0.03)	-0.01 (0.03)	0.03 (0.03)	0.05 (0.04)	-0.12** (0.04)	0.02 (0.02)	-0.02 (0.02)	-0.00 (0.00)
Age (continuous)	0.00** (0.00)	0.00 (0.00)	-0.00* (0.00)	-0.00** (0.00)	-0.00 (0.00)	0.00 (0.00)	-0.00 (0.00)	-0.00* (0.00)	-0.00 (0.00)
White (ind)	0.00 (0.07)	0.06 (0.09)	0.14+ (0.08)	0.17* (0.08)	0.16+ (0.10)	-0.06 (0.07)	-0.11+ (0.05)	-0.02 (0.02)	-0.00 (0.00)
Black (ind)	-0.02 (0.07)	0.15 (0.11)	0.24* (0.10)	0.23* (0.10)	0.27* (0.12)	-0.06 (0.07)	-0.10+ (0.05)	-0.01 (0.02)	-0.00 (0.00)
Hispanic (ind)	-0.04 (0.05)	0.06 (0.07)	0.12+ (0.07)	0.12+ (0.07)	0.07 (0.08)	-0.07 (0.05)	0.00 (0.02)	-0.03 (0.02)	-0.00 (0.00)
Asian (ind)	-0.06 (0.08)	0.14 (0.12)	0.16+ (0.09)	0.26** (0.10)	0.21+ (0.12)	-0.14* (0.07)	-0.08 (0.05)	0.02 (0.04)	0.01 (0.01)
Native American (ind)	-0.09 (0.08)	-0.11 (0.21)	-0.23 (0.16)	-0.24 (0.15)	-0.10 (0.21)	0.18 (0.12)	0.03 (0.04)	-0.03 (0.03)	-0.01 (0.01)

continued

TABLE A2.2. (Continued)

Did the respondent agree with the statement . . . ?	Vote	Contact elected officials	Volun. for camp. orgs.	Volun. for civic groups	Vol. for comm. orgs.	Donate money to polit. causes	Work for a gov.-related business	Work for a camp.	Work for a sitting pol.
Pacific Islander (ind)	0.02 (0.07)	0.06 (0.13)	0.05 (0.09)	0.09 (0.08)	0.27 (0.19)	-0.18* (0.07)	-0.09+ (0.05)	0.05 (0.11)	-0.00 (0.00)
Other race (ind)	0.16* (0.07)	0.03 (0.14)	0.14 (0.13)	0.14 (0.12)	0.03 (0.15)	-0.19** (0.06)	-0.06 (0.07)	-0.05+ (0.03)	-0.00 (0.00)
Married (omitted)	—	—	—	—	—	—	—	—	—
Not married (ind)	0.03 (0.03)	-0.04 (0.04)	0.00 (0.03)	-0.04 (0.03)	0.04 (0.04)	0.03 (0.04)	-0.03 (0.02)	0.02 (0.01)	-0.00 (0.00)
Children (omitted)	—	—	—	—	—	—	—	—	—
No children (ind)	0.03 (0.03)	-0.03 (0.04)	-0.02 (0.03)	-0.05 (0.03)	-0.04 (0.04)	-0.11* (0.04)	0.00 (0.03)	0.00 (0.01)	-0.00 (0.00)
Intercept	0.66** (0.16)	0.20 (0.13)	0.12 (0.13)	0.08 (0.13)	0.01 (0.14)	0.48** (0.14)	0.29* (0.13)	0.08+ (0.04)	0.01 (0.00)
N	818	818	818	818	818	818	818	818	818
R^2	0.141	0.065	0.114	0.103	0.051	0.085	0.113	0.064	0.015

Source: Broockman et al. 2014a.

Note: Cells report coefficients (with clustered standard errors in parentheses). $+p < 0.10$, $*p < 0.05$, $**p < 0.01$, two-tailed.

TABLE A2.3. Auxiliary Regression Models for Figure 2.6

	Change in Population	Change in Revenue	Change in School Spending	Change in Debt
Majority worker council in 1996 (ind)	−589.62 (1136.74)	591.16 (4369.73)	535.07 (2493.87)	−4696.13 (11902.11)
Female propor-tion on council	3787.45 (3366.49)	7885.11 (13900.29)	28433.08 (23514.62)	20121.76 (37873.39)
Native American proportion on council	−580.79 (1389.18)	414.53 (6709.79)	−7855.83 (6723.39)	8559.76 (16967.03)
Hispanic propor-tion on council	−20450.11+ (11965.87)	−23744.15 (18706.02)	8559.36 (19230.65)	−142015.72* (57367.23)
Asian proportion on council	−2425.31 (13378.07)	−174483.54 (190091.84)	−15970.72 (23710.21)	−541216.99 (591839.03)
Black proportion on council	9643.88 (8810.82)	−28006.13 (41239.48)	−62754.86 (56655.42)	−118030.27 (125787.92)
Latino percent in city	23669.38* (11793.39)	43670.04+ (23549.40)	13078.93 (12057.58)	227069.94** (75491.36)
Black percent in city	−8684.59 (7943.53)	22160.96 (39656.76)	40501.38 (36907.30)	133689.65 (128237.06)
Asian percent in city	34949.13* (16820.74)	193865.00* (95855.66)	34556.06 (40359.09)	300336.82 (268488.42)
Other races per-cent in city	67761.41* (26369.08)	87921.67 (108315.24)	165073.98 (139697.59)	52470.96 (290944.21)
Female percent in city	5419.51 (13994.58)	76669.94 (63235.67)	−58648.71 (71818.11)	81629.49 (160720.10)
Percent below poverty line in city	−16236.87+ (9177.29)	−58399.21 (39509.58)	−47468.20 (44472.45)	−144064.89 (90490.69)
Percent college grads in city	8566.11* (4218.13)	53794.05+ (27666.97)	−20249.26 (21097.93)	145383.74+ (82113.70)
City council elected by dis-trict (prop)	1543.59 (1576.16)	6041.07 (4181.72)	5979.06 (6980.73)	3462.94 (9075.43)

continued

Table A2.3. (Continued)

	Change in Population	Change in Revenue	Change in School Spending	Change in Debt
City council re-election rate	510.73 (1398.01)	3796.52 (6324.70)	−1217.30 (5614.28)	−3865.69 (17100.50)
Council Meetings: > Once a week	13624.34** (3573.12)	−137067.39** (13920.98)	−19840.17 (19825.08)	1123316.17** (38296.63)
Council Meetings: Once a week	−1011.32 (2812.33)	23731.64 (17652.51)	−4952.69 (8884.80)	120425.56* (58690.73)
Council Meetings: Three times a month	−8412.91 (5858.42)	35274.59+ (20105.73)	57374.33 (42704.34)	90910.47* (40547.17)
Council Meetings: Twice a month	−841.14 (2068.41)	8854.82 (9617.66)	−4226.38 (7027.82)	62519.73+ (33150.85)
Council Meetings: Once a month	−1669.73 (1984.06)	9811.49 (9562.61)	−1933.65 (6591.21)	59782.82+ (32798.65)
Council Meetings: < Once a month	—	—	—	—
Council Meetings: As needed	—	—	—	—
Alabama	155.56 (2614.98)	18319.02 (15426.01)	19507.43 (16828.00)	13825.90 (84549.90)
Alaska	−11618.70* (4778.42)	−23285.09 (31088.34)	−22041.02 (21637.92)	−64896.20 (113668.06)
Arizona	626.40 (3288.16)	12340.63 (22510.87)	−5731.68 (5710.71)	−44247.15 (84747.34)
Arkansas	—	—	—	—
California	—	—	—	—
Colorado	−137.40 (2697.67)	17665.16 (14564.11)	2507.45 (5169.90)	−27022.83 (83581.74)
Connecticut	−3493.30 (2824.62)	9669.15 (15538.44)	15298.82* (6386.03)	−15999.63 (85004.60)

continued

TABLE **A2.3.** *(Continued)*

	Change in Population	Change in Revenue	Change in School Spending	Change in Debt
Delaware	—	—	—	—
DC	—	—	—	—
Florida	3002.92 (2742.63)	12992.20 (16534.40)	6759.97 (11517.66)	219.94 (87840.85)
Georgia	2529.79 (2898.25)	19847.99 (15139.10)	6735.79 (8954.94)	28550.01 (86779.39)
Hawaii	—	—	—	—
Idaho	−1906.81 (2378.39)	3773.66 (15957.10)	13957.30 (12707.25)	−16874.24 (83220.40)
Illinois	−1715.47 (2419.77)	−699 (15162.98)	3894.49 (6041.42)	−38786.82 (84754.78)
Indiana	1050.49 (1978.28)	36019.81* (16083.26)	11379.76 (10115.09)	5087.64 (84234.72)
Iowa	127.06 (2029.66)	14791.77 (15574.02)	11923.35 (9546.67)	11414.65 (86520.82)
Kansas	—	—	—	—
Kentucky	1388.85 (2503.39)	23447.44 (18209.44)	15243.34 (13615.95)	41400.12 (91663.00)
Louisiana	−15364.60 (14509.74)	35853.21 (26198.94)	−8951.81 (18952.18)	26621.61 (91335.18)
Maine	−201.74 (1955.24)	16524.43 (14999.86)	12337.01+ (7267.80)	41170.10 (87004.52)
Maryland	—	—	—	—
Massachusetts	−1026.69 (1957.59)	7402.91 (13492.00)	26249.42** (8017.89)	19839.16 (83477.16)
Michigan	−2564.45 (3452.92)	16902.45 (19795.89)	4987.77 (7839.98)	72690.54 (94773.07)

continued

TABLE **A2.3.** *(Continued)*

	Change in Population	Change in Revenue	Change in School Spending	Change in Debt
Minnesota	−674.61 (1994.66)	6126.32 (14161.93)	6571.08 (6914.63)	−19303.66 (85520.48)
Mississippi	1585.38 (3678.80)	17761.37 (15454.76)	21861.17 (18942.01)	17509.99 (84636.88)
Missouri	1455.65 (2361.17)	23327.19 (17676.13)	−1404.94 (8411.76)	110238.62 (101230.39)
Montana	—	—	—	—
Nebraska	−681.77 (1866.58)	11109.46 (14177.86)	8587.51 (7286.67)	−1924.17 (84376.35)
Nevada	32669.21 (27504.79)	42914.81+ (24245.03)	6049.50 (7203.73)	73640.38 (98428.47)
New Hampshire	−722.03 (6583.95)	−13873.71 (17208.69)	−16588.74 (28187.57)	−30023.74 (87247.21)
New Jersey	23.10 (2092.82)	12855.07 (14184.99)	7731.05 (8615.69)	7374.94 (83502.55)
New Mexico	6821.73 (5338.50)	23078.84 (20005.40)	−7762.09 (13501.40)	21834.72 (91954.18)
New York	−27.32 (2341.80)	10086.34 (14604.71)	9578.16 (9913.94)	7420.87 (84842.02)
North Carolina	15227.17 (10889.51)	27080.97+ (15892.08)	5299.42 (8222.07)	−24563.93 (86832.85)
North Dakota	−2347.97 (3162.96)	21364.36 (18483.81)	2676.32 (9354.25)	15301.82 (90878.57)
Ohio	−936.46 (3151.17)	21279.51 (16173.18)	11759.29 (11368.72)	31102.89 (87477.69)
Oklahoma	−2421.94 (2190.48)	23608.32 (17441.00)	1975.95 (6414.25)	31387.83 (87075.90)

continued

TABLE **A2.3.** *(Continued)*

	Change in Population	Change in Revenue	Change in School Spending	Change in Debt
Oklahoma	−2421.94 (2190.48)	23608.32 (17441.00)	1975.95 (6414.25)	31387.83 (87075.90)
Oregon	454.95 (2573.39)	20959.18 (18226.82)	5286.71 (6984.36)	32729.79 (92793.49)
Pennsylvania	—	—	—	—
Rhode Island	−1910.42 (1703.62)	23392.94 (16910.36)	30525.66** (10520.44)	54513.89 (86638.79)
South Carolina	—	—	—	—
South Dakota	−1138.08 (1816.48)	12799.62 (13540.01)	6766.35 (5879.40)	16984.08 (83495.21)
Tennessee	3241.37 (2399.61)	23299.78 (16548.34)	14116.87 (10479.23)	23565.88 (87003.51)
Texas	4595.17 (2956.88)	16871.89 (16458.60)	2514.68 (7687.49)	7264.60 (88369.43)
Utah	—	—	—	—
Vermont	—	—	—	—
Virginia	14.51 (2502.25)	22001.59 (17744.67)	35703.29 (24631.82)	21375.38 (86441.17)
Washington	8112.85 (7859.42)	112495.34 (99434.46)	6304.87 (10981.85)	317747.63 (335034.13)
West Virginia	1222.09 (2606.71)	24474.06 (17745.57)	12385.21 (11370.85)	40865.26 (89503.99)
Wisconsin	57.30 (1764.46)	10377.69 (14850.02)	5813.87 (5972.98)	18392.72 (85883.96)
Wyoming	−2190.23 (2007.11)	3109.96 (14285.20)	7343.59 (7388.24)	−11693.84 (84918.91)

continued

TABLE A2.3. *(Continued)*

	Change in Population	Change in Revenue	Change in School Spending	Change in Debt
Form of gov't: Not sure	—	—	—	—
Form of gov't: Mayor-Council	—	—	—	—
Form of gov't: Council-Manager	−534.54 (790.30)	−3412.09 (5835.41)	3816.37 (3859.76)	−22056.73 (18252.32)
Form of gov't: Commission	−698.73 (2026.32)	−4889.87 (6878.97)	4802.23 (6454.07)	5836.44 (17259.72)
Form of gov't: Town Meeting	—	—	—	—
Form of gov't: Rep. Town Meeting	—	—	—	—
Central City	—	—	—	—
Suburban	−2047.25 (1933.35)	−15352.29** (4983.07)	−5579.37 (4536.68)	−30740.72* (12710.46)
Independent	−911.80 (1620.75)	−11190.54* (5393.48)	−4897.54 (4448.00)	−12474.24 (13823.63)
Intercept	−4193.73 (8609.85)	−63487.91 (46425.18)	27129.47 (36174.81)	−118072.13 (150636.59)
N	253	253	253	253
R^2	0.468	0.466	0.379	0.581

Source: Trounstine and Valdini 2008.

Note: Cells report coefficients (with standard errors in parentheses). $+p < 0.10$, $*p < 0.05$, $**p < 0.01$, two-tailed.

Tᴀʙʟᴇ **A3.1. Auxiliary Regression Models for Figure 3.2**

	free time	income or job	raising money
Worker (ind)	0.06	0.11+	0.03
	(0.06)	(0.06)	(0.06)
Democrat (omitted)	—	—	—
Republican (ind)	−0.01	−0.32**	0.09
	(0.08)	(0.08)	(0.09)
Independent (ind)	−0.05	−0.11	0.06
	(0.07)	(0.07)	(0.07)
Other party (ind)	−0.38	0.21	−0.03
	(0.26)	(0.26)	(0.27)
Extremely liberal (omitted)	—	—	—
Liberal (ind)	0.17	0.03	0.15
	(0.13)	(0.13)	(0.13)
Slightly liberal (ind)	0.25+	0.05	0.11
	(0.13)	(0.13)	(0.14)
Moderate (ind)	0.28*	0.09	0.03
	(0.12)	(0.13)	(0.13)
Slightly conservative (ind)	0.13	−0.05	−0.22
	(0.14)	(0.14)	(0.14)
Conservative (ind)	0.20	0.21	0.00
	(0.14)	(0.14)	(0.14)
Extremely conservative (ind)	0.26	0.34*	0.28+
	(0.16)	(0.16)	(0.17)
Male (omitted)	—	—	—
Female (ind)	−0.06	−0.02	0.00
	(0.05)	(0.05)	(0.05)
White (ind)	−0.15	−0.07	0.30**
	(0.11)	(0.11)	(0.11)

continued

TABLE A3.1. *(Continued)*

	free time	income or job	raising money
Black (ind)	−0.21+	−0.26*	0.20+
	(0.11)	(0.11)	(0.11)
Hispanic (ind)	0.01	0.04	0.13
	(0.08)	(0.08)	(0.09)
Asian (ind)	0.13	−0.11	0.07
	(0.15)	(0.15)	(0.16)
Native American (ind)	−0.63**	−0.38+	0.08
	(0.22)	(0.22)	(0.23)
Pacific Islander (ind)	0.24	0.26	0.16
	(0.31)	(0.32)	(0.33)
Other race (ind)	0.06	0.13	0.29*
	(0.11)	(0.11)	(0.11)
Married (omitted)	—	—	—
Not married (ind)	0.13*	−0.13*	0.00
	(0.06)	(0.06)	(0.06)
Has children (omitted)	—	—	—
No children (ind)	0.12*	0.20**	−0.08
	(0.06)	(0.06)	(0.06)
Intercept	0.11	0.40*	0.38*
	(0.15)	(0.16)	(0.16)
N	343	343	343
R^2	0.155	0.200	0.100

Source: Broockman et al. 2014a.

Note: Cells report coefficients (with standard errors in parentheses). $+p < 0.10$, $*p < 0.05$, $**p < 0.01$, two-tailed.

TABLE A3.2. Auxiliary Regression Models for Figure 3.5

Income gap between profs. and workers (in $10,000s)	−0.80** (0.19)	−0.31+ (0.16)
Legislative salaries (in 2007 $10,000s)		−0.28+ (0.14)
Session length (in days)		0.00 (0.01)
Average staff size		−0.09 (0.07)
Term limits (indicator)		−1.20+ (0.68)
Black population (percentage)		−0.08* (0.03)
Urban population (percentage)		−0.03 (0.02)
Poverty (percentage)		−0.05 (0.07)
Republican percentage of two-party vote		−0.01 (0.03)
Intercept	7.00** (0.81)	10.87* (2.49)
N	200	200
R^2	0.109	0.276

Source: Carnes and Hansen 2016; Flood et al. 2015; Insurance Information Institute 1979; National Conference of State Legislatures 2015.

Note: Cells report coefficients (with standard errors clustered by state in parentheses). $+p < 0.10$, $*p < 0.05$, $**p < 0.01$, two-tailed.

TABLE A3.3. Auxiliary Regression Models for Figure 3.6

	Qualified to Run	Qualified to Hold Office
Worker (ind)	0.07	−0.00
	(0.06)	(0.06)
Male (omitted)	—	—
Female (ind)	−0.26**	−0.38**
	(0.05)	(0.05)
Democrat (omitted)	—	—
Republican (ind)	0.15+	0.22*
	(0.08)	(0.09)
Independent (ind)	−0.04	−0.00
	(0.06)	(0.07)
Other party (ind)	−0.36	0.25
	(0.25)	(0.27)
Extremely liberal (omitted)	—	—
Liberal (ind)	0.02	0.04
	(0.12)	(0.13)
Slightly liberal (ind)	−0.06	−0.15
	(0.13)	(0.14)
Moderate (ind)	−0.13	−0.18
	(0.12)	(0.13)
Slightly conservative (ind)	−0.12	−0.29*
	(0.13)	(0.14)
Conservative (ind)	−0.10	−0.21
	(0.13)	(0.14)
Extremely conservative (ind)	−0.24	−0.42*
	(0.16)	(0.17)
Age (continuous)	−0.00	−0.00
	(0.00)	(0.00)
White (ind)	0.41**	0.42**
	(0.10)	(0.11)

continued

TABLE **A3.3.** *(Continued)*

	Qualified to Run	Qualified to Hold Office
Black (ind)	0.41**	0.40**
	(0.11)	(0.11)
Hispanic (ind)	0.13	0.15+
	(0.08)	(0.09)
Asian (ind)	0.10	−0.02
	(0.15)	(0.16)
Native American (ind)	0.43+	0.38
	(0.22)	(0.24)
Pacific Islander (ind)	0.67*	0.47
	(0.30)	(0.32)
Other race (ind)	0.34**	0.21+
	(0.11)	(0.11)
Married (omitted)	—	—
Not married (ind)	0.03	0.06
	(0.06)	(0.06)
Has children (omitted)	—	—
No children (ind)	−0.16*	−0.14*
	(0.06)	(0.07)
Intercept	0.20	0.39*
	(0.18)	(0.20)
N	343	343
R^2	0.216	0.252

Source: Broockman et al. 2014a.

Note: Cells report coefficients (with standard errors in parentheses). $+p < 0.10$, $*p < 0.05$, $**p < 0.01$, two-tailed.

Table A3.4. Auxiliary Regression Models for Figures 3.9 and 3.10

Self-reported measure of attitudes about working-class candidates	Percentage of workers recruited	Workers less qualified? (ind)	Workers less recruitable? (ind)	Workers less fundable? (ind)	Workers less runnable? (ind)	Workers less electable? (ind)
Demographics						
Party: Democrat (omitted)	—	—	—	—	—	—
Republican	2.39 (4.54)	0.05 (0.07)	-0.12 (0.08)	-0.04 (0.08)	-0.08 (0.08)	-0.01 (0.08)
Gender: Female (omitted)	—	—	—	—	—	—
Male	4.58* (2.15)	-0.01 (0.03)	-0.04 (0.04)	0.06 (0.04)	0.00 (0.04)	-0.02 (0.04)
Skipped	9.68 (9.62)	-0.05 (0.15)	-0.04 (0.17)	-0.24 (0.16)	-0.30 (0.16)	-0.31* (0.15)
Race: White	-8.00 (6.27)	-0.03 (0.10)	0.09 (0.11)	0.01 (0.10)	0.05 (0.11)	-0.08 (0.10)
Black	-4.63 (8.20)	-0.06 (0.13)	-0.08 (0.15)	-0.06 (0.14)	0.06 (0.15)	-0.04 (0.14)
Hispanic	-3.08 (8.12)	0.14 (0.12)	0.09 (0.13)	0.23 (0.12)	0.12 (0.13)	0.08 (0.12)
Asian/Pacific Islander	-10.16 (13.84)	0.16 (0.22)	-0.13 (0.25)	0.09 (0.23)	0.12 (0.23)	0.11 (0.23)

	(1)	(2)	(3)	(4)	(5)	(6)
Native American	-0.16 (0.11)	-0.20 (0.12)	-0.11 (0.11)	0.10 (0.12)	-0.02 (0.11)	-2.15 (6.45)
Other Race	-0.02 (0.12)	0.04 (0.12)	-0.03 (0.12)	0.11 (0.12)	-0.13 (0.12)	-11.89 (7.39)
Income: 0–30k (omitted)	—	—	—	—	—	—
30–50k	0.09 (0.08)	0.05 (0.08)	-0.05 (0.08)	-0.02 (0.09)	-0.04 (0.08)	-3.10 (5.01)
50–75k	0.15 (0.08)	-0.01 (0.08)	0.02 (0.08)	0.01 (0.08)	-0.01 (0.07)	-9.79* (4.88)
75–100k	0.14 (0.08)	0.01 (0.08)	-0.01 (0.08)	0.04 (0.08)	0.02 (0.07)	-3.78 (4.93)
100–150k	0.12 (0.08)	0.11 (0.08)	0.08 (0.08)	-0.02 (0.08)	0.06 (0.07)	-11.20* (4.91)
150k +	0.17* (0.08)	0.04 (0.09)	0.01 (0.09)	-0.02 (0.09)	0.05 (0.08)	-7.72 (5.23)
Rather not say	0.05 (0.08)	-0.02 (0.08)	-0.07 (0.08)	-0.10 (0.09)	-0.03 (0.08)	-5.69 (5.23)
No answer	0.21 (0.21)	0.10 (0.21)	0.01 (0.22)	-0.14 (0.23)	-0.13 (0.20)	-1.55 (12.90)
Ideology: Very liberal (omitted)	—	—	—	—	—	—
Liberal	0.04 (0.06)	0.03 (0.06)	0.09 (0.06)	-0.05 (0.06)	0.09 (0.05)	-0.66 (3.48)

continued

Table A3.4. (Continued)

Self-reported measure of attitudes about working-class candidates	Percentage of workers recruited	Workers less qualified? (ind)	Workers less recruitable? (ind)	Workers less fundable? (ind)	Workers less runnable? (ind)	Workers less electable? (ind)
Slightly liberal	3.16 (4.40)	0.05 (0.07)	-0.08 (0.08)	0.08 (0.07)	0.02 (0.08)	-0.05 (0.07)
Moderate	3.65 (4.30)	0.12 (0.07)	-0.10 (0.08)	-0.01 (0.07)	0.04 (0.08)	0.08 (0.07)
Slightly cons.	-0.41 (6.06)	0.14 (0.10)	-0.03 (0.11)	0.09 (0.10)	0.14 (0.10)	0.10 (0.10)
Conservative	7.83 (5.43)	0.03 (0.09)	-0.05 (0.10)	0.10 (0.09)	0.13 (0.10)	-0.04 (0.09)
Very conservative	12.87* (5.98)	0.01 (0.10)	0.00 (0.11)	0.05 (0.10)	0.11 (0.10)	-0.04 (0.10)
No answer	4.80 (12.37)	0.06 (0.18)	0.17 (0.21)	-0.16 (0.20)	-0.06 (0.19)	0.39* (0.19)
Elections						
Cost: $0–5k (omitted)	—	—	—	—	—	—
$5–10k	0.78 (2.93)	0.03 (0.05)	-0.15** (0.05)	0.08 (0.05)	-0.01 (0.05)	0.02 (0.05)
$10–15k	4.71 (4.40)	-0.11 (0.07)	0.12 (0.08)	0.02 (0.08)	-0.03 (0.08)	0.01 (0.07)

$15–20k	-0.12 (4.97)	-0.09 (0.08)	-0.18* (0.09)	-0.03 (0.08)	-0.07 (0.08)	-0.11 (0.08)
$20–25k	0.54 (4.43)	0.04 (0.07)	0.07 (0.08)	0.27*** (0.08)	0.08 (0.08)	0.12 (0.08)
$25k+	0.22 (2.80)	0.01 (0.05)	-0.09 (0.05)	0.11* (0.05)	-0.09 (0.05)	0.05 (0.05)
Don't know/No answer	-1.53 (3.04)	0.06 (0.05)	-0.05 (0.05)	0.08 (0.05)	0.07 (0.05)	0.14** (0.05)
Safe seats: 0–25% (omitted)	—	—	—	—	—	—
26–50%	0.53 (2.74)	0.08 (0.05)	-0.05 (0.05)	-0.01 (0.05)	-0.04 (0.05)	-0.02 (0.05)
51–75%	-0.21 (2.72)	0.02 (0.04)	-0.04 (0.05)	-0.07 (0.05)	-0.07 (0.05)	-0.02 (0.05)
75–100%	-1.96 (2.68)	0.01 (0.04)	0.02 (0.05)	0.02 (0.04)	-0.10* (0.05)	-0.01 (0.04)
Don't know/No answer	-11.18 (10.69)	0.04 (0.14)	-0.09 (0.15)	-0.14 (0.15)	-0.29 (0.15)	-0.18 (0.14)
Does the party organization LACK . . .						
Year-round physical office	3.23 (2.34)	-0.02 (0.04)	-0.13** (0.04)	-0.00 (0.04)	0.02 (0.04)	-0.02 (0.04)

continued

TABLE A3.4. (Continued)

Self-reported measure of attitudes about working-class candidates	Percentage of workers recruited	Workers less qualified? (ind)	Workers less recruitable? (ind)	Workers less fundable? (ind)	Workers less runnable? (ind)	Workers less electable? (ind)
Campaign headquarters	-0.00 (2.10)	0.01 (0.03)	-0.03 (0.04)	-0.03 (0.04)	-0.01 (0.04)	0.05 (0.03)
Website	5.01* (2.37)	-0.03 (0.04)	-0.06 (0.04)	-0.09* (0.04)	-0.01 (0.04)	-0.14*** (0.04)
Constitution/charter	4.79 (2.91)	-0.02 (0.05)	-0.05 (0.05)	-0.04 (0.05)	-0.03 (0.05)	0.03 (0.05)
Monthly meetings	-1.43 (2.28)	-0.00 (0.04)	-0.05 (0.04)	0.00 (0.04)	-0.03 (0.04)	0.02 (0.04)
(Skipped the above items)	21.23** (7.41)	-0.07 (0.11)	-0.18 (0.12)	-0.17 (0.11)	0.00 (0.11)	0.04 (0.11)
Worker(s) on exec committee	-6.94*** (2.07)	0.04 (0.03)	0.06 (0.04)	-0.02 (0.04)	-0.02 (0.04)	0.08* (0.03)
(Skipped the above item)	-1.85 (3.46)	-0.05 (0.05)	0.01 (0.06)	-0.12* (0.05)	-0.05 (0.06)	0.01 (0.05)
Formal candidate recruitment	0.91 (2.02)	0.03 (0.03)	0.03 (0.04)	0.04 (0.03)	0.04 (0.04)	0.02 (0.03)
(Skipped the above item)	-14.73 (11.41)	0.37* (0.15)	0.24 (0.17)	0.23 (0.16)	0.31 (0.16)	0.30 (0.16)

Sometimes/often recruits candidates from

People active in elections	1.80 (3.17)	0.00 (0.05)	-0.05 (0.06)	0.05 (0.05)	-0.07 (0.05)	-0.06 (0.05)
Current officeholders	11.03** (3.53)	-0.04 (0.06)	0.06 (0.06)	0.03 (0.06)	0.03 (0.06)	-0.03 (0.06)
Business groups	-2.41 (2.39)	0.01 (0.04)	0.02 (0.04)	0.06 (0.04)	-0.00 (0.04)	0.01 (0.04)
High-skilled occupations	1.59 (2.38)	0.04 (0.04)	0.02 (0.04)	-0.00 (0.04)	-0.03 (0.04)	-0.03 (0.04)
Education organizations	1.59 (2.38)	0.04 (0.04)	0.02 (0.04)	-0.00 (0.04)	-0.03 (0.04)	-0.03 (0.04)
Labor unions	8.31** (2.61)	-0.14** (0.04)	-0.10* (0.05)	-0.08 (0.04)	-0.12* (0.05)	-0.06 (0.04)
Ethnic or civil rights groups	-1.83 (2.37)	0.05 (0.04)	-0.04 (0.04)	-0.01 (0.04)	0.01 (0.04)	0.03 (0.04)
Service or fraternal organizations	2.70 (2.18)	-0.05 (0.04)	-0.04 (0.04)	-0.01 (0.04)	0.01 (0.04)	-0.01 (0.04)
Recommend. from officeholders	-2.37 (3.16)	-0.03 (0.05)	-0.01 (0.06)	-0.06 (0.05)	0.06 (0.06)	0.09 (0.05)

continued

TABLE A3.4. (Continued)

Self-reported measure of attitudes about working-class candidates	Percentage of workers recruited	Workers less qualified? (ind)	Workers less recruitable? (ind)	Workers less fundable? (ind)	Workers less runnable? (ind)	Workers less electable? (ind)
Recommendations from donors	-5.22* (2.18)	0.03 (0.04)	0.04 (0.04)	-0.02 (0.04)	0.06 (0.04)	-0.03 (0.04)
Recommendations from friends	-0.10 (2.66)	0.01 (0.04)	0.05 (0.05)	0.07 (0.05)	-0.00 (0.05)	0.04 (0.05)
Posting ads or sending emails	2.23 (2.45)	0.00 (0.04)	-0.03 (0.05)	-0.11* (0.04)	0.04 (0.04)	-0.00 (0.04)
Using voter lists	4.37* (2.13)	-0.00 (0.03)	-0.03 (0.04)	-0.02 (0.04)	0.00 (0.04)	0.02 (0.04)
(None of the above)	2.65 (10.21)	-0.17 (0.10)	-0.18 (0.12)	-0.04 (0.11)	-0.21 (0.11)	-0.09 (0.11)
Intercept	18.01 (9.63)	0.25 (0.15)	0.77*** (0.17)	0.54*** (0.16)	0.30 (0.16)	0.26 (0.15)
N	709	882	877	881	821	878
R^2	0.171	0.078	0.092	0.122	0.083	0.098

Source: Broockman et al. 2013.

Note: Cells report estimates from ordinary least squares regression models. $^+ p < 0.10$, $^* p < 0.05$, $^{**} p < 0.01$, two-tailed.

TABLE A3.5. Auxiliary Regression Models for Figure 3.11

Measure	Encourage to run?	Win the primary?	Win the general election?	Raise enough money?	Recruit enough volunteers?	Stay loyal to the party?	Be effective?
Demographics							
Occupation: Worker	−0.06+ (0.03)	−0.08* (0.03)	−0.13** (0.03)	−0.21** (0.03)	0.04 (0.03)	0.01 (0.03)	−0.03 (0.03)
Professional (omitted)	—	—	—	—	—	—	—
Gender: Female	0.06* (0.02)	0.03 (0.02)	0.00 (0.02)	0.04 (0.02)	0.02 (0.02)	0.01 (0.02)	0.02 (0.02)
Male (omitted)	—	—	—	—	—	—	—
Age: 47	0.03 (0.03)	−0.02 (0.03)	0.02 (0.03)	−0.03 (0.03)	−0.01 (0.03)	0.04 (0.03)	0.06 (0.03)
43 (omitted)	—	—	—	—	—	—	—
Experience							
None (omitted)	—	—	—	—	—	—	—
Active in county party	0.23** (0.04)	0.21** (0.04)	0.19** (0.04)	0.15** (0.04)	0.27** (0.04)	0.23** (0.04)	0.20** (0.04)
Active in important groups	0.15** (0.04)	0.18** (0.04)	0.14** (0.04)	0.11* (0.04)	0.21** (0.04)	0.16** (0.04)	0.16** (0.04)

continued

Table A3.5. (Continued)

Measure	Encourage to run?	Win the primary?	Win the general election?	Raise enough money?	Recruit enough volunteers?	Stay loyal to the party?	Be effective?
Frequent campaign volunteer	0.18** (0.04)	0.11* (0.04)	0.10* (0.04)	0.07 (0.04)	0.28** (0.04)	0.18** (0.04)	0.15** (0.04)
Recent campaign volunteer	0.13** (0.04)	0.08+ (0.04)	0.10* (0.04)	0.06 (0.04)	0.21** (0.04)	0.16** (0.04)	0.12** (0.04)
Ideology (Republicans)							
Very conservative (omitted)	—	—	—	—	—	—	—
Somewhat conservative	-0.02 (0.06)	-0.09 (0.05)	-0.04 (0.06)	-0.11 (0.06)	-0.05 (0.06)	-0.05 (0.05)	-0.03 (0.06)
Middle of the road	0.09 (0.05)	-0.05 (0.05)	0.11+ (0.05)	-0.08 (0.05)	-0.05 (0.06)	-0.07 (0.05)	0.04 (0.05)
Somewhat liberal	-0.33** (0.06)	-0.39** (0.05)	-0.21** (0.06)	-0.19** (0.06)	-0.17** (0.06)	-0.47** (0.05)	-0.39** (0.05)
Very liberal	-0.53** (0.05)	-0.52** (0.05)	-0.34** (0.06)	-0.26** (0.06)	-0.29** (0.06)	-0.59** (0.05)	-0.51** (0.05)
Ideology (Democrats)							
Very conservative	-0.37** (0.05)	-0.36** (0.05)	-0.17** (0.05)	-0.12+ (0.05)	-0.24** (0.05)	-0.42** (0.04)	-0.39** (0.05)
Somewhat conservative	-0.13* (0.05)	-0.21** (0.05)	-0.02 (0.05)	-0.13* (0.05)	-0.11+ (0.05)	-0.33** (0.05)	-0.14* (0.05)

Middle of the road	−0.01 (0.05)	−0.04 (0.05)	0.05 (0.05)	−0.09 (0.05)	−0.03 (0.05)	−0.06 (0.05)	−0.03 (0.05)
Somewhat liberal	−0.07 (0.05)	−0.16** (0.05)	−0.11+ (0.05)	−0.13* (0.05)	−0.05 (0.05)	−0.10+ (0.04)	−0.08 (0.05)
Very liberal	−0.20** (0.05)	−0.23** (0.05)	−0.19** (0.05)	−0.16** (0.05)	−0.12+ (0.05)	−0.21** (0.05)	−0.19** (0.05)
Life circumstances							
Has a great deal of free time (omitted)	—	—	—	—	—	—	—
Has flexible work hours	−0.04 (0.04)	−0.08+ (0.04)	−0.08+ (0.04)	0.00 (0.04)	−0.05 (0.04)	−0.07 (0.04)	0.00 (0.04)
Has two young children	−0.10+ (0.04)	−0.10* (0.04)	−0.10+ (0.04)	−0.09+ (0.04)	−0.05 (0.04)	−0.09+ (0.04)	−0.03 (0.04)
Is independently wealthy	−0.06 (0.04)	−0.05 (0.04)	−0.04 (0.04)	0.22** (0.04)	−0.12** (0.04)	−0.12* (0.04)	−0.03 (0.04)
Military veteran	0.07* (0.04)	0.04 (0.04)	0.04 (0.04)	0.02 (0.04)	−0.02 (0.04)	−0.01 (0.03)	0.08* (0.04)
Talents							
Assertive (omitted)	—	—	—	—	—	—	—
Experienced fundraiser	0.04 (0.04)	0.07 (0.04)	0.05 (0.04)	0.17** (0.04)	0.12* (0.04)	0.05 (0.04)	−0.00 (0.04)

continued

TABLE A3.5. *(Continued)*

Measure	Encourage to run?	Win the primary?	Win the general election?	Raise enough money?	Recruit enough volunteers?	Stay loyal to the party?	Be effective?
Hard worker	0.05	0.05	0.04	-0.04	0.08$^+$	0.08$^+$	0.05
	(0.04)	(0.04)	(0.04)	(0.04)	(0.04)	(0.04)	(0.04)
Physically attractive	0.01	0.01	0.02	-0.03	0.08	0.06	-0.00
	(0.04)	(0.04)	(0.04)	(0.04)	(0.04)	(0.04)	(0.04)
Talented public speaker	0.06	0.10$^+$	0.09$^+$	0.00	0.11*	0.04	0.04
	(0.04)	(0.04)	(0.04)	(0.04)	(0.04)	(0.04)	(0.04)
Well-known	0.05	0.02	0.06	0.02	0.14**	0.03	0.01
	(0.04)	(0.04)	(0.04)	(0.04)	(0.04)	(0.04)	(0.04)
Level of office							
County board (omitted)	—	—	—	—	—	—	—
State legislature	-0.00	0.01	0.00	0.00	0.01	0.01	0.00
	(0.01)	(0.01)	(0.01)	(0.01)	(0.01)	(0.01)	(0.01)
U.S. House	0.01	0.01	-0.00	0.00	0.01	0.01	0.01
	(0.01)	(0.01)	(0.01)	(0.01)	(0.01)	(0.01)	(0.01)
Intercept	0.48**	0.60**	0.50**	0.55**	0.36**	0.56**	0.50**
	(0.06)	(0.06)	(0.06)	(0.06)	(0.06)	(0.06)	(0.06)
N	1480	1688	1676	1660	1654	1660	1614
R^2	0.177	0.140	0.107	0.125	0.090	0.181	0.157

Source: Broockman et al. 2013.

Note: Cells report estimates from ordinary least squares regression models relating the outcome in question to indicators for the hypothetical candidate's characteristics. Standard errors are clustered by respondent. $^+ p < 0.10$, $^* p < 0.05$, $^{**} p < 0.01$, two-tailed.

TABLE A4.1. Auxiliary Regression Model for Figure 4.1

Population (in 100,000s)	−0.25
	(0.31)
Citywide elections (omitted)	—
District elections (ind)	1.43*
	(0.62)
Meetings > once a week (omitted)	—
Meetings = once a week (ind)	−2.74
	(1.71)
Meetings = 3 times a month (ind)	−1.51
	(1.68)
Meetings = 2 times a month (ind)	−0.23
	(1.48)
Meetings = 1 time a month (ind)	−1.01
	(1.56)
Meetings < once a month (ind)	−7.68***
	(1.92)
Meetings as needed	−7.34*
	(2.89)
Year = 1996	−0.24
	(0.43)
Women on council (proportion)	−0.02
	(1.29)
Native Americans on council (proportion)	−1.18
	(1.87)
Hispanics on council (proportion)	0.58
	(2.63)
Asians on council (proportion)	−9.71
	(5.43)
Blacks on council (proportion)	1.82
	(2.66)

continued

TABLE **A4.1.** *(Continued)*

Latinos in city (proportion)	−2.77
	(3.01)
Blacks in city (proportion)	−10.03***
	(3.04)
Asians in city (proportion)	2.34
	(5.12)
Other races in city (proportion)	17.93
	(10.87)
Women in city (proportion)	7.51
	(8.79)
Poverty rate in city (proportion)	7.89
	(4.51)
College grads in city (proportion)	−18.03***
	(1.58)
Re-election rate in city (proportion)	−1.77
	(0.99)
Alabama	0.56
	(2.58)
Alaska	−4.31
	(4.65)
Arizona	0.42
	(2.77)
Arkansas	−3.69
	(2.73)
California	−2.92
	(2.06)
Colorado	3.01
	(2.73)
Connecticut	−1.75
	(4.39)

continued

TABLE A4.1. *(Continued)*

Delaware	−0.77
	(3.60)
Florida	−4.16*
	(2.02)
Georgia	−2.30
	(2.44)
Hawaii	0.00
	(.)
Idaho	−1.98
	(2.89)
Illinois	2.11
	(2.04)
Indiana	0.84
	(2.58)
Iowa	−0.34
	(2.27)
Kansas (omitted)	
Kentucky	0.39
	(2.45)
Louisiana	0.83
	(3.38)
Maine	0.87
	(3.78)
Maryland	−2.66
	(2.77)
Massachusetts	−0.02
	(2.74)
Michigan	−0.39
	(2.04)

continued

TABLE **A4.1.** *(Continued)*

Minnesota	2.50
	(2.27)
Mississippi	−0.17
	(2.60)
Missouri	0.87
	(2.30)
Montana	6.39
	(4.10)
Nebraska	1.47
	(2.64)
Nevada	−10.38***
	(1.92)
New Hampshire	−1.32
	(4.37)
New Jersey	0.25
	(2.30)
New Mexico	−0.89
	(3.74)
New York	1.86
	(2.21)
North Carolina	−2.97
	(2.10)
North Dakota	−2.12
	(3.89)
Ohio	0.37
	(2.06)
Oklahoma	−2.01
	(2.50)
Oregon	−1.47
	(2.57)

continued

TABLE A4.1. *(Continued)*

Pennsylvania	2.57
	(2.25)
Rhode Island	−7.91**
	(2.82)
South Carolina	−2.55
	(2.19)
South Dakota	0.32
	(2.72)
Tennessee	−3.00
	(2.22)
Texas	−1.08
	(2.06)
Utah	−0.29
	(2.71)
Vermont	−0.12
	(5.68)
Virginia	−2.36
	(2.14)
Washington	−2.03
	(2.26)
West Virginia	−3.70
	(2.75)
Wisconsin	0.22
	(2.04)
Wyoming	−1.39
	(4.78)
Center city (omitted)	—
Suburb (ind)	1.17
	(0.82)

continued

TABLE A4.1. *(Continued)*

Independent town (ind)	0.84
	(0.85)
Intercept	10.59*
	(5.34)
N	5205
R²	0.063

Source: Trounstine and Valdini 2008.

Note: Cells report estimates from ordinary least squares regression models. [+]$p < 0.10$, [*]$p < 0.05$, [**]$p < 0.01$, two-tailed.

TABLE A4.2. Auxiliary Regression Models for Figure 4.2

Campaign costs ($10,000s per seat)	−0.02+	—
	(0.01)	
Population (10,000 per seat)	—	−0.22**
		(0.07)
Session length (in days)	—	−0.00
		(0.01)
Year = 1993 (omitted)	—	—
Year = 1995	—	−0.13
		(0.62)
Year = 2007	—	−0.00
		(0.01)
Term limits (ind)	−0.19	—
	(0.82)	
Average citizen partisanship (ANES seven-point scale)	0.12	1.66
	(1.07)	(1.09)
Unionization rate (proportion)	6.24	8.99
	(7.51)	(5.26)
Poverty rate (proportion)	−0.06	−0.18
	(0.15)	(0.13)
South (ind)	0.84	−0.50
	(0.98)	(0.80)
Per capita personal income (in thousands)	0.04	−0.51**
	(0.06)	(0.17)
Democratic control of state legislature (ind)	−0.07	1.91**
	(0.80)	(0.71)
Intercept	1.17	12.05*
	(4.78)	(6.05)
N	46	100
R^2	0.145	0.335

Source: Insurance Information Institute 1979; National Conference of State Legislatures 2015; Carnes and Hansen 2016.

Note: Cells report estimates from ordinary least squares regression models. $^+p < 0.10$, $^*p < 0.05$, $^{**}p < 0.01$, two tailed.

TABLE A4.3. Auxiliary Regression Model for Figure 4.4

Campaign spending (in $100,000s)	−0.002
	(0.002)
Population (in 100,000s)	−0.01*
	(0.01)
Senator (indicator)	0.90
	(0.47)
106th Congress (omitted)	—
107th Congress (indicator)	0.39
	(0.44)
108th Congress (indicator)	0.66
	(0.44)
109th Congress (indicator)	0.66
	(0.45)
110th Congress (indicator)	0.74
	(0.45)
Republican legislator (indicator)	−0.62
	(0.35)
Female legislator (indicator)	1.68***
	(0.41)
Republican % of two-party vote in last presidential election	−0.02
	(0.02)
District: Union percentage	0.04
	(0.02)
District: Percent urban	−0.00
	(0.01)
District: Percent white	−0.01
	(0.01)
Intercept	2.42
	(1.33)
N	2678
R^2	0.025

Sources: Insurance Information Institute 1979; National Conference of State Legislatures 2015; Carnes and Hansen 2016.

Note: Cells report estimates from ordinary least squares regression models. $^+p < 0.10$, $^*p < 0.05$, $^{**}p < 0.01$, two-tailed.

TABLE **A5.1. Auxiliary Regression Models for Figure 5.5**

DV: Probability of being a worker among	. . . candidates	. . . winners
No public financing (omitted)	—	—
Public financing for other offices	0.016	0.012
	(0.010)	(0.010)
Public financing for state legislature (matching)	−0.001	0.019
	(0.016)	(0.025)
Public financing for state legislature (clean elections)	0.026**	−0.010
	(0.009)	(0.006)
Term limits for state legislature	0.002	0.004
	(0.009)	(0.008)
State legislator compensation ($)	0.000	0.000
	(0.000)	(0.000)
Session length (in days)	−0.000*	−0.000**
	(0.000)	(0.000)
Average legislative staff size	−0.003	−0.003
	(0.002)	(0.002)
Percent of income going top 1% (state-level measure)	−0.001	0.001
	(0.001)	(0.001)
Per capita personal income (state-level measure)	0.001	−0.002
	(0.002)	(0.002)
Republican share of two-party presidential vote (state-level measure)	0.000	−0.001
	(0.001)	(0.001)
# of state legislative chambers with Democratic majority (state-level measure)	0.001	−0.002
	(0.006)	(0.006)
Unionization rate (state-level measure)	0.001	0.002*
	(0.001)	(0.001)
Percent urban (state-level measure)	0.000	−0.000
	(0.000)	(0.000)
Percent black (state-level measure)	−0.001	−0.000
	(0.001)	(0.001)
Percent in poverty (state-level measure)	0.003	0.003
	(0.003)	(0.004)

continued

TABLE A5.1. *(Continued)*

DV: Probability of being a worker among	. . . candidates	. . . winners
Intercept	−0.020	0.109
	(0.100)	(0.117)
N	3178	1526
R²	0.005	0.008

Sources: Broockman et al. 2012, 2014b; Carnes and Hansen 2016.

Note: Cells report coefficients (with standard errors clustered by state in parentheses) from regression models relating an indicator for whether the candidate was a blue-collar worker to the controls listed here. $*p < 0.05$, $**p < 0.01$, $***p < 0.001$, two-tailed.

TABLE A5.2. Auxiliary Regression Model for Figure 5.9

New Jersey (indicator)	4.42[+]
	(2.60)
Change in percent Democrat in the general public	−9.69*
	(4.45)
Change in average 7-point ideology score in the public	1.52
	(1.32)
Change in unionization rate	17.00[+]
	(8.70)
Change in legislative professionalization score	8.42
	(9.41)
Southern state (indicator)	0.54
	(1.00)
Change in Republican presidential candidate's share of the two-party vote	−0.08
	(0.07)
Intercept	−1.31
	0.79
N	49
R²	0.2446

Source: Carnes and Hansen 2016.

Note: Cells report coefficients (with standard errors clustered by state in parentheses) from regression models relating the change in the percentage of candidates from the working class in each state's legislature between 1995 and 2007 to the controls listed here. $+p < 0.10$, $*p < 0.05$, two-tailed.

QUESTION WORDING

FIGURE 1.3

STATE LEGISLATORS

» Abolish all federal welfare programs (% who agree)

Do you agree or disagree with the following statements? (We have kept these choices simple and realize that there are shades of gray on many issues. Please check the option that most accurately reflects your views.) . . . Abolish all federal welfare programs.

Agree, disagree

» Reduce government regulation of the private sector (% who agree)

Do you agree or disagree with the following statements? (We have kept these choices simple and realize that there are shades of gray on many issues. Please check the option that most accurately reflects your views.) . . . Reduce government regulation of the private sector.

Agree, disagree

» The government should attempt to reduce economic inequality (% who disagree)

Do you agree or disagree with the following statements? (We have kept these choices simple and realize that there are shades of gray on many issues. Please check the option that most accurately reflects your views.) . . . The government should attempt to reduce economic inequality.

Agree, *disagree*

» Providing health care is not the responsibility of the government (% who agree)

Do you agree or disagree with the following statements? (We have kept these choices simple and realize that there are shades of gray on many issues. Please check the option that most accurately reflects your views.) . . . Providing health care is not a responsibility of the government.

Agree, disagree

THE GENERAL PUBLIC

» Increase federal spending on aid to poor people (% who disagree)

If you had a say in making up the federal budget this year, for which of the following programs would you like to see spending increased and for which would you like to see spending decreased? Should federal spending on aid to poor people be increased, decreased, or kept about the same?

Increased, *same*, *decreased or cut out entirely*

» Increase the minimum wage (% who disagree)
Do you favor or oppose increasing the $5.15 minimum wage employers now must pay their workers?

Strongly favor, somewhat favor, neither favor nor oppose, *somewhat oppose*, *strongly oppose*

» The government should attempt to reduce economic inequality (% who disagree)
The federal government trying to reduce the income differences between rich and poor Americans—do you favor or oppose the federal government doing this?

Strongly favor, somewhat favor, neither favor nor oppose, *somewhat oppose*, *strongly oppose*

» There should be a government health insurance plan that covers all expenses (% who disagree)

There is much concern about the rapid rise in medical and hospital costs. Some people feel there should be a government insurance plan which would cover all medical and hospital expenses for everyone. Suppose these people are at one end of a scale, at point 1. Others feel that medical expenses should be paid by individuals, and through private insurance plans like Blue Cross or other company paid plans. Suppose these people are at the other end, at point 7. And of course, some people have opinions somewhere in between at points 2, 3, 4, 5, or 6. Where would you place yourself on this scale, or haven't you thought much about this?

1, 2, 3, *4*, *5*, *6*, *7*

FIGURE 2.1

COUNTY-LEVEL PARTY LEADERS SAY . . .

» In a perfect world, what personal qualities would all of your party's political candidates have? Please list as many as you would like.

(open-ended responses)

THE PUBLIC SAYS . . .

» In an ideal world, what personal qualities would all political candidates have? Please list as many as you would like.

(open-ended responses)

FIGURE 2.2

» In your opinion, how important is it that a nominee for elected office from your party have the following qualifications? (check one per row: Not important, Somewhat important, Very important)

General:

Has previously held office

Is an active political activist/volunteer

Is an active community activist/volunteer

Has held a community leadership position (e.g., leader of Kiwanis, a board, or a commission)

Has close ties with or is active in groups important to the party

Professional background:

Is a businessperson

Is an educator

Is a lawyer

Personal qualities:

Is assertive

Is a hard worker

Is personable

Is physically attractive

Life circumstances:

Has a flexible work schedule

Has a great deal of free time

Is independently wealthy

Is able to raise money from friends and associates

FIGURE 2.3

» Do any of the following statements describe you? (check all that apply)

I'm assertive

I'm a hard worker

I'm outgoing and personable

I have a flexible work schedule

I have lots of free time

I'm honest

I'm good at public speaking

I'm dedicated to my political party

FIGURE 2.4

» In the last few years, have you done any of the following? (check all that apply)

Regularly vote

Regularly contact elected officials to express your views

Volunteer for a campaign organization, like your party or a candidate's campaign

Volunteer for a civic group (e.g., the Chamber of Commerce, a union, or the Sierra Club)

Volunteer for other community organizations like churches or community service organizations

Donate money to political causes or campaigns

Work for a business that closely works with government (e.g., an election law firm)

Work (paid or full-time) for a campaign organization like your party or a candidate's campaign

Work for a sitting politician in an official capacity (e.g., chief of staff for a state legislator)

FIGURE 2.8

» In races for county and local office in your area, relative to candidates with professional backgrounds, do you think candidates from working-class backgrounds (e.g., factory workers, restaurant servers, receptionists) tend to be more or less . . . (options: more, the same, less)

Qualified

qualified to hold office

Recruitable

easy to convince to run

Good at fundraising

good at fundraising

Good at campaigning

good at campaigning

Electable

preferred by voters

FIGURE 3.1

» People from a variety of backgrounds are less likely to run for office in the United States—for example, women are less likely to run for office than are men. One regular pattern is that people who work in working-class jobs (manual labor jobs, service industry work) are relatively rare in public office in the United States. Based on your experiences deciding to run for office and in speaking to others, why do you think that is?

FIGURE 3.2

» Imagine you were thinking about running for public office in the next few years. What would you be concerned about? (check all that apply)

. . .

giving up my income or job to run for office

. . .

the need to raise lots of money

. . .

giving up my free time

. . .

FIGURE 3.4

» Screener question: We've been asking about recent political activity. Was there a time in the past when you were more politically active than you are at present?

» If yes: Here is a list of reasons people give us for not being very active politically. Please tell me if each of these reasons is *very important*, somewhat important, or not at all important in explaining why you are not very politically active? How about . . . ?

I think I should take care of myself and my family before I worry about the welfare of the community and nation.

FIGURE 3.6

» Overall, how qualified do you feel you are to run for public office? *Very qualified, Qualified,* Somewhat qualified, Not at all qualified

» Overall, how qualified do you feel you are to do the job of an elected official? *Very qualified, Qualified,* Somewhat qualified, Not at all qualified

FIGURE 3.7

» Which of the following options do you think is the most effective way for you to get government to address a political issue?

Run for office and become a policymaker

Form a grassroots organization to lobby government

Make monetary contributions to appropriate political leaders

Support a candidate who shares your views

» In the last few years, have you ever thought about running for political office?

No, I've never really thought about it

Yes, I've sometimes thought about running

Yes, I've thought a lot about running

Yes, I've seriously investigated the possibility of running

Yes, I've run for public office

Yes, I've held an elected office

» Would you be more likely to consider running for office if:

. . .

You had more experience working in politics (e.g., on a campaign)?

» Imagine you were thinking about running for public office in the next few years. What would you be concerned about? (check all that apply)

. . .

the difficulty of holding office

losing the election

I don't think I could make a difference in politics

I don't think I would make a good politician

. . .

FIGURE 3.8

» Sometimes politics and government seem so complicated that a person like me can't really understand what's going on.

Agree

Disagree

Neither

Don't Know, Depends

FIGURE 3.9

» In the last few elections, what percentage of the following groups would you estimate were employed in working-class jobs (e.g., factory workers, restaurant servers, receptionists) at the time? . . . The potential candidates your party tried to recruit.

» In the last few elections, what percentage of the following groups would you estimate were women? . . . The potential candidates your party tried to recruit.

FIGURE 3.10

» In races for county and local office in your area, relative to candidates with professional backgrounds, do you think candidates from working-class jobs (e.g., factory workers, restaurant servers, receptionists) tend to be [options: more, the same, less] . . . Qualified to hold office? Easy to convince to run? Preferred by voters? Good at fundraising? Good at campaigning?

» In races for county and local office in your area, relative to male candidates, do you think female candidates tend to be [options: more, the same, less] . . . Qualified to hold office? Easy to convince to run? Preferred by voters? Good at fundraising? Good at campaigning?

FIGURE 3.11

» Suppose there is a primary for an open [county board/state legislative/U.S. House] seat in your county and the two individuals below are considering running. We'd like you to consider the following two potential candidates for this office.

» Which of the above candidates would you be more likely to encourage to run for office? (circle one)

» Which of the above candidates do you believe would be more likely to

   . . . Win the primary election

   . . . Win the general election if they won the primary

   . . . Raise enough money

   . . . Recruit enough volunteers

   . . . Stay loyal to the party's positions if elected

   . . . Be an effective elected official

FIGURE 3.12

» When you first ran for political office, did any of the following people encourage or discourage you from running? (check all that apply)

   . . .

   Sitting politicians

   Other local community leaders

   . . .

   Local interest or community groups

A formal candidate training program

. . .

Members of the media

. . .

FIGURE 3.13

» Did you do any (other) work for one of the parties or candidates?

No

Yes

Don't Know, No Answer, Inappropriate, Question Not Used

FIGURE 4.5

» In races for county and local office in your area, relative to candidates with professional backgrounds, do you think candidates from working-class jobs (e.g., factory workers, restaurant servers, receptionists) tend to be [options: more, the same, less] . . . Qualified to hold office? Easy to convince to run? Preferred by voters? Good at fundraising? Good at campaigning?

» In the last few elections, what percentage of the following groups would you estimate were employed in working-class jobs (e.g., factory workers, restaurant servers, receptionists) at the time? . . . The potential candidates your party tried to recruit.

» Does your party organization have (check all that apply):

A year-round physical office

A physical campaign headquarters during election season

A website

A constitution, charter, or other set of formal rules

Meetings at least once a month

» Does your party organization have a *formal* process, committee, or person in charge of identifying and encouraging candidates to run for office (at any level)?

　Yes

　No

FIGURE 4.6

» In races for county and local office in your area, relative to candidates with professional backgrounds, do you think candidates from working-class jobs (e.g., factory workers, restaurant servers, receptionists) tend to be [options: more, the same, less] . . . Qualified to hold office? Easy to convince to run? Preferred by voters? Good at fundraising? Good at campaigning?

» In the last few elections, what percentage of the following groups would you estimate were employed in working-class jobs (e.g., factory workers, restaurant servers, receptionists) at the time? . . . The potential candidates your party tried to recruit.

» In your area, about what proportion of political offices would you consider safe for your party or are almost certain your party will win?

　0–25%

　26–50%

　51–75%

　75–100%

» Running for political office can be expensive these days. Thinking about elections over the last few years in your area, about how much would a candidate for the following offices have to spend, on average, to win both the primary and general elections for the following offices?

　County legislative office (e.g., county supervisor or commissioner)

FIGURE 4.7

» In races for county and local office in your area, relative to candidates with professional backgrounds, do you think candidates from working-class jobs (e.g., factory workers, restaurant servers, receptionists) tend to be [options: more, the same, less] . . . Qualified to hold office? Easy to convince to run? Preferred by voters? Good at fundraising? Good at campaigning?

» In the last few elections, what percentage of the following groups would you estimate were employed in working-class jobs (e.g., factory workers, restaurant servers, receptionists) at the time? . . . The potential candidates your party tried to recruit.

» What is your current annual household income?

Under $30,000

$30,000–49,999

$50,000–74,999

$75,000–99,999

$100,000–149,999

Over $150,000

Rather not say

» We're interested in knowing who gets active in politics in your area. Thinking about the executive committee of your county party, to the best of your knowledge, how many current members are . . .

Occupation (currently, or before retirement)

Business owners ___

Farm owners ___

Lawyers ___

Teachers ___

Doctors ___

Manual laborers or service workers ___

Other (please specify_____) ___

FIGURE 5.1

» What is your primary occupation? (If holding a political office is currently your primary occupation, what was your primary occupation before you got into politics?) _____

» Which ELECTED offices have you RUN FOR, HELD, or are you running for THIS YEAR? (check all that apply)

   . . .

   State Legislature

   . . .

FIGURE 5.2

» What is your primary occupation? (If holding a political office is currently your primary occupation, what was your primary occupation before you got into politics?) _____

» Many people who think about running for office choose not to because of the many personal challenges entailed in seeking office. When you first ran for elected political office, did you feel seriously concerned about any of the following? (check all that apply)

   . . .

   Losing out on income while campaigning

   Losing out on income while serving in office

   . . .

FIGURE 5.3

» What is your primary occupation? (If holding a political office is currently your primary occupation, what was your primary occupation before you got into politics?) _____

» Imagine you were thinking about running for public office in the next few years. What would you be concerned about? (check all that apply)

   . . .

   Giving up my income or job to run for office

   . . .

FIGURE 5.5

» What is your primary occupation? (If holding a political office is currently your primary occupation, what was your primary occupation before you got into politics?) _____

» Which ELECTED offices have you RUN FOR, HELD, or are you running for THIS YEAR? (check all that apply)

    . . .

    State Legislature

    . . .

FIGURE 5.7

» What is your primary occupation? (If holding a political office is currently your primary occupation, what was your primary occupation before you got into politics?) _____

» Before running for office for the first time, did you feel seriously concerned about any of the following political challenges? (check all that apply)

    . . .

    The need to raise lots of money

    . . .

    The difficulty of running a campaign

    . . .

» How many hours per week do you typically spend on the following campaign activities?

    Personally contacting voters one-on-one (e.g., knocking on their doors)

    Raising money

    Attending public community meetings to speak to groups of voters (e.g., at civics clubs)

    Meeting voters one-on-one at public events (e.g., county fairs)

Meeting privately with community leaders (e.g., civic club presidents, church pastors)

FIGURE 5.8

» In the last few elections, what percentage of the following groups would you estimate were employed in working-class jobs (e.g., factory workers, restaurant servers, receptionists) at the time? . . . The potential candidates your party tried to recruit.

» In the last few elections, what percentage of the following groups would you estimate were women? . . . The potential candidates your party tried to recruit.

FIGURE 5.10

» How would you rate yourself on the following skills? (above average, average, below average)

Speaking in public

Describing your core values

Working long hours on a project

Asking other people for help

Making quick decisions

» In the last few years, have you done any of the following? (check all that apply)

Regularly vote

Regularly contact elected officials to express your views

Volunteer for a campaign organization, like your party or a candidate's campaign

Volunteer for a civic group (e.g., the Chamber of Commerce, a union, or the Sierra Club)

Volunteer for other community organizations like churches or community service organizations

Donate money to political causes or campaigns

Work for a business that closely works with government (e.g., an election law firm)

Work (paid or full-time) for a campaign organization like your party or a candidate's campaign

Work for a sitting politician in an official capacity (e.g., chief of staff for a state legislator)

SURVEY DETAILS

The 2012 National Candidate Study

In August 2012, I worked with my co-Principal Investigators (David Broockman, Melody Crowder-Meyer, and Chris Skovron; from here, I'll refer to them as my co-PIs) to survey the 10,131 people running for state legislature nationwide at that time. We first collected email or physical mailing addresses for every registered candidate from Project Vote Smart. Most legislators had both; 306 (3 percent) had neither, leaving a total of 9,825 candidates who could be contacted. In mid-August, we sent three waves of email solicitations to the 7,444 candidates with known email addresses. After receiving 1,318 responses to the emailed version of the survey, we then sent a print version of the survey to a randomly selected sample of 5,000 candidates who had not responded (and for whom a physical address was known). An additional 589 candidates returned this paper survey, which left us with a total sample of 1,907 state legislative candidates.

The survey's response rate (19 percent) was roughly double the response rate of a typical public opinion survey conducted at that time. And the responses appeared to capture the views of a representative sample of candidates. About half of respondents were Republican, about half won their races, and there were no obvious regional differences. The only potential nonresponse bias detected was that candidates running unopposed were less likely to complete the survey, perhaps because they were not checking email or physical mail at their campaign addresses.

The survey's response rate did not seem to be higher among the affluent (a common concern in survey research): the survey's respondents included 52 workers (3 percent of respondents), a sample about as large as we would expect based on other exhaustive studies of the social class backgrounds of state legislators and large enough to make at least simple inferences about candidates from the working class.

The 2013 National Survey of Party Leaders (NSPL)

Following Crowder-Meyer's (2010) research on elite biases against women, my co-PIs and I began the 2013 NSPL by first collecting the email and/or physical mailing addresses of the leaders or chairs of every county-level (or equivalent) branch of the Republican and Democratic parties nation-wide in the spring of 2013. (Nine states were excluded because neither party posted contact information for county-level officials: GA, IN, IA, KY, MI, NH, NM, OK, and WI.) Again, we were able to get both email and phys-ical mailing addresses for most party chairs; in this survey, we sent mate-rials simultaneously to both sets of addresses. We first sent postcards and pre-survey emails to each party chair, then followed up a week later with a full letter and/or email inviting the chair to complete the survey. (If both a mailing address and an email address were available, the study attempted to contact party leaders both ways.)

Of the 6,219 chairs who were contacted, 1,118 completed the survey (18 percent), a response rate comparable to recent self-completed surveys of sitting politicians, although somewhat lower than Crowder-Meyer's (2010) comparable survey in 2008. There were no obvious regional differences in response rates, and rates were nearly identical for Republican and Demo-cratic party chairs (18 and 17.9 percent, respectively) and for party leaders previously identified as men and women (18.2 and 18.5 percent; among party leaders whose genders were not known, the response rate was 16.5 percent).

The 2014 Public Opinion Follow-Up

In January 2014, my co-PIs and I conducted an online survey of ordinary citizens that asked many of the same kinds of questions that were asked on the 2013 NSPL. The survey was fielded by a polling company called Survey

Sampling International, which administers surveys to a pool of online respondents selected to resemble the demographic makeup of the entire country. The survey was completed by 1,240 respondents, generating a large enough sample to make generalizations about the population as a whole.

The 2014 National Candidate Study

In August 2014, I worked with my co-PIs to survey the 10,226 people running for state legislature nationwide at that time. The study first collected email or physical mailing addresses for every registered candidate from Project Vote Smart. Again, most legislators had both. In mid-August the study sent three waves of email solicitations to the 6,892 candidates with known email addresses; 1,175 responded. Around that time, we also sent a print version of the survey to the candidates who had not responded (and for whom a physical address was known). An additional 694 candidates responded, which left the researchers with a total sample of 1,869 state legislative candidates.

The survey's response rate (18 percent) was again roughly double the response rate of a typical public opinion survey conducted at that time. And the responses appeared to capture the views of a representative sample of candidates. About half of respondents were Democrats, over 40 percent won their races, and there were no obvious regional differences in response rates.

The survey's response rate did not seem to be higher among the affluent (a common concern in survey research): the survey's respondents included 73 workers (4 percent of respondents), a sample about as large as we would expect based on other exhaustive studies of the social class backgrounds of state legislators and large enough to make at least simple inferences about candidates from the working class.

Notes

CHAPTER 1

1. Throughout this book, I define someone as belonging to the *working class* (or having a *blue-collar job*, or as simply a *worker*) if he or she is employed in a manual labor job (e.g., factory worker), a service industry job (e.g., restaurant server), a clerical job (e.g., receptionist), or a job within a labor union (e.g., field organizer). This definition excludes people who *manage* workers (e.g., front-line managers at fast-food restaurants) or who own their own businesses (e.g., self-employed contractors). I define a person as having a white-collar job if she is not a part of the working class. Of course, there are other ways to disaggregate occupations (e.g., some people might not classify clerical jobs as "working class") and other ways to measure class (e.g., education, income, wealth, family background, subjective perceptions of class, etc.). Most modern class analysts agree, however, that any measure of class should be rooted in occupational data, that is, information about how a person earns a living (e.g., Weeden and Grusky 2005; Wright 1997). And the distinction I draw between working-class jobs and white-collar jobs seems to be the major class-based dividing line in political opinion in the United States (Hout 2008; Hout, Manza, and Brooks 1995). Research on politicians (Carnes 2012, 2013) squares with both intuitions: lawmakers from working-class jobs tend to vote significantly differently than legislators from white-collar jobs; however, legislators with higher net worths, more formal education, or well-to-do parents tend not to behave as differently (Grumbach 2015; Carreri and Teso 2016). Of course, there are also important differences between the many jobs that fall in the working-class and white-collar categories (e.g., teachers and social workers tend to be slightly more progressive than business owners). However, the major dividing line seems to be between workers, who tend to support more progressive economic policies, and professionals, who tend to support a more conservative role for government in economic affairs.
2. Carnes 2012, 2013; see also Domhoff 1967; Matthews 1954a, 1954b; Mills 1956.
3. Carnes 2012, 2013, 2016a; Grose 2013; Griffin and Anewalt-Remsburg 2013; Kraus and Callaghan 2014; see also Carnes and Lupu 2015; O'Grady, n.d.
4. Ajbaili 2012.

5. Morocco's constitution actually mandates that women hold at least 60 of the 395 seats in its Parliament.

6. Pitkin 1967.

7. Burrell 2006; Crowder-Meyer 2010a; Darcy, Welch, and Clark 1994; Gaddie and Bullock 1995; Lawless and Fox 2005, 2010b; Niven 1998; Palmer and Simon 2010; Pimlott 2010; Sanbonmatsu 2002, 2006a, 2006b, 2006c; Trounstine and Valdini 2008.

8. Aldrich 1995; Arnold 1990; Austin-Smith and Wright 1994; Hall and Deardorff 2006; Hall and Wayman 1990; Mayhew 1974; Rohde 1991.

9. See, for instance, Arnold 1990; Delli Carpini and Keeter 1996; Gelman and King 1990; Hall 1996; Jacobs and Shapiro 2000; Kingdon 1981, ch. 10; Mettler 2011.

10. For a useful overview, see Burden 2007. On race, see, for instance, Anwar, Bayer, and Hjalmarsson 2012; Canon 1999; Griffin and Newman 2008; Whitby 1997. On gender, see Berkman and O'Connor 1993; Swers 2002; Thomas 1991; Thomas and Welch 1991. On military service, see Gelpi and Feaver 2002. And on religion, education, and smoking, see Burden 2007.

11. The available data on politicians differ slightly from branch to branch. Most city council members and state legislators continue working while serving in office, so the best available data simply record their main occupations outside of public office. Members of Congress, governors, Supreme Court justices, and presidents, on the other hand, usually stop working when they take office; the best available data focus either on their last main occupations before holding office or, in the case of members of Congress, the proportions of their pre-congressional careers that they spent in different occupations (although looking at their most recent occupations gives roughly the same result; the average member spent 2 percent of his pre-congressional career in a working-class job, and about 2 percent of members had working-class jobs when they first got involved in politics).

12. Carnes 2015.

13. Hamilton 1788.

14. Bartels 2006b; Cramer 2016; Gilens 2009; McCall and Manza 2010; Page, Bartels, and Seawright 2013; Suhay, Klasnja, and Rivero, n.d.; Thal 2017; Walsh 2012.

15. Scholars have many hunches about why that might be. People from different classes might have different views about economic issues because they have different experiences, material interests, and social networks. Or it may be because people with different political views go into different lines of work. For a useful review, see Hout 2008 or Hout, Manza, and Brooks 1995.

16. Carnes 2012, 2013, 2016a. See also Bellemare and Carnes 2015; Carnes and Lupu 2015.

17. Carnes 2013, figure 2.1 and table 2.1.

18. Carnes 2012, figure 5.

19. Griffin and Anewalt-Remsburg 2013; Kirkland, n.d.; Kraus and Callaghan 2014; Grose 2013. See also Carreri and Teso 2016; Eulau and Sprague 1964; Miller 1995; Robinson 2015; Witko and Friedman 2008.

20. Carnes 2013, ch. 5.

21. The shortage of politicians from the working class may also have important *symbolic* effects. In Latin American countries with fewer working-class politicians, citizens are less likely to trust the government—and democracy itself (Barnes and Saxton, n.d.).
22. Thompson and 24/7 Wall Street 2010.
23. It wouldn't have been unprecedented; see, for instance, Brands 2000; Pessen 1984.
24. Choma 2014.
25. Acosta 2013.
26. Robertson 2015.
27. Matthews 1954a, 1954b.
28. Carnes 2013, ch. 6; Sadin 2012.
29. Bartels 2008, ch. 9; Gilens 2005, 2013; Gilens and Page 2014; Hayes 2013; Jacobs and Druckman 2011; Rigby and Wright 2013; Sances 2016. See also Hill and Leighley 1992; Schumaker and Getter 1977. For a contrasting perspective, see Ura and Ellis 2008.
30. Bartels 2005; Faricy and Ellis 2014; Flavin 2012; Franko 2015; Franko, Tolbert, and Witko 2013; Kelly and Enns 2010; Levine 2015; McCall 2013, 2014; McCall and Kenworthy 2009; Page and Jacobs 2009; Schlozman et al. 2005, 69.
31. Flavin 2014a, 2014b, 2014c; Gilens 2015; Gilens and Page 2014; Hacker and Pierson 2010; Hertel-Fernandez 2014, 2016; Powell forthcoming; Powell and Grimmer 2016; Schattschneider [1960] 1975, 35; Winters 2011, ch. 5; Witko 2012, 2013a, 2013b.
32. Enns et al. 2014; Faricy 2011, 2015, 2016; Flavin 2015; Jusko 2014, 2017; Kelly 2009; Kelly and Witko 2012, 2014; Mettler 2010, 2011; Witko 2013a.
33. Mansbridge 2015, 262.
34. I discuss this *civic voluntarism model* of participation in more detail in chapter 3. For a complete discussion, see Verba, Schlozman, and Brady 1995.
35. This point about intersectionality deserves more attention in itself. As a first cut at this problem, this book foregrounds class, but I hope future research will investigate the intersection between class, race, gender, and other characteristics. The experiences of workers who are women and/or people of color undoubtedly differ from the experiences of workers who are white men. I do not have the space or data to expand on this point here, but I hope future research will do so.
36. I group individual occupations using the same classification system I have used in other research; see Carnes 2013, table A.1.

CHAPTER 2

1. Quoted in Wilson 1999, 239.
2. Goings 1990.
3. As one group of Anti-Federalists pointedly noted in *The Address and Reasons of Dissent of the Minority of the Convention of the State of Pennsylvania to Their Constituents*, under the Constitution, "men of the most elevated rank in life will alone be chosen" for office. "The other orders of society, such as farmers, traders, and mechanics, who

all ought to have a competent number of their best informed men in the legislature, shall be totally unrepresented. . . . [Congress] will consist of the lordly and high minded; of men who will have no congenial feelings with the people, but a perfect indifference for, and contempt of them; [it] will consist of those harpies of power that prey upon the very vitals, that riot on the miseries of the community."

4. See Hamilton 1788.

5. Henry 1995, 21; Reston 2012; http://huff.to/1rweqrp (accessed December 10, 2013); http://politicalhotwire.com/political-discussion/91717-kasich-president .html (accessed October 1, 2015); http://www.npr.org/2012/08/30/160357612/ transcript-mitt-romneys-acceptance-speech (accessed October 1, 2015).

6. Cohen 1981, 5.

7. Kotakorpi and Poutvaara 2011, 879; De Benedetto and De Paola 2014, 6. See also Baltrunaite et al. 2014; Besley and Reynal-Querol 2011.

8. Zernike and Thee-Brenan 2010.

9. Anonymous review, *Journal of Politics*, March 6, 2016.

10. For a useful review, see Llavador 2017.

11. There is another perspective, moreover, that regards economic adversity not as a mark of deficiency but rather a breeding ground of talent. Gladwell's (2008, 36) discussion of this point is worth quoting at length:

> If you wanted to end up on top, the thinking went, it was better to start at the bottom, because it was there that you learned the discipline and motivation essential for success. "New York merchants preferred to hire country boys, on the theory that they worked harder, and were more resolute, obedient, and cheerful than native New Yorkers," Irvin G. Wyllie wrote in his 1954 study "The Self-Made Man in America." Andrew Carnegie, whose personal history was the defining self-made-man narrative of the nineteenth century, insisted that there was an advantage to being "cradled, nursed and reared in the stimulating school of poverty." According to Carnegie, "It is not from the sons of the millionaire or the noble that the world receives its teachers, its martyrs, its inventors, its statesmen, its poets, or even its men of affairs. It is from the cottage of the poor that all these spring."

12. Lawless and Fox 2005, 2010b.

13. E.g., Norris and Lovenduski 1995.

14. Norris and Lovenduski 1995, 15. See also Gaddie and Bullock 1995; Palmer and Simon 2010.

15. On *recruitment*, see Crowder-Meyer 2010a, 2010b; Lawless and Fox 2005, 2010b; Niven 1998; Pimlott 2010. On *voters*, see Darcy, Welch, and Clark 1994. On *institutions*, see Trounstine and Valdini 2008.

16. Ganzach 2011; Nettle 2003.

17. Baron, Albright, and Malloy 1995; Cozzarelli, Wilkinson, and Tagler 2001; Fiske et al. 1999.

18. http://newerawindows.com/about-us/our-story (accessed March 3, 2018). See also Dewan 2014; Mead-Lucero 2008.

19. Carnes and Lupu 2016b.

20. One other proxy that is unfortunately impossible to use in the U.S. context is directly measuring *intellectual ability and leadership potential*. To my knowledge, this is only possible in Sweden, where the military conducted IQ and leadership testing on every male citizen between 1951 and 1980. Using these data, Dal Bó et al. (2017, 1907) find that every class of citizens has many qualified people, and that working-class politicians tend to be about as qualified as others thanks to *positive selection*, that is, the fact that political candidates tend to be the most competent members of their social groups.

21. For a useful introduction, see Jacobson 2012.

22. See Broockman et al. 2014c.

23. Ganzach 2011; Nettle 2003.

24. Beatty 1988.

25. Brady, Verba, and Schlozman 1995; Verba 1987; Verba, Schlozman, and Brady 1995.

26. Piff et al. 2012; Piff 2013.

27. See, for instance, Besley, Montalvo, and Reynal-Querol 2011; Carnes and Lupu 2016b; Jones and Olken 2005.

28. See, for instance, Trounstine and Valdini 2008.

29. I independently coded the open-ended occupations listed under "other."

30. I controlled for each city's centrality (center city, suburb, or independent township), racial makeup (percent Latino, percent Black, percent Asian, and percent other non-white races), education level (percent with a college degree), whether city council members were elected by district or in at-large races, the re-election rate among council members, the frequency of city council meetings, the form of government (mayor-council, council-manager, commission, or town meeting), the state the city was located in, the percent of the city in poverty, and the percentage of women and racial minorities on the city council.

31. Outside of political science, scholars who study the class backgrounds of politicians often skip over Matthews and take as their intellectual starting points the groundbreaking sociological work that emerged a few years after Matthews wrote, like C. Wright Mills's 1956 book *The Power Elite* and William Domhoff's 1967 book *Who Rules America?*

32. Matthews 1954b, 14.

33. Matthews 1954a, 1954b, [1960] 1974, 11, 1985, 24.

34. Matthews 1954a, 32, emphasis in original.

35. Matthews (1954a, 32) also suggested other explanations, including "the obvious fact that the money and time necessary for sustained political activity are possessed by only a minority of the American people."

36. Darcy, Welch, and Clark 1994; Philpot and Walton 2007; Sanbonmatsu 2003.

37. Baron, Albright, and Malloy 1995; Cozzarelli, Wilkinson, and Tagler 2001; Fiske et al. 1999.

38. Fiske et al. 1999.

39. Jacobson 2012.

40. Pessen 1984.

41. Joseph 2014, 1.
42. Sadin 2012.
43. Carnes and Lupu 2016a.
44. For further details, see Carnes and Lupu 2016a.
45. Hainmueller, Hopkins, and Yamamoto (2014) also document biases *within* white-collar jobs—in hypothetical candidate experiments, they find, for instance, that farmers and car dealers are less popular with voters than business owners and teachers—and biases against extremely wealthy candidates. However, their study does not include hypothetical candidates from the working class. Griffin, Newman, and Burh (n.d.) also find that voters evaluate middle-income candidates about as favorably as (and sometimes more favorably than) millionaire candidates. Again, however, their study does not include hypothetical working-class candidates, although its findings are consistent with the research discussed here.
46. There are lots of data on the social class backgrounds of ordinary citizens and elected politicians. But it's harder to find good data on the candidates who ran and lost. Especially at the state and local levels, many candidates are political newcomers whose biographies aren't well-documented. Many aren't covered extensively in the media, and many take down campaign websites shortly after election day. As a result, it can be difficult to obtain representative data on the entire candidate pool. If we want to know whether workers really are screened out at the Running stage, though, those are exactly the data we need: we need to know how many workers run for office and how many win.
47. The complete LEAP data set includes partisanship for many elections, but the extract I requested did not, unfortunately.

CHAPTER 3

1. Of course, this kind of attrition raises questions about whether we can generalize from this sample to the larger universe of candidates. Figure 3.1 is only illustrative and not meant to be representative of the views of all candidates.
2. Bianco 1984; Black 1972; Kang, Niemi, and Powell 2003; Rogers 2015; Stone, Maisel, and Maestas 2004.
3. Adams and Squire 1997; Hogan 2008; Lazarus 2008; Krasno and Green 1988; on term limits, see Rogers, n.d.
4. When this book discusses ambition, it is referring to *nascent* ambition, the intrinsic desire to hold political office. Historically, political scientists have also used the term "ambition" to refer to the act of running for office (or what is sometimes called *expressive ambition*) or to distinguish between the desire to run for just one term (*discrete ambition*), multiple terms (*static ambition*), or higher office (*progressive ambition*). This book is not primarily concerned with the question of whether workers exhibit discrete, static, and/or progressive ambition—with so few workers at any level of government, the first question is why workers exhibit less expressive ambition, that is, why they run less often. And to answer that question, we must consider the possibility that workers have less *nascent* ambition.
5. Fowler and McClure 1989; Schlesinger 1966.

6. Fox and Lawless 2005, 643.

7. Carroll 1985; Lawless and Fox 2005, 2010a.

8. Gaddie 2004; Lawless 2012.

9. For a useful review, see Broockman 2014. See also Carroll and Sanbonmatsu 2013; Crowder-Meyer 2010a, 2013; Fox and Lawless 2004; Lawless 2011, 2012; Lawless and Fox 2005, 2010b; Niven 1998; Pimlott 2010; Sanbonmatsu 2002, 2006c.

10. Brady, Verba, and Schlozman 1995; Verba, Schlozman, and Brady 1995.

11. As Levine (2015) has recently shown, just *thinking* about economic insecurity can discourage less affluent people from participating in politics.

12. Of course, people's self-reports of their personal qualities aren't perfect. However, this approach has the virtue that it at least excludes respondents who *admit* that they don't have most of the qualities that voters and party leaders want in a politician, which should leave us with a more qualified sample than if we simply analyzed all respondents.

13. To illustrate that workers are just as likely to be *extremely* qualified, Figure 2.3 focuses on respondents who have *five* or more traits. The analysis in the rest of this book is concerned more with respondents who are generally well qualified, however, so I use four traits as the cutoff.

14. It's important to note that the question posed to respondents asked them about running for political office without specifying the level (e.g., school board versus Congress). In a sense, the question tapped not ability to run in a particular race, but rather social class differences in respondents' general or *nascent* ability to run for public office. Of course, it is always possible that respondents' perceptions of their ability to run are somehow skewed; for instance, people might generalize from the news about grueling congressional campaigns and think that *all* political campaigns are beyond their reach. Future research could find out: workers express general concerns about the practical burdens associated with campaigns, but are those concerns exaggerated by the fact that federal campaigns dominate popular thought?

15. Lawless and Fox 2005, 42.

16. The results were similar when I tried other economic measures, like average per capita income in each state.

17. Carroll and Jenkins 2005; Jacobson 2012.

18. Darcy, Welch, and Clark 1994.

19. Lawless and Fox also noted that women were less likely to be encouraged to run, a point that the next section will return to.

20. Fox and Lawless 2004, 2005, 2011a, 2011b, 2014a, 2014b; Lawless and Fox 2005, 2010b. See also Kanthak and Woon 2015; Moore 2005.

21. Elder 2004; Fulton et al. 2006; Johnson, Oppenheimer, and Selin 2012; Maestas et al. 2006; Moore 2005; Palmer and Simon 2003; Shah 2014; Thomsen 2017; Windett 2011.

22. Thomsen 2014, 2015.

23. As chapter 2 noted, we often hear—even from experts—that workers aren't fit to be politicians. It isn't true, but some workers might believe it.

24. Gaddie 2004; Karpowitz and Mendelberg 2014; Lawless 2012.

25. Interestingly, respondents said they felt more qualified to govern than to campaign.

26. So, too, do data from the American Citizen Participation Study (the 1990 survey used in Figure 3.4). When I analyzed responses to a question that asked people who had not been politically active lately whether the reason was "It's not my place to be involved in politics," workers were far less likely to cite this reason as very important (11 percent) than they were to cite the need to take care of themselves (40 percent).

27. The results were similar when I reversed the numerator and denominator, that is, when I analyzed the share of workers among the politically efficacious, rather than the share of politically efficacious among workers.

28. Quoted in Hohmann 2013.

29. Indeed, in my 2014 public opinion survey, we asked respondents whether they would be more likely to consider running for office if "someone involved in politics suggested [they] run." Among high-potential respondents (defined the same as in the previous sections), approximately half said that recruitment would make them more likely to run.

30. For a useful review, see Broockman 2014. See also Ocampo 2018.

31. There is another slightly different school of thought on this subject (perhaps best exemplified by Bawn et al. 2017 and DeMora et al. 2017) that argues that many candidates are self-starters, and that they aren't *recruited* so much as *supported*. In this view, would-be candidates aren't usually induced to run by political and civic groups but rather want to run and try to tap into existing organizational networks, political parties, and so on. In this view, the groups I have labeled candidate recruiters would be thought of more as candidate *screeners* or *facilitators*. This perspective, however, still acknowledges that civic leaders are crucial to the success of would-be candidates and that any biases they have against a social group would reduce the number of candidates from that group.

32. Lawless and Fox 2005, 2010b.

33. Crowder-Meyer 2010a, 2013. See also Niven 1998; Pimlott 2010; Sanbonmatsu 2002, 2006c.

34. Crowder-Meyer 2010a.

35. Of course, candidate recruiters can offset these burdens by supplying candidates with campaign funds, volunteers, and other resources; see, for instance, Bawn et al. 2012; Masket 2011; Masket and McGhee 2013. But a recruiter's resources are limited, and candidates who need less campaign support are more appealing, other things equal.

36. Louisiana's parties are organized by parish, Alaska's are organized by borough, North Dakota's are organized by district, Connecticut's are organized by city, and the Democratic Party in Massachusetts is organized by sub-city unit. Nine states were excluded because neither party posted contact information for county-level officials: Georgia, Indiana, Iowa, Kentucky, Michigan, New Hampshire, New Mexico, Oklahoma, and Wisconsin.

37. Aldrich 2000; Cotter et al. 1984; Crowder-Meyer 2010b; Gibson et al. 1983; Sanbon-matsu 2006c.
38. Masket 2011.
39. No single measure of bias is bulletproof, of course, but by using three different approaches, the NSPL helped ensure that we wouldn't be led astray by a single faulty measure.
40. Of course, party leaders' responses reflected what they *believed* about each group, not how the group actually performed.
41. The level of office in the question was randomly assigned. The results reported here hold regardless.
42. The estimates in this figure are taken from regression models (presented in their entirety in Table A3.5 in the appendix) in which I treated each hypothetical candidate as an independent observation (following Hainmueller, Hopkins, and Yamamoto 2014), then regressed the probability that a party leader would choose that candidate as the one they would encourage (then, separately, the one more likely to win the primary, and so on) on each of the independent, randomly assigned candidate attributes (clustering standard errors by a unique identifier for each respondent, to account for the fact that each candidate was a part of a two-candidate head-to-head comparison). I also conducted the diagnostic tests recommended by Hainmueller, Hopkins, and Yamamoto 2014; see Carnes, n.d.
43. The two concerns may well have been related. The research design did not allow me to say whether party leaders' views about fundraising drove their views about general election success, unfortunately, but it seems likely that that the two were connected.
44. There were no comparable penalties for female candidates on any of these measures.
45. Results were similar when I reversed the numerator and denominator, that is, when I computed the share of campaign staff and volunteers who were workers, rather than the share of workers who were staff/volunteers.
46. These analyses control for a wide range of potential explanations for working-class representation, including how much income workers earn, how much political interest they exhibit, how actively they participate in politics, how knowledgeable and confident they are, the share of voters from the working class, the partisan difference between workers and other voters in a given state, the share of campaign staff from the working class, union density, and the state legislature's professionalization score; see Carnes 2016b.
47. Personal email from Blaine Stum, April 25, 2016.
48. Brady, Schlozman, and Verba 1999.

CHAPTER 4

1. Austen 2015.
2. Taber 2016, 1.
3. On this point, I am in full agreement. Race, class, and gender are very different social constructs, and scholars should treat them as such. As chapter 3 showed,

for instance, the barriers that keep women out of office are not the same as the barriers that keep working-class Americans out. But there *are* structural barriers keeping workers out of politics, and the shortage of workers *is* an important topic, just as the shortages of women and people of color are driven by structural barriers and are normatively important. Apples and oranges have many differences, but they have things in common, too.

4. Fox and Lawless 2005, 2014b; Lawless 2012.

5. Of course, it's possible that other forms of leadership selection (say, for instance, letting politicians in other branches appoint new leaders) would also create barriers to working-class officeholding. My argument is that our electoral process disadvantages workers in absolute terms, not that it disadvantages them relative to other electoral processes we might imagine.

6. Edward Beard, interview with the author, March 12, 2010.

7. Gelman 2013.

8. Even uncontested races take time and energy; they are often uncontested *because* a candidate has worked hard to scare away potential challengers.

9. E.g., Trounstine and Valdini 2008.

10. I independently coded the open-ended occupations listed under "other."

11. Most research on representation in district versus at-large councils has focused on the geographic concentration of groups (e.g., Trounstine and Valdini 2008). My argument here is different; whereas past studies have noted that large concentrated groups can benefit from district elections, I argue that district elections may also benefit groups that suffer resource shortages.

12. Importantly, the gaps in Figure 4.1 didn't appear to be the result of differences in the practical burdens associated with *holding office* (a point chapter 5 will take up in its discussion of one common but misguided reform proposal, namely, raising legislative salaries). In larger cities, for instance, elections take more time and energy *and* politicians have more work to do (more roads to maintain, more constituents to serve, etc.). However, when I compared city councils based on the best available measure of the burdens associated with holding office—how often the city council met—the differences in working-class representation between cities that met monthly or less and cities that met weekly or more were small (around two percentage points) and disappeared when I controlled for the characteristics in Figure 4.1 (see Table A4.1 in the appendix).

13. The regression models controlled for the year, whether the state had term limits, the partisanship of citizens in that state (from the NES), the state's unionization rate, the state's poverty rate, per capita personal income in the state, whether the state was in the South, and whether Democrats controlled the state legislature.

14. Again, controlling for the practical burdens associated with *holding* office did not appear to change the findings reported in Figure 4.2: when I compared states where the legislature met for fewer than thirty-five days a year and those where it met for 120+ days, the difference in the share of workers who held office was smaller than the gaps in Figure 4.2 (and was not statistically distinguishable from zero).

15. http://www.cfinst.org/pdf/vital/VitalStats_t2c.pdf (accessed October 13, 2016).

16. Etzioni 1984; Hall and Wayman 1990; Jackson 1988.

17. Hall and Wayman 1990; Hacker and Pierson 2010; Hall and Deardorff 2006; Broockman and Kalla 2015; Powell and Grimmer 2016; Skocpol and Hertel-Fernandez 2016; see also Sclar et al., n.d.

18. The one exception, to my knowledge, is Bonica's (2017) recent work on fundraising and the number of attorneys in public office.

19. Broockman 2014; Carroll and Sanbonmatsu 2013; Lawless 2011.

20. Bawn et al. 2012; Masket 2011; Masket and McGhee 2013.

21. Crowder-Meyer 2010a, 2013; Lawless and Fox 2005, 2010b; Niven 1998; Pimlott 2010; Sanbonmatsu 2002, 2006b.

22. Aldrich 1995.

23. Bawn et al. 2012; Masket 2011; Masket and McGhee 2013.

24. These kinds of social shortcuts show up vividly in the 2013 National Survey of Party Leaders. The survey included an item that asked party leaders, "Thinking about elections over the past five years, how often have your party officials looked for new state legislative, county, or local office candidates . . . ," then listed a variety of options, allowing party leaders to respond "Rarely or never," "Sometimes," or "Often." Party leaders overwhelmingly said that they look for people among those who are already connected to themselves or the party in some way. Of the 899 county-level party leaders who answered the question, 82 percent said that they often/sometimes search for candidates "among people active in election and issue campaigns (e.g., volunteers, activists, campaign managers)," 84 percent said they search "among those already holding other offices," 81 percent said they search "based on recommendations from current officeholders," and 82 percent said they search for candidates "based on recommendations from people in party members' personal networks." In sharp contrast, only about half as many said they sometimes or often recruit candidates "using voter lists" (41 percent) or outside organizations like "labor unions" (35 percent), "service and fraternal organizations" (40 percent), or "ethnic, nationality, or civil rights organizations" (35 percent).

25. Rivera 2012.

26. Crowder-Meyer 2010a.

27. Sinyai 2006.

28. Carnes 2016b.

29. Giese 2015.

30. Berr 2016.

CHAPTER 5

1. Hoxby and Avery 2012.

2. Ibid.

3. Avery et al. 2006; but see Angrist et al. 2014.

4. Pérez-Peña 2014.

5. Vedantam 2013.

6. Sojourner 2013, 484.
7. McElwee 2015, 1. See also Roberson 2018.
8. Clawson and Clawson 1999.
9. Godard 2009, 82.
10. Schrad 2010.
11. Kauffman 2017, 1.
12. Email to the author, December 10, 2014; Fitzsimon 2010, 1. See also Lehman 2016.
13. See, for instance, Maddox's (2004) work on economic threshold models, and Mattozzi and Merlo's (2008) work on the relative boost in salary associated with holding office.
14. Besley 2004; Besley and Coate 1997; Osborne and Slivinski 1996.
15. For complete details, see Carnes and Hansen 2016.
16. In follow-up analyses, I focused only on candidates who had never run or held public office before, that is, candidates for whom the current state legislative race was the first political campaign referenced in the question. The results were unchanged from the findings presented in Figure 5.2.
17. Maine Citizens for Clean Elections 2016, 1.
18. https://www.bostonglobe.com/ideas/2014/01/12/america-white-collar-congress/nsFNlQ7LAZgJpdmzQji80O/story.html#comments (accessed January 31, 2017).
19. http://talkingpointsmemo.com/cafe/of-course-the-u-s-is-an-oligarchy-we-keep-electing-the-rich (accessed January 31, 2017).
20. Ibid.
21. Several major cities have implemented public financing, and some states have adopted public financing for non-legislative races, like North Carolina's recently repealed system of public financing for judicial elections.
22. Francia and Herrnson 2003; Miller 2011b, 2014.
23. Mayer 2013.
24. Malhotra 2008; Mayer, Werner, and Williams 2006; Miller 2014.
25. Miller 2014.
26. Miller 2008.
27. Osborne 2012; United States Government Accountability Office 2010.
28. Miller and Panagopoulos 2011.
29. Mayer 2013; Mayer and Wood 1995; Miller 2011a; United States Government Accountability Office 2010.
30. Mayer 2013, 366. See also Hamm and Hogan 2009.
31. Besley 2004; Bowen and Mo, n.d.; Carnes and Hansen 2016; Diermeier, Keane, and Merlo 2005; Hoffman and Lyons, n.d.; Maddox 2004.
32. Bellafante 2013, 1.
33. Ari Kamen, interview with the author, March 2, 2017.
34. Neuman 2017.
35. See, for instance, Yong 2017.
36. Carnes 2018.
37. http://www.emilyslist.org/pages/entry/women-we-helped-elect (accessed February 21, 2017).

38. http://www.emilyslist.org/pages/entry/candidate-recruitment (accessed February 21, 2017).
39. Charles Wowkanech, interview with the author, July 14, 2011.
40. Broockman 2014.
41. Matthew Brokman, interview with the author, December 16, 2011.
42. See Carnes 2018.
43. Kamen interview.
44. Bonica (2017) finds that early fundraising advantages are one of the most important reasons attorneys are overrepresented in Congress.
45. Kamen interview.

CHAPTER 6

1. Quoted in Truthout 2011, 1.
2. The table does not include instances when one of the book's empirical claims was also supported with citations to other studies. For instance, the claim that workers bring different perspectives to public office is only tested briefly (in Figure 1.3) because other studies have already used many of the data sets listed to test that claim.
3. Task Force on Inequality and American Democracy 2004, 651.
4. E.g., Weissberg 2006.
5. Jacobs and Skocpol 2006; Hauck 2006; Weissberg 2006; Jacobs and Skocpol 2006; Brandolini and Smeeding 2006; Macedo and Karpowitz 2006; Schlozman 2006; Bennett 2006; Hacker 2006; Piven 2006; Bartels 2006a.
6. Bartels 2005; Faricy and Ellis 2014; Flavin 2012; Franko 2015; Franko, Tolbert, and Witko 2013; Kelly and Enns 2010; Levine 2015; McCall 2013, 2014; McCall and Kenworthy 2009; Page and Jacobs 2009; Schlozman et al. 2005, 69.
7. Flavin 2014a, 2014b, 2014c; Gilens 2015; Gilens and Page 2014; Hacker and Pierson 2010; Hertel-Fernandez 2014, 2016; Powell forthcoming; Schattschneider [1960] 1975, 35; Winters 2011, ch. 5; Witko 2012, 2013a.
8. Enns et al. 2014; Faricy 2011, 2015, 2016; Flavin 2015; Jusko 2014, 2017; Kelly 2009; Kelly and Witko 2012, 2014; Mettler 2010, 2011; Witko 2013a.
9. Bartels 2008; Gilens 2013.
10. Hill and Leighley 1992; Schumaker and Getter 1977.
11. Gilens and Page 2014; Hayes 2013; Jacobs and Druckman 2011; Rigby and Wright 2013; Sances 2016. But see Ura and Ellis 2008.
12. https://www.fordfoundation.org/work/challenging-inequality/civic-engagement-and-government/our-strategy/ (accessed June 2, 2017).
13. https://www.russellsage.org/research/funding/social-inequality (accessed June 2, 2017).
14. Gilens 2013, 248.
15. Hacker and Pierson 2010, 303.
16. http://www.electproject.org/national-1789-present (accessed June 7, 2017).
17. https://www.opensecrets.org/overview/cost.php?display=T&infl=Y (accessed June 7, 2017).

18. Carnes 2015.

19. Smith [1776] 2007, 220.

20. http://www.huffingtonpost.ca/2017/02/07/melania-trump-lawsuit_n_14636538 .html (accessed March 4, 2018).

21. See Carnes and Lupu 2017.

22. https://twitter.com/BraddJaffy/status/877689992658767872 (accessed June 27, 2017).

23. The preceding text in this section draws on an article I published in *Forum* (2017, volume 15, issue 1, 151–165). I am grateful to the article's publishers for permission to draw upon it here.

24. Remarks at the Maine Democratic Party Convention, May 30, 2014. https://www .youtube.com/watch?v=UD9GAqKX53Y (accessed June 8, 2017).

References

Acosta, Jim. 2013. "Meet the 113th Congress: More Diverse than Ever." *CNN.com*, January 13. http://inamerica.blogs.cnn.com/2013/01/03/meet-the-113th-congress-more-diverse-than-ever/?hpt=hp_c2 (accessed August 20, 2015).

Adams, Greg D., and Peverill Squire. 1997. "Incumbent Vulnerability and Challenger Emergence in Senate Elections." *Political Behavior* 19(2): 97–111.

Ajbaili, Mustapha. 2012. "Moroccan Female Lawmakers Protest Lack of Representation in Islamist-Led Cabinet." *Al Arabiya News*, January 20. http://english.alarabiya.net/articles/2012/01/20/189421.html (accessed August 3, 2015).

Aldrich, John. 1995. *Why Parties?* Chicago: University of Chicago Press.

———. 2000. "Southern Parties in State and Nation." *Journal of Politics* 62(3): 643–70.

American National Election Studies. 2014. *Time Series Cumulative Data File* [data set]. Stanford, CA: Stanford University; Ann Arbor: University of Michigan [producers and distributors].

Angrist, Joshua, David Autor, Sally Hudson, and Amanda Pallais. 2014. "Leveling Up: Early Results from a Randomized Evaluation of Post-Secondary Aid." School Effectiveness and Inequality Initiative Discussion Paper #2014.04. https://seii.mit.edu/wp-content/uploads/2015/03/SEII-Discussion-Paper-2014.04-Angrist-Autor-Hudson-Pallais.pdf (accessed February 27, 2018).

Annenberg Public Policy Center. 2004. *National Annenberg Election Survey: National Rolling Cross Section* [data set]. Philadelphia: University of Pennsylvania [producer and distributor].

Ansolabehere, Stephen, and Brian Schaffner. 2013. *CCES Common Content, 2012* [database]. Harvard University [distributor].

Anwar, Shamena, Patrick Bayer, and Randi Hjalmarsson. 2012. "The Impact of Jury Race in Criminal Trials." *Quarterly Journal of Economics* 127(2): 1017–55.

Arnold, R. Douglas. 1990. *The Logic of Congressional Action.* New Haven: Yale University Press.

Austen, Ian. 2015. "Accidental Lawmaker in Canada Defies Critics, and Liberal Party Resurgence." *New York Times*, October 26. http://www.nytimes.com/2015/10/27/world/americas/ruth-ellen-brosseau-canada-quebec.html?emc=eta1&_r=0 (accessed July 22, 2016).

Austin-Smith, David, and John R. Wright. 1994. "Counteractive Lobbying." *American Journal of Political Science* 38: 25–44.

Avery, Christopher, Caroline Hoxby, Clement Jackson, Kaitlin Burek, Glenn Pope, and Mridula Raman. 2006. "Cost Should Be No Barrier: An Evaluation of the First Year of Harvard's Financial Aid Initiative." NBER Working Paper No. 12029. http://www.nber.org/papers/w12029 (accessed February 27, 2018).

Baltrunaite, Audinga, Piera Bello, Alessandra Casarico, and Paola Profeta. 2014. "Gender Quotas and the Quality of Politicians." *Journal of Public Economics* 118: 62–74.

Barnes, Tiffany D., and Gregory W. Saxton. n.d. "Class and Unequal Representation in Latin America: Linking Descriptive and Symbolic Representation." Working paper. http://gregorywsaxton.weebly.com/uploads/5/4/3/0/54300059/classrep_bbs.pdf (accessed February 27, 2018).

Baron, Reuben M., Linda Albright, and Thomas E. Malloy. 1995. "Effects of Behavioral and Social Class Information on Social Judgement." *Personality and Social Psychology Bulletin* 21(4): 308–15.

Bartels, Larry M. 2005. "Homer Gets a Tax Cut: Inequality and Public Policy in the American Mind." *Perspectives on Politics* 3(1): 15–31.

———. 2006a. "Is the Water Rising? Reflections on Inequality and American Democracy." *PS: Political Science & Politics* 39(1): 39–42.

———. 2006b. "What's the Matter with *What's the Matter with Kansas?*" *Quarterly Journal of Political Science* 1(2): 201–26.

———. 2008. *Unequal Democracy: The Political Economy of the New Gilded Age.* Princeton: Princeton University Press.

Bawn, Kathleen, Knox Brown, Angela Ocampo, Shawn Patterson, John Ray, and John Zaller. 2017. "Social Choice and Coordination Problems in Open House Primaries." Working paper.

Bawn, Kathleen, Martin Cohen, David Karol, Seth Masket, Hans Noel, and John Zaller. 2012. "A Theory of Political Parties: Groups, Policy Demands, and Nominations in American Politics." *Perspectives on Politics* 10(3): 571–97.

Beatty, Michael J. 1988. "Situational and Predispositional Correlates of Public Speaking Anxiety." *Communication Education* 37(1): 28–39.

Bellafante, Ginia. 2013. "A New Era for Progressives: De Blasio's Win Is Sign of Working Families Party's Advance." *New York Times*, November 15. http://www.nytimes.com/2013/11/17/nyregion/de-blasios-win-is-sign-of-working-families-partys-advance.html (accessed March 4, 2018).

Bellemare, Marc F., and Nicholas Carnes. 2015. "Why Do Members of Congress Support Agricultural Protection?" *Food Policy* 50: 20–34.

Bennett, Stephen Earl. 2006. "Comment on 'American Democracy in an Age of Inequality.'" *PS: Political Science & Politics* 39(1): 51–54.

Berkman, Michael B., and Robert E. O'Connor. 1993. "Do Women Legislators Matter? Female Legislators and State Abortion Policy." *American Politics Quarterly* 21(1): 102–24.

Berr, Jonathan. 2016. "Election 2016's Price Tag: $6.8 Billion." CBS News, November 8. http://www.cbsnews.com/news/election-2016s-price-tag-6-8-billion/ (accessed June 28, 2017).

Besley, Timothy. 2004. "Paying Politicians: Theory and Evidence." *Journal of the European Economic Association* 2(2–3): 85–114.

Besley, Timothy, and Stephen Coate. 1997. "An Economic Model of Representative Democracy." *Quarterly Journal of Economics* 112(1): 85–114.

Besley, Timothy, Jose G. Montalvo, and Marta Reynal-Querol. 2011. "Do Educated Leaders Matter?" *Economic Journal* 121(554): 205–27.

Besley, Timothy, and Marta Reynal-Querol. 2011. "Do Democracies Select More Educated Leaders?" *American Political Science Review* 105(3): 552–66.

Bianco, William T. 1984. "Strategic Decisions on Candidacy in US Congressional Districts." *Legislative Studies Quarterly* 9(2): 351–64.

Black, Gordon S. 1972. "A Theory of Political Ambition." *American Political Science Review* 66: 144–59.

Bonica, Adam. 2013. *Database on Ideology, Money in Politics, and Elections: Public Version 1.0* [computer file]. Stanford, CA: Stanford University Libraries. http://data.stanford.edu/dime (accessed June 22, 2016).

———. 2017. "Why Are There So Many Lawyers in Congress? Professional Networks, Early Fundraising, and Electoral Success." Working paper. https://papers.ssrn.com/sol3/papers.cfm?abstract_id=2898140 (accessed February 27, 2018).

Bowen, T. Renee, and Cecilia Hyunjung Mo. n.d. "The Voter's Blunt Tool." Working paper. https://www.gsb.stanford.edu/gsb-cmis/gsb-cmis-download-auth/311661 (accessed June 5, 2015).

Brady, Henry E., Kay Lehman Schlozman, and Sidney Verba. 1999. "Prospecting for Participants: Rational Expectations and the Recruitment of Political Activists." *American Political Science Review* 93(1): 153–68.

Brady, Henry E., Sidney Verba, and Kay Lehman Schlozman. 1995. "Beyond SES: A Resource Model of Political Participation." *American Political Science Review* 89(2): 271–94.

Brandolini, Andrea, and Timothy M. Smeeding. 2006. "Patterns of Economic Inequality in Western Democracies." *PS: Political Science & Politics* 39(1): 21–26.

Brands, H. W. 2000. *Traitor to His Class.* New York: Anchor.

Broockman, David. 2014. "Mobilizing Candidates: Political Actors Strategically Shape the Candidate Pool with Personal Appeals." *Journal of Experimental Political Science* 1(2): 104–19.

Broockman, David E., and Joshua L. Kalla. 2015. "Campaign Contributions Facilitate Access to Congressional Officials: A Randomized Field Experiment." *American Journal of Political Science* 60(3): 545–58.

Broockman, David, Nicholas Carnes, Melody Crowder-Meyer, and Christopher Skovron. 2012. *The 2012 National Candidate Study* [data file].

———. 2013. *The 2013 National Survey of Party Leaders* [data file].

———. 2014a. *The 2013 National Survey of Party Leaders: Mass Public Supplement* [data file].

———. 2014b. *The 2014 National Candidate Study* [data file].

———. 2014c. "Who's a Good Candidate? How Party Gatekeepers Evaluate Potential Nominees." Working paper.

Burden, Barry C. 2007. *The Personal Roots of Representation.* Princeton: Princeton University Press.

Burrell, Barbara. 1994. *A Woman's Place Is in the House: Campaigning for Congress in the Feminist Era*. Ann Arbor: University of Michigan Press.

——. 2006. "Political Parties and Women's Organizations: Bringing Women into the Electoral Arena." In *Gender and Elections: Shaping the Future of American Politics*, ed. Susan J. Carroll and Richard L. Fox. New York: Cambridge University Press.

Canon, David T. 1999. *Race, Redistricting and Representation: The Unintended Consequences of Black Majority Districts*. Chicago: University of Chicago Press.

Carnes, Nicholas [producer and distributor]. 2011. *Congressional Leadership and Social Status* [data set].

——. 2012. "Does the Numerical Underrepresentation of the Working Class in Congress Matter?" *Legislative Studies Quarterly* 37: 5–34.

——. 2013. *White-Collar Government: The Hidden Role of Class in Economic Policy Making*. Chicago: University of Chicago Press.

——. 2015. "Does the Descriptive Representation of the Working Class 'Crowd Out' Women and Minorities (and Vice Versa)? Evidence from the Local Elections in America Project." *Politics, Groups, and Identities* 3(2): 350–65.

——. 2016a. "Who Votes for Inequality?" In *Congress and Policy Making in the 21st Century*, ed. Jeffrey Jenkins and Eric Patashnik. New York: Cambridge University Press.

——. 2016b. "Why Are There So Few Working-Class People in Political Office? Evidence from State Legislatures." *Politics, Groups, and Identities* 4(1): 84–109.

——. 2018. "Candidate Training Programs in the United States." Working paper.

——. n.d. "Keeping Workers off the Ballot: Gatekeeper Biases and the Shortage of Candidates from the Working Class." Working paper.

Carnes, Nicholas, and Eric Hansen. 2016. "Does Paying Politicians More Promote Economic Diversity in Legislatures?" *American Political Science Review* 110(4): 699–716.

Carnes, Nicholas, and Noam Lupu. 2014. "The Rich Are Running Latin America—And Why That Matters." http://www.washingtonpost.com/blogs/monkey-cage/wp/2014/04/08/the-rich-are-running-latin-america-and-why-that-matters/ (accessed September 30, 2015).

——. 2015. "Rethinking the Comparative Perspective on Class and Representation: Evidence from Latin America." *American Journal of Political Science* 59(1): 1–18.

——. 2016a. "Do Voters Dislike Working-Class Candidates? Voter Biases and the Descriptive Underrepresentation of the Working Class." *American Political Science Review* 110(4): 832–44.

——. 2016b. "What Good Is a College Degree? Education and Leader Quality Reconsidered." *Journal of Politics* 78(1): 35–49.

——. 2017. "It's Time to Bust the Myth: Most Trump Voters Were Not Working Class." *Washington Post* Monkey Cage blog, June 5. https://www.washingtonpost.com/news/monkey-cage/wp/2017/06/05/its-time-to-bust-the-myth-most-trump-voters-were-not-working-class/?utm_term=.a1e2e91b8a89 (accessed November 9, 2017).

Carreri, Maria, and Edoardo Teso. 2016. "Economic Recessions and Congressional Preferences for Redistribution." Working paper. https://papers.ssrn.com/sol3/papers.cfm?abstract_id=2813588 (accessed June 8, 2017).

Carroll, Susan J. 1985. "Political Elites and Sex Differences in Political Ambition: A Reconsideration." *Journal of Politics* 47(4): 1231–43.

Carroll, Susan J., and Krista Jenkins. 2005. "Increasing Diversity or More of the Same? Term Limits and the Representation of Women, Minorities, and Minority Women in State Legislatures." *National Political Science Review* 10: 71–84.

Carroll, Susan J., and Kira Sanbonmatsu. 2013. *More Women Can Run*. New York: Oxford University Press.

Center for American Women and Politics. 2012. "History of Women in State Legislatures." http://www.cawp.rutgers.edu/sites/default/files/resources/stleghist.pdf (accessed August 7, 2015).

Choma, Russ. 2014. "Millionaires' Club: For First Time, Most Lawmakers Are Worth $1 Million-Plus." *OpenSecrets.Org.* http://www.opensecrets.org/news/2014/01/millionaires-club-for-first-time-most-lawmakers-are-worth-1-million-plus/ (accessed August 28, 2015).

Clawson, Dan, and Mary Ann Clawson. 1999. "What Has Happened to the US Labor Movement? Union Decline and Renewal." *Annual Review of Sociology* 25(1): 95–119.

Cohen, Abner. 1981. *The Politics of Elite Culture: Explorations in the Dramaturgy of Power in a Modern African Society*. Berkeley: University of California Press.

Cotter, Cornelius, James Gibson, John Bibby, and Robert Huckshorn. 1984. *Party Organizations in American Politics*. New York: Praeger.

Cozzarelli, Catherine, Anna V. Wilkinson, and Michael J. Tagler. 2001. "Attitudes toward the Poor and Attributions for Poverty." *Journal of Social Issues* 57(2): 207–27.

Cramer, Kathy. 2016. *The Politics of Resentment: Rural Consciousness in Wisconsin and the Rise of Scott Walker*. Chicago: University of Chicago Press.

Crowder-Meyer, Melody. 2010a. "Local Parties, Local Candidates, and Women's Representation: How County Parties Affect Who Runs for and Wins Political Office." PhD diss., Princeton University.

——. 2010b. "The Party's Still Going: County Party Strength, Activity, and Influence." In *The State of the Parties: The Changing Role of Contemporary American Parties*, ed. J. Green and D. Coffey. Lanham, MD: Rowman and Littlefield.

——. 2013. "Gendered Recruitment without Trying: How Local Party Recruiters Affect Women's Representation." *Politics & Gender* 9(4): 390–413.

Dal Bó, Ernesto, Frederico Finan, Olle Folke, Torsten Persson, and Johanna Rickne. 2017. "Who Becomes a Politician?" *Quarterly Journal of Economics* 132(4): 1877–1914.

Darcy, Robert, Susan Welch, and Janet Clark. 1994. *Women, Elections, and Representation*. 2nd ed. Lincoln: University of Nebraska Press.

De Benedetto, Marco Alberto, and Maria De Paola. 2014. "Candidates' Quality and Electoral Participation: Evidence from Italian Municipal Elections." Working paper.

Delli Carpini, Michael X., and Scott Keeter. 1996. *What Americans Know about Politics and Why It Matters*. New Haven: Yale University Press.

DeMora, Stephanie, Andrew Dowdle, Mark Myers, Spencer Hall, Angela Ocampo, Shawn Patterson, and John Zaller. 2017. "Who Owns Nominations for the House of Representatives? Evidence from Four Case Studies." Working paper.

Desilver, Drew. 2015. "Women Have Long History in Congress, but Until Recently There Haven't Been Many." *Pew Research Center FactTank*, January 14. http://www.pewresearch.org/fact-tank/2015/01/14/women-have-long-history-in-congress-but-until-recently-there-havent-been-many/ (accessed August 7, 2015).

Dewan, Shaila. 2014. "Who Needs a Boss?" *New York Times Magazine*, March 25. http://www.nytimes.com/2014/03/30/magazine/who-needs-a-boss.html?hp&pagewanted=all&_r=2 (accessed October 19, 2015).

Diermeier, Daniel, Michael Keane, and Antonio Merlo. 2005. "A Political Economy Model of Congressional Careers." *American Economic Review* 95(1): 347–73.

Domhoff, G. William. 1967. *Who Rules America?* Englewood Cliffs, NJ: Prentice-Hall.

Elder, Laurel. 2004. "Why Women Don't Run: Explaining Women's Underrepresentation in America's Political Institutions." *Women & Politics* 26(2): 27–56.

Enns, Peter K., Nathan J. Kelly, Jana Morgan, Thomas Volscho, and Christopher Witko. 2014. "Conditional Status Quo Bias and Top Income Shares: How U.S. Political Institutions Have Benefited the Rich." *Journal of Politics* 76(2): 289–303.

Etzioni, Amitai. 1984. *Capital Corruption: The New Attack on American Democracy*. New York: Harcourt, Brace, Jovanovich.

Eulau, Heinz, and John D. Sprague. 1964. *Lawyers in Politics: A Study in Professional Convergence*. Indianapolis: Bobbs-Merrill.

Faricy, Christopher. 2011. "The Politics of Social Policy in America: The Causes and Effects of Indirect versus Direct Social Spending." *Journal of Politics* 73(1): 74–83.

———. 2015. *Welfare for the Wealthy: Parties, Social Spending, and Inequality in the U.S.* New York: Cambridge University Press.

———. 2016. "The Distributive Politics of Tax Expenditures: How Parties Use Policy Tools to Distribute Revenue to the Rich and the Poor." *Politics, Groups, and Identities* 4(1): 110–25.

Faricy, Christopher, and Christopher Ellis. 2014. "Public Attitudes towards Direct Spending vs. Tax Expenditures in the United States." *Political Behavior* 36(1): 53–76.

Fiske, Susan T., Juan Xu, Amy C. Cuddy, and Peter Glick. 1999. "(Dis)respecting versus (Dis)liking." *Journal of Social Issues* 55(3): 473–89.

Fitzsimon, Chris. 2010. "Legislative Pay the Latest Distortion of the Right." NC Policy Watch. http://www.ncpolicywatch.com/2010/09/02/legislative-pay-the-latest-distortion-of-the-right/#sthash.fwV5WxYS.dpuf (accessed April 2, 2015).

Flavin, Patrick. 2012. "Does Higher Voter Turnout among the Poor Lead to More Equal Policy Representation?" *Social Science Journal* 49(4): 405–12.

———. 2014a. "Campaign Finance Laws, Policy Outcomes, and Political Equality in the American States." *Political Research Quarterly* 68(1): 77–88.

———. 2014b. "Lobbying Regulations and Political Equality in the American States." *American Politics Research* 43(2): 304–26.

———. 2014c. "State Campaign Finance Laws and the Equality of Political Representation." *Election Law Journal* 13(3): 362–74.

———. 2015. "Direct Democracy and Political Equality in the American States." *Social Science Quarterly* 96(1): 119–32.

Flood, Sarah, Miriam King, Steven Ruggles, and J. Robert Warren. 2015. *Integrated Public Use Microdata Series, Current Population Survey: Version 4.0.* [data set]. Minneapolis: University of Minnesota.

Fowler, Linda L., and Robert D. McClure. 1989. *Political Ambition.* New Haven: Yale University Press.

Fox, Richard L. 2001. "Congressional Elections: Women's Candidacies and the Road to Gender Parity." In *Gender and Elections: Shaping the Future of American Politics*, ed. Susan J. Carroll and Richard L. Fox, 187–209. New York: Cambridge University Press.

Fox, Richard L., and Jennifer Lawless. 2004. "Entering the Arena: Gender and the Decision to Run for Office." *American Journal of Political Science* 48(2): 264–80.

———. 2005. "To Run or Not to Run for Office: Explaining Nascent Political Ambition." *American Journal of Political Science* 49(3): 642–59.

———. 2011a. "Gaining and Losing Interest in Running for Public Office: The Concept of Dynamic Political Ambition." *Journal of Politics* 73(2): 443–62.

———. 2011b. "Gendered Perceptions and Political Candidacies: A Central Barrier to Women's Equality in Electoral Politics." *American Journal of Political Science* 55(1): 59–73.

———. 2014a. "Reconciling Family Roles with Political Ambition: The New Normal for Women in Twenty-First-Century U.S. Politics." *Journal of Politics* 76(2): 398–414.

———. 2014b. "Uncovering the Origins of the Gender Gap in Political Ambition." *American Political Science Review* 108(3): 499–519.

Francia, Peter L., and Paul S. Herrnson. 2003. "The Impact of Public Finance Laws on Fundraising in State Legislative Elections." *American Politics Research* 31(5): 520–39.

Franko, William W. 2015. "More Equal than We Thought? Using Vote Validation to Better Understand Participation Inequality in the States." *State Politics & Policy Quarterly* 15(1): 91–114.

Franko, William F., Caroline Tolbert, and Christopher Witko. 2013. "Inequality, Self-Interest, and Public Support for 'Robin Hood' Tax Policies." *Political Research Quarterly* 66(4): 922–36.

Fulton, Sarah A., Cherie D. Maestas, L. Sandy Maisel, and Walter J. Stone. 2006. "The Sense of a Woman: Gender, Ambition, and the Decision to Run for Congress." *Political Research Quarterly* 59(2): 235–48.

Gaddie, Ronald Keith. 2004. *Born to Run: Origins of the Political Career.* New York: Rowman and Littlefield.

Gaddie, Ronald Keith, and Charles S. Bullock III. 1995. "Congressional Elections and the Year of the Woman." *Social Science Quarterly* 76: 749–62.

Ganzach, Yoav. 2011. "A Dynamic Analysis of the Effects of Intelligence and Socioeconomic Background on Job-Market Success." *Intelligence* 39: 120–29.

Gelman, Andrew. 2013. "The Average American Knows How Many People?" *New York Times*, February 18. http://www.nytimes.com/2013/02/19/science/the-average-american-knows-how-many-people.html?mcubz=0 (accessed June 30, 2017).

Gelman, Andrew, and Gary King. 1990. "Estimating Incumbency Advantage without Bias." *American Journal of Political Science* 34(4): 1142–64.

Gelpi, Christopher, and Peter D. Feaver. 2002. "Speak Softly and Carry a Big Stick? Veterans in the Political Elite and the American Use of Force." *American Political Science Review* 96(4): 779–93.

Gibson, James, Cornelius Cotter, John Bibby, and Robert Huckshorn. 1983. "Assessing Party Organizational Strength." *American Journal of Political Science* 27(2): 193–222.

Giese, Rachel. 2015. "Ruth Ellen Brosseau: From 'Vegas Girl' to NDP Vice-chair." *Chatelaine*, July 27. http://www.chatelaine.com/living/politics/ruth-ellen-brosseau -from-vegas-girl-to-ndp-vice-chair/ (accessed October 10, 2016).

Gilens, Martin. 2005. "Inequality and Democratic Responsiveness." *Public Opinion Quarterly* 69(5): 778–896.

———. 2009. "Preference Gaps and Inequality in Representation." *PS: Political Science & Politics* 42(2): 335–41.

———. 2013. *Affluence and Influence: Economic Inequality and Political Power in America.* Princeton: Princeton University Press.

———. 2015. "Descriptive Representation, Money, and Political Inequality in the United States." *Swiss Political Science Review* 21(2): 222–28.

Gilens, Martin, and Benjamin I. Page. 2014. "Testing Theories of American Politics: Elites, Interest Groups, and Average Citizens." *Perspectives on Politics* 12(3): 564–81.

Gladwell, Malcolm. 2008. *Outliers: The Story of Success.* New York: Little, Brown, and Company.

Godard, John. 2009. "The Exceptional Decline of the American Labor Movement." *Industrial and Labor Relations Review* 63(1): 82–108.

Goings, Kenneth W. 1990. *The NAACP Comes of Age: The Defeat of Judge John J. Parker.* Bloomington: Indiana University Press.

Griffin, John D., and Claudia Anewalt-Remsburg. 2013. "Legislator Wealth and the Effort to Repeal the Estate Tax." *American Politics Research* 41(4): 599–622.

Griffin, John D., and Brian Newman. 2008. *Minority Report: Evaluating Political Equality in America.* Chicago: University of Chicago Press.

Griffin, John D., Brian Newman, and Patrick Burh. n.d. "Bias against High Income Candidates in the U.S." Working paper.

Grose, Christian. 2013. "Risk and Roll Calls: How Legislators' Personal Finances Shape Congressional Decisions." Working paper. https://papers.ssrn.com/sol3/papers .cfm?abstract_id=2220524 (accessed February 27, 2018).

Grumbach, Jacob M. 2015. "Does the American Dream Matter for Members of Congress? Social-Class Backgrounds and Roll-Call Votes." *Political Research Quarterly* 68(2): 306–23.

Hacker, Jacob S. 2006. "Inequality, American Democracy, and American Political Science: The Need for Cumulative Research." *PS: Political Science & Politics* 39(1): 47–49.

Hacker, Jacob S., and Paul Pierson. 2010. *Winner-Take-All Politics: How Washington Made the Rich Richer—and Turned Its Back on the Middle Class.* New York: Simon and Schuster.

Hainmueller, Jens, Dan Hopkins, and Teppei Yamamoto. 2014. "Causal Inference in Conjoint Analysis: Understanding Multi-Dimensional Choices via Stated Preference Experiments." *Political Analysis* 22(1): 1–30.

Hall, Richard L. 1996. *Participation in Congress.* New Haven: Yale University Press.

Hall, Richard L., and Alan V. Deardorff. 2006. "Lobbying as Legislative Subsidy." *American Political Science Review* 100(1): 69–84.

Hall, Richard L., and Frank W. Wayman. 1990. "Buying Time: Moneyed Interests and the Mobilization of Bias in Congressional Committees." *American Political Science Review* 84(3): 797–820.

Hamilton, Alexander. 1788. "Federalist 35." In *The Federalist.* http://thomas.loc.gov/home/histdox/fedpapers.html (accessed March 16, 2016).

Hamm, Keith, and Robert W. Hogan. 2009. "Perspectives of State Legislative Candidates on Connecticut's Implementation of Clean Elections." Working paper. https://papers.ssrn.com/sol3/papers.cfm?abstract_id=1450959 (accessed February 27, 2018).

Hauck, Robert J-P. 2006. "Editor's Note—Let Them Eat Beignets: Inequality and American Democracy." *PS: Political Science & Politics* 39(1): 19–20.

Hayes, Thomas J. 2013. "Responsiveness in an Era of Inequality: The Case of the U.S. Senate." *Political Research Quarterly* 66(3): 585–99.

Henry, William A. III. 1995. *In Defense of Elitism.* New York: Doubleday.

Hertel-Fernandez, Alexander. 2014. "Who Passes Business's 'Model Bills'? Policy Capacity and Corporate Influence in U.S. State Politics." *Perspectives on Politics* 12(3): 582–602.

———. 2016. "Explaining Durable Business Coalitions in the States: Conservatives and Corporate Interests across America's Statehouses." *Studies in American Political Development* 30(1): 1–18.

Hill, Kim Quaile, and Susan Leighley. 1992. "The Policy Consequences of Class Bias in State Electorates." *American Journal of Political Science* 36(2): 351–65.

Hirsch, Barry T., and David A. Macpherson. 2003. "Union Membership and Coverage Database: Note." *Industrial and Labor Relations Review* 56(2): 349–54.

Hoffman, Mitchell, and Elizabeth Lyons. 2014. "Do Higher Salaries Lead to Higher Performance? Evidence from State Politicians." Working paper. http://www-2.rotman.utoronto.ca/facbios/file/PoliticianSalaries.pdf (accessed December 10, 2014).

Hogan, Robert E. 2008. "Policy Responsiveness and Incumbent Reelection in State Legislatures." *American Journal of Political Science* 52(4): 858–73.

Hohmann, James. 2013. "Rick Santorum: Why Mitt Romney Didn't Win." *Politico,* June 13. http://www.politico.com/story/2013/06/rick-santorum-mitt-romney-92783.html (accessed June 18, 2013).

Hout, Michael. 2008. "How Class Works: Objective and Subjective Aspects of Class since the 1970s." In *Social Class: How Does It Work?* ed. Annette Lareau and Dalton Conley. New York: Russell Sage Foundation.

Hout, Michael, Jeff Manza, and Clem Brooks. 1995. "The Democratic Class Struggle in the United States, 1948–1992." *American Sociological Review* 60(6): 805–28.

Hoxby, Caroline M., and Christopher Avery. 2012. "The Missing 'One-offs': The Hidden Supply of High-Achieving, Low Income Students." NBER Working Paper 18586. http://www.nber.org/papers/w18586 (accessed October 26, 2016).

Insurance Information Institute. 1979. *Occupational Profile of State Legislatures.* New York: Insurance Information Institute.

International City/County Management Association. 2001. *Municipal Form of Government Survey* [computer file]. Washington, DC: International City/County Management Association [producer and distributor].

Inter-university Consortium for Political and Social Research (ICPSR) and Carroll McKibbin. 1997. *Roster of United States Congressional Officeholders and Biographical Characteristics of Members of the United States Congress, 1789–1996: Merged Data* [computer file] (Study #7803). Ann Arbor, MI: Inter-university Consortium for Political and Social Research [producer and distributor].

Jackson, Brooks. 1988. *Honest Graft*. New York: Knopf.

Jacobs, Lawrence R., and James N. Druckman. 2011. "Segmented Representation: The Reagan White House and Disproportionate Responsiveness." In *Who Gets Represented?* ed. Peter Enns and Christopher Wlezien. New York: Russell Sage Foundation.

Jacobs, Lawrence R., and Robert Y. Shapiro. 2000. *Politicians Don't Pander: Political Manipulation and the Loss of Democratic Responsiveness*. Chicago: University of Chicago Press.

Jacobs, Lawrence R., and Theda Skocpol. 2006. "Restoring the Tradition of Rigor and Relevance to Political Science." *PS: Political Science & Politics* 39(1): 27–31.

Jacobson, Gary. 2012. *The Politics of Congressional Elections*. 8th ed. New York: Pearson.

Johnson, Gbemende, Bruce I. Oppenheimer, and Jennifer L. Selin. 2012. "The House as a Stepping Stone to the Senate: Why Do So Few African American House Members Run?" *American Journal of Political Science* 56(4): 387–99.

Jones, Benjamin F., and Benjamin A. Olken. 2005. "Do Leaders Matter? National Leadership and Growth since World War II." *Quarterly Journal of Economics* 120(3): 835–64.

Joseph, Cameron. 2014. "GOP Bets on Execs to Help Retake Senate." *The Hill*, February 26. http://thehill.com/blogs/ballot-box/house-races/199267-businessmen-a-boon-or-bust-for-senate-gop (accessed February 11, 2016).

Jusko, Karen. 2014. "Electoral Geography and Redistributive Politics." *Journal of Theoretical Politics* 27(2): 269–87.

———. 2017. *Who Speaks for the Poor? Electoral Geography and the Political Representation of Low-Income and Working Class Voters*. New York: Cambridge University Press.

Kang, Insung, Richard G. Niemi, and Lynda W. Powell. 2003. "Strategic Candidate Decisionmaking and Competition in Gubernatorial Nonincumbent-Party Primaries." *State Politics & Policy Quarterly* 3(4): 353–66.

Kanthak, Kristin, and Jonathan Woon. 2015. "Women Don't Run? Election Aversion and Candidate Entry." *American Journal of Political Science* 59(3): 595–612.

Karpowitz, Christopher F., and Tali Mendelberg. 2014. *The Silent Sex: Gender, Deliberation, and Institutions*. Princeton: Princeton University Press.

Kauffman, Johnny. 2017. "Low Pay in State Legislatures Means Some Can't Afford the Job." *NPR Morning Edition*, January 9. http://www.npr.org/2017/01/09/508237086/low-pay-in-state-legislatures-means-some-cant-afford-the-job (accessed January 9, 2017).

Kelly, Nathan J. 2009. *The Politics of Income Inequality in the United States*. New York: Cambridge University Press.

Kelly, Nathan J., and Peter K. Enns. 2010. "Inequality and the Dynamics of Public Opinion: The Self-Reinforcing Link between Economic Inequality and Mass Preferences." *American Journal of Political Science* 54(4): 855–70.

Kelly, Nathan J., and Christopher Witko. 2012. "Federalism and American Inequality." *Journal of Politics* 74(2): 414–26.

———. 2014. "Government Ideology and Unemployment in the U.S. States." *State Politics & Policy Quarterly* 14(4): 389–413.

Kingdon, John W. 1981. *Congressmen's Voting Decisions.* 2nd ed. New York: Harper and Row.

Kirkland, Patricia A. n.d. "The Business of Being Mayor: Mayors and Fiscal Policy in U.S. Cities." Working paper. https://patriciaakirkland.files.wordpress.com/2016/05/business_mayors_0517.pdf (accessed June 16, 2017).

Kotakorpi, Kaisa, and Panu Poutvaara. 2011. "Pay for Politicians and Candidate Selection: An Empirical Analysis." *Journal of Public Economics* 95(8): 877–85.

Krasno, Jonathan S., and Donald Philip Green. 1988. "Preempting Quality Challengers in House Elections." *Journal of Politics* 50(4): 920–36.

Kraus, Michael W., and Bennett Callaghan. 2014. "Noblesse Oblige? Social Status and Economic Inequality Maintenance among Politicians." *PLoS One* 9(1): 1–6.

Lawless, Jennifer L. 2011. "The State of the Field: Studying Women, Gender, and Politics." *Politics & Gender* 7(1): 91–93.

———. 2012. *Becoming a Candidate.* New York: Cambridge University Press.

Lawless, Jennifer L., and Richard L. Fox. 2005. *It Takes a Candidate: Why Women Don't Run for Office.* New York: Cambridge University Press.

———. 2010a. "If Only They'd Ask: Gender, Recruitment and Political Ambition." *Journal of Politics* 72(2): 310–26.

———. 2010b. *It Still Takes a Candidate: Why Women Don't Run for Office.* New York: Cambridge University Press.

Lazarus, Jeffrey. 2008. "Buying In: Testing the Rational Model of Candidate Entry." *Journal of Politics* 50(3): 837–50.

Lehman, E. Philip. 2016. "Congressional Staffers' $225 Shoes Reveal a Major Problem on Capitol Hill." *Washington Post*, January 7. https://www.washingtonpost.com/opinions/congressional-staffers-225-shoes-reveal-a-major-problem-on-capitol-hill/2016/01/07/6705d0aa-adb0-11e5-b711-1998289ffcea_story.html?utm_term=.1e4c2602fd83 (accessed January 9, 2017).

Levine, Adam Seth. 2015. *American Insecurity: Why Our Economic Fears Lead to Political Inaction.* Princeton: Princeton University Press.

Lewis, John D., ed. 1961. *Anti-Federalists versus Federalists: Selected Documents.* Scranton, PA: Chandler Publishing Company.

Llavador, Humberto. 2017. "Suffrage Rights." In *Oxford Research Encyclopedia of Politics.* doi.org/10.1093/acrefore/9780190228637.013.5 (accessed November 27, 2017).

Macedo, Stephen, and Christopher F. Karpowitz. 2006. "The Local Roots of American Inequality." *PS: Political Science & Politics* 39(1): 59–64.

Maddox, H. W. Jerome. 2004. "Opportunity Costs and Outside Careers in U.S. State Legislatures." *Legislative Studies Quarterly* 29(4): 517–44.

Maestas, Cherie D., Sarah Fulton, L. Sandy Maisel, and Walter J. Stone. 2006. "When to Risk It? Institutions, Ambitions, and the Decision to Run for the U.S. House." *American Political Science Review* 100(2): 195–208.

Maine Citizens for Clean Elections. 2016. "Understanding Maine Clean Elections." https://www.mainecleanelections.org/sites/default/files/fact_sheets/ 160804_Clean ElectionsBasicFactSheet.pdf (accessed January 31, 2017).

Malhotra, Neil. 2008. "The Impact of Public Financing on Electoral Competition: Evidence from Arizona and Maine." *State Politics & Policy Quarterly* 8(3): 263–81.

Manin, Bernard. 1997. *The Principles of Representative Government.* New York: Cambridge University Press.

Mansbridge, Jane. 2015. "Should Workers Represent Workers?" *Swiss Political Science Review* 21(2): 261–70.

Marschall, Melissa, and Paru Shah [producers and distributors]. 2013. *The Local Elections in American Project* [database].

Masket, Seth. 2011. "The Circus That Wasn't: The Republican Party's Quest for Order in California's 2003 Gubernatorial Recall Election." *State Politics & Policy Quarterly* 11(2): 123–47.

Masket, Seth, and Eric McGhee. 2013. "Party Power and the Causal Effect of Endorsements." Paper presented at the American Political Science Association 2013 Annual Meeting.

Matthews, Donald R. [1960] 1974. *U.S. Senators and Their World.* New York: W. W. Norton.

———. 1954a. *The Social Background of Political Decision Makers.* New York: Random House.

———. 1954b. "United States Senators and the Class Structure." *Public Opinion Quarterly* 18: 5–22.

———. 1985. "Legislative Recruitment and Legislative Careers." In *Handbook of Legislative Research*, ed. Gerhard Loewenberg, Samuel C. Patterson, and Malcolm E. Jewell. Cambridge, MA: Harvard University Press.

Mattozzi, Andrea, and Antonio Merlo. 2008. "Political Careers or Career Politicians?" *Journal of Public Economics* 92(3): 597–608.

Mayer, Kenneth R. 2013. "Public Election Funding: An Assessment of What We Would Like to Know." *The Forum* 11(3): 365–84.

Mayer, Kenneth R., and John M. Wood. 1995. "The Impact of Public Financing on Electoral Competitiveness: Evidence from Wisconsin, 1964–1990." *Legislative Studies Quarterly* 20(1): 69–88.

Mayer, Kenneth R., Timothy Werner, and Amanda Williams. 2006. "Do Funding Programs Enhance Electoral Competition?" In *The Marketplace of Democracy: Electoral Competition and American Politics*, ed. Michael P. McDonald and John Samples, 245–67. Washington, DC: Brookings Institution.

Mayhew, David R. 1974. *Congress: The Electoral Connection.* New Haven: Yale University Press.

McCall, Leslie. 2013. *The Undeserving Rich: American Beliefs about Inequality, Opportunity, and Redistribution.* New York: Cambridge University Press.

———. 2014. "The Political Meanings of Social Class Inequality." *Social Currents* 1(1): 25–34.

McCall, Leslie, and Lane Kenworthy. 2009. "Americans' Social Policy Preferences in the Era of Rising Inequality." *Perspectives on Politics* 7(3): 459–84.

McCall, Leslie, and Jeff Manza. 2010. "Class Differences in Social and Political Attitudes." In *The Oxford Handbook of American Public Opinion and the Media*, ed. R. Shapiro and Larry Jacobs, 552–70. New York: Oxford University Press.

McElwee, Sean. 2015. "Unions Still Matter." *Al Jazeera America*, April 15. http://america.aljazeera.com/opinions/2015/4/why-unions-matter.html (accessed December 14, 2016).

Mead-Lucero, Jerry. 2008. "Chicago Sitdown Strike Produces Win for Workers, Not Banks." *Broadcast Union News*, December 30. http://broadcastunionnews.blogspot.com/2008/12/chicago-sitdown-strike-produces-win-for.html (accessed October 19, 2015).

Mettler, Suzanne. 2010. "Reconstituting the Submerged State: The Challenges of Social Policy Reform in the Obama Era." *Perspectives on Politics* 8(3): 803–24.

——. 2011. *The Submerged State: How Invisible Government Policies Undermine American Democracy*. Chicago: University of Chicago Press.

Miller, Mark C. 1995. *The High Priests of American Politics*. Knoxville: University of Tennessee Press.

Miller, Michael G. 2008. "Gaming Arizona: Public Money and Shifting Candidate Strategies." *PS: Political Science & Politics* 41(3): 527–32.

——. 2011a. "After the GAO Report: What Do We Know about Public Election Funding?" *Election Law Journal* 10(3): 273–90.

——. 2011b. "Public Money, Candidate Time, and Electoral Outcomes in State Legislative Elections." In *Public Financing in American Elections*, ed. Costas Panagopoulos, 205–24. Philadelphia: Temple University Press.

——. 2014. *Subsidizing Democracy*. Ithaca, NY: Cornell University Press.

Miller, Michael G., and Costas Panagopoulos. 2011. "Public Financing, Attitudes toward Government and Politics, and Efficacy." In *Public Financing in American Elections*, ed. Costas Panagopoulos. Philadelphia: Temple University Press.

Mills, C. Wright. 1956. *The Power Elite*. New York: Oxford University Press.

Moore, Gregory. 2005. "Religion, Race, and Gender Differences in Political Ambition." *Politics and Gender* 1(4): 577–96.

National Conference of State Legislatures. 2015. "Legislators' Occupations in All States." http://www.ncsl.org/research/about-state-legislatures/legislator-occupations-national-data.aspx (accessed August 6, 2015).

National Institute of Latino Elected and Appointed Officials. 2008. "How Much Help? Public Financing and Latino Candidates." Washington, DC: NALEO Educational Fund.

Nettle, Daniel. 2003. "Intelligence and Class Mobility in the British Population." *British Journal of Psychology* 94(4): 551–61.

Neuman, William. 2017. "Working Families Party Starts Small, but Thinks Big." *New York Times*, December 25. https://www.nytimes.com/2017/12/25/nyregion/working-families-party-new-york.html?rref=collection%2Fbyline%2Fwilliam-neuman&action=click&contentCollection=undefined&region=stream&module

=stream_unit&version=latest&contentPlacement=1&pgtype=collection&_r=1 (accessed March 4, 2018).

Niven, David. 1998. "Party Elites and Women Candidates: The Shape of Bias." *Women and Politics* 19(2): 57–80.

Norris, Pippa, and Joni Lovenduski. 1995. *Political Recruitment.* New York: Cambridge University Press.

O'Grady, Tom. n.d. "Careerists versus Coal-Miners: Welfare Reforms and the Substantive Representation of Social Groups in the British Labour Party." Working paper. https://www.dropbox.com/s/8bldral713elt5j/new.pdf?dl=0 (accessed November 20, 2017).

Ocampo, Angela X. 2018. "The Wielding Influence of Political Networks: Representation in Majority-Latino Districts." *Political Research Quarterly* 71(1): 184–98.

Osborne, Anne. 2012. "Clean Elections: How Has Public Election Funding in Maine and Arizona Influenced the Behavior of Non-candidate Political Actors?" Undergraduate honors thesis, Duke University. https://dukespace.lib.duke.edu/dspace /bitstream/handle/10161/6451/Clean%20Elections-%20How%20has%20public %20election%20funding%20in%20Maine%20and%20Arizona%20influenced%20 the%20behavior%20of%20non-candidate%20political%20actors_.pdf?sequence=1 (accessed February 2, 2017).

Osborne, Martin J., and Al Slivinski. 1996. "A Model of Political Competition with Citizen-Candidates." *Quarterly Journal of Economics* 111(5): 65–96.

Page, Benjamin I., Larry M. Bartels, and Jason Seawright. 2013. "Democracy and the Policy Preferences of Wealthy Americans." *Perspectives on Politics* 11(1): 51–73.

Page, Benjamin, and Lawrence Jacobs. 2009. *Class War? What Americans Really Think about Economic Inequality.* Chicago: University of Chicago Press.

Palmer, Barbara, and Dennis Simon. 2003. "Political Ambition and Women in the U.S. House of Representatives, 1916–2000." *Political Research Quarterly* 56(2): 127–38.

———. 2010. *Women and Congressional Elections: A Century of Change.* Boulder, CO: Lynne Rienner Publishers.

Pérez-Peña, Richard. 2014. "Generation Later, Poor Are Still Rare at Elite Colleges." *New York Times,* August 25. http://www.nytimes.com/2014/08/26/education/despite -promises-little-progress-in-drawing-poor-to-elite-colleges.html?_r=0 (accessed October 27, 2016).

Pessen, Edward. 1984. *The Log Cabin Myth: The Social Backgrounds of the Presidents.* New Haven: Yale University Press.

Philpot, Tasha S., and Hanes Walton Jr. 2007. "One of Our Own: Black Female Candidates and the Voters Who Support Them." *American Journal of Political Science* 51(1): 49–62.

Piff, Paul K. 2013. "Wealth and the Inflated Self: Class, Entitlement, and Narcissism." *Personality and Social Psychology Bulletin* 40(1): 34–43.

Piff, Paul K., Daniel M. Stancato, Stéphane Côté, Rodolfo Mendoza-Denton, and Dacher Keltner. 2012. "Higher Social Class Predicts Increased Unethical Behavior." *Proceedings of the National Academy of Sciences* 109(11): 4086–91.

Pimlott, Jamie Pamelia. 2010. *Women and the Democratic Party: The Evolution of EMILY's List.* Amherst, NY: Cambria Press.

Pitkin, Hannah Fenichel. 1967. *The Concept of Representation*. Berkeley: University of California Press.

Piven, Frances Fox. 2006. "Response to 'American Democracy in an Age of Inequality.'" *PS: Political Science & Politics* 39(1): 43–46.

Powell, Eleanor Neff. Forthcoming. *Where Money Matters in Congress*. New York: Cambridge University Press.

Powell, Eleanor Neff, and Justin Grimmer. 2016. "Money in Exile: Campaign Contributions and Committee Access." *Journal of Politics* 78(4): 974–88.

Reston, Maeve. 2012. "Protesters Raise Cloud of Sand as Romney Raises $3 Million in N.Y." *Los Angeles Times*, June 8. http://www.latimes.com/news/nationworld/nation /la-na-romney-protests-20120709,0,5308609.story (accessed September 30, 2015).

Rigby, Elizabeth, and Gerald C. Wright. 2013. "Political Parties and Representation of the Poor in the American States." *American Journal of Political Science* 57(3): 552–65.

Rivera, Lauren A. 2012. "Hiring as Cultural Matching: The Case of Elite Professional Service Firms." *American Sociological Review* 77(6): 999–1022.

Roberson, Alex. 2018. "Welcome to the Family: Adoption in 2018." Working paper.

Robertson, Campbell. 2015. "Chosen by Mississippi Democrats, Shy Trucker Is at a Crossroad." *New York Times*, September 7. http://www.nytimes.com/2015/09/08 /us/shy-trucker-emerges-as-democrats-pick-for-mississippi-governor.html (accessed September 10, 2015).

Robinson, Nick. 2015. "The Declining Dominance of Lawyers in U.S. Federal Politics." HLS Center on the Legal Profession Research Paper No. 2015-10. http://papers .ssrn.com/sol3/papers.cfm?abstract_id=2684731 (accessed April 28, 2016).

Rogers, Steve M. 2015. "Strategic Challenger Entry in a Federal System: The Role of Economic and Political Conditions in State Legislative Competition." *Legislative Studies Quarterly* 40(4): 539–70.

——. n.d. "Term Limits: Keeping Incumbents in Office." Working paper. http://www .stevenmrogers.com/Conferences/StatePolitics/Rogers-SPPC-TermLimits.pdf (accessed February 29, 2016).

Rohde, David W. 1991. *Parties and Leaders in the Postreform House*. Chicago: University of Chicago Press.

Sadin, Meredith. 2012. "Campaigning with Class: The Effect of Candidate Social Class on Voter Evaluations." Unpublished manuscript.

Sanbonmatsu, Kira. 2002. *Democrats, Republicans, and the Politics of Women's Place*. Ann Arbor: University of Michigan Press.

——. 2003. "Gender-Related Political Knowledge and the Descriptive Representation of Women." *Political Behavior* 25(4): 367–88.

——. 2006a. "Do Parties Know That 'Women Win'? Party Leader Beliefs about Women's Electoral Chances." *Politics & Gender* 2 (December): 431–50.

——. 2006b. "State Elections: Where Do Women Run? Where Do Women Win?" In *Gender and Elections: Shaping the Future of American Politics*, ed. Susan J. Carroll and Richard L. Fox, 189–214. New York: Cambridge University Press.

——. 2006c. *Where Women Run: Gender and Party in the American States*. Ann Arbor: University of Michigan Press.

Sances, Michael. 2016. "The Distributional Impact of Greater Responsiveness: Evidence from New York Towns." *Journal of Politics* 78(1): 105–19.

Schattschneider, E. E. [1960] 1975. *The Semisovereign People: A Realist's View of Democracy in America*. New York: Wadsworth Publishing.

Schlesinger, Joseph A. 1966. *Ambition and Politics: Political Careers in the United States*. Chicago: Rand McNally.

Schlozman, Kay Lehman. 2006. "On Inequality and Political Voice: Response to Stephen Earl Bennett's Critique." *PS: Political Science & Politics* 39(1): 55–57.

Schlozman, Kay Lehman, Nancy Burns, and Sidney Verba. 1994. "Gender and the Pathways to Participation: The Role of Resources." *Journal of Politics* 56(4): 963–90.

Schlozman, Kay Lehman, Benjamin I. Page, Sidney Verba, and Morris P. Fiorina. 2005. "Inequalities of Political Voice." In *Inequality and American Democracy*, ed. Lawrence R. Jacobs and Theda Skocpol. New York: Russell Sage Foundation.

Schrad, Mark Lawrence. 2010. *The Political Power of Bad Ideas*. New York: Oxford University Press.

Schumaker, Paul D., and Russell W. Getter. 1977. "Responsiveness Bias in 51 American Communities." *American Journal of Political Science* 21(2): 247–81.

Schwarz, Henry. 2014. "What Jobs You Should Have If You Want to Be Elected Governor." *Washington Post GovBeat*, September 12. http://www.washingtonpost.com /blogs/govbeat/wp/2014/09/12/what-jobs-you-should-have-if-you-want-to-be -elected-governor/ (accessed August 6, 2015).

Sclar, Jason, Alexander Hertel-Fernandez, Theda Skocpol, and Vanessa Williamson. n.d. "Donor Consortia on the Left and Right." Working paper. http://terrain.gov .harvard.edu/files/terrain/files/donor_consortia_on_the_left_and_right_com paring_the_membership_activities_and_impact_of_the_democracy_alliance_and _the_koch_seminars.pdf?m=1463891744 (accessed October 14, 2016).

Shah, Paru. 2014. "It Takes a Black Candidate: A Supply-Side Theory of Minority Representation." *Political Research Quarterly* 67(2): 266–79.

Sinyai, Clayton. 2006. *Schools of Democracy: A Political History of the American Labor Movement*. Ithaca, NY: ILR Press.

Skocpol, Theda, and Alexander Hertel-Fernandez. 2016. "The Koch Network and Republican Party Extremism." *Perspectives on Politics* 14(3): 681–99.

Smith, Adam. [1776] 2007. *Wealth of Nations*. New York: Cosimo Classics.

Smith, Tom W., Peter V. Marsden, and Michael Hout. 2015. *General Social Surveys, 1972–2014* [machine-readable data file]. Chicago: National Opinion Research Center [distributor].

Sojourner, Aaron. 2013. "Do Unions Promote Electoral Office-Holding? Evidence from Correlates of State Legislatures' Occupational Shares." *Industrial and Labor Relations Review* 66(2): 467–86.

Stone, Walter J., L. Sandy Maisel, and Cherie D. Maestas. 2004. "Quality Counts." *American Journal of Political Science* 48(3): 479–95.

Suhay, Elizabeth, Marko Klasnja, and Gonzalo Rivero. 2017. "American Aristocracy: How the Wealthy Explain Inequality, and Why It Matters." Working paper.

Swers, Michele. 2002. *The Difference Women Make*. Chicago: University of Chicago Press.

Taber, Jane. 2016. "From 'Vegas Girl' to MP, Ruth Ellen Brosseau Had to Prove Her Legitimacy." *Globe and Mail*, February 18. http://www.theglobeandmail.com/news/politics/from-vegas-girl-to-mp-ruth-ellen-brosseau-had-to-prove-her-legitimacy/article28807480/ (accessed July 22, 2016).

Task Force on Inequality and American Democracy. 2004. "American Democracy in an Age of Rising Inequality." *Perspectives on Politics* 2(4): 651–66.

Thal, Adam. 2017. "Class Isolation and Affluent Americans' Perceptions of Social Conditions." *Political Behavior* 39(2): 401–24.

Thomas, Sue. 1991. "The Impact of Women on State Legislative Policies." *Journal of Politics* 53(4): 958–76.

Thomas, Sue, and Susan Welch. 1991. "The Impact of Gender on Activities and Priorities of State Legislators." *Western Political Quarterly* 44(2): 445–56.

Thompson, Derek, and 24/7 Wall St. 2010. "The Net Worth of the U.S. Presidents: From Washington to Obama." *Atlantic*. http://www.theatlantic.com/business/archive/2010/05/the-net-worth-of-the-us-presidents-from-washington-to-obama/57020/ (accessed August 18, 2015).

Thomsen, Danielle M. 2014. "Ideological Moderates Won't Run: How Party Fit Matters for Partisan Polarization in Congress." *Journal of Politics* 76(3): 786–97.

———. 2015. "Why So Few (Republican) Women? Explaining the Partisan Imbalance of Women in the U.S. Congress." *Legislative Studies Quarterly* 40(2): 295–323.

———. 2017. *Opting Out of Congress: Partisan Polarization and the Decline of Moderate Candidates.* New York: Cambridge University Press.

Trounstine, Jessica, and Melody E. Valdini. 2008. "The Context Matters: The Effects of Single-Member versus At-Large Districts on City Council Diversity." *American Journal of Political Science* 52(3): 554–69.

Truthout. 2011. "The 99 Percent Takes Office: Lessons from a Rhode Island Special Election." http://www.truth-out.org/news/item/5323:the-99-percent-takes-office-lessons-from-a-rhode-island-special-election (accessed March 22, 2017).

United States Government Accountability Office. 2010. "Campaign Finance Reform: Experiences of Two States That Offered Full Public Funding for Political Candidates." GAO-10-390.

Ura, Joseph Daniel, and Christopher R. Ellis. 2008. "Income, Preferences, and the Dynamics of Policy Responsiveness." *PS: Political Science & Politics* 41(4): 785–94.

US Census Bureau. 2013. "Median Earnings by Occupation." http://www.census.gov/people/io/files/Median%20earnings%20by%20occupation%20031015.xlsx (accessed August 6, 2015).

Vedantam, Shankar. 2013. "Elite Colleges Struggle to Recruit Smart, Low-Income Kids." *NPR Morning Edition*, January 9. http://www.npr.org/2013/01/09/168889785/elite-colleges-struggle-to-recruit-smart-low-income-kids (accessed October 27, 2016).

Verba, Sidney. 1987. *Participation in America: Political Democracy and Social Equality.* Chicago: University of Chicago Press.

Verba, Sidney, Nancy Burns, and Kay Lehman Schlozman. 2003. "Unequal at the Starting Line: Creating Participatory Inequalities across Generations and among Groups." *American Sociologist* 34(1): 45–69.

Verba, Sidney, Kay Lehman Schlozman, and Henry E. Brady. 1995. *Voice and Equality: Civic Voluntarism in American Politics.* Cambridge, MA: Harvard University Press.

Verba, Sidney, Kay Lehman Schlozman, Henry E. Brady, and Norman Nie. 1990. *American Citizen Participation Study.* ICPSR06635-v1. Ann Arbor, MI: Inter-university Consortium for Political and Social Research [distributor].

———. 1993. "Race, Ethnicity, and Political Resources: Participation in the United States." *British Journal of Political Science* 93(4): 453–97.

Walsh, Katherine Cramer. 2012. "Putting Inequality in Its Place: Rural Consciousness and the Power of Perspective." *American Political Science Review* 106(3): 517–32.

Weeden, Kim A., and David B. Grusky. 2005. "The Case for a New Class Map." *American Journal of Sociology* 111(1): 141–212.

Weissberg, Robert. 2006. "Politicized Pseudo Science." *PS: Political Science & Politics* 39(1): 21–26.

Whitby, Kenny J. 1997. *The Color of Representation: Congressional Behavior and Black Interests.* Ann Arbor: University of Michigan Press.

Wilson, Sondra Kathryn, ed. 1999. *In Search of Democracy.* New York: Oxford University Press.

Windett, Jason Harold. 2011. "State Effects and the Emergence and Success of Female Gubernatorial Candidates." *State Politics & Policy Quarterly* 11(4): 460–82.

Winters, Jeffrey A. 2011. *Oligarchy.* New York: Cambridge University Press.

Witko, Christopher. 2012. "The Impact of Campaign Contributions on Congressional Behavior." In *Oxford Bibliographies in Political Science*, ed. Rick Valelly. New York: Oxford University Press.

———. 2013a. "Party Government and Variation in Corporate Influence on Agency Decisionmaking: OSHA Regulation, 1981–2006." *Social Science Quarterly* 94(4): 894–911.

———. 2013b. "When Does Money Buy Votes? Campaign Contributions and Policymaking." In *New Directions in Interest Group Politics*, ed. Matt Grossmann. New York: Routledge.

Witko, Christopher, and Sally Friedman. 2008. "Business Backgrounds and Congressional Behavior." *Congress & the Presidency* 35(1): 71–86.

Wright, Erik Olin. 1997. "Rethinking, Once Again, the Concept of Class Structure." In *Reworking Class*, ed. John Hall. Ithaca, NY: Cornell University Press.

Wyatt, Benjamin J. 2002. "The Origins of State Public Financing of Elections." Honors thesis, Wesleyan University. http://www.octobernight.com/bwyatt/index.htm (accessed December 22, 2016).

Yong, Ed. 2017. "Professor Smith Goes to Washington." *Atlantic*, January 25. https://www.theatlantic.com/science/archive/2017/01/thanks-to-trump-scientists-are-planning-to-run-for-office/514229/ (accessed February 21, 2017).

Zernike, Kate, and Megan Thee-Brenan. 2010. "Poll Finds Tea Party Backers Wealthier and More Educated." http://www.nytimes.com/2010/04/15/us/politics/15poll.html?_r=0 (accessed October 1, 2015).

Index

advertising, 77

AFL-CIO, 9, 139, 192, 193, 195

African Americans, 27–28. *See also* racial minorities

ambition. *See* political ambition

American Citizen Participation Study, 86, 292n26

"American Democracy in an Age of Rising Inequality," 211–12, 226

American National Election Studies (NES), 12, 97, 113–14

American Political Science Association (APSA), 211, 214

Annenberg National Election Study, 12

Anti-Federalists, 30

antistructural theory, 124–25, 126, 136, 140

Arizona, 183, 184, 195–96

assertiveness, 43, 44, 47, 83, 111

Bartels, Larry, 215

Beard, Edward P., 126–27, 128–29, 136, 138, 157

Benkirane, Abdelilah, 3

Bloc Québécois, 120

Blue-Collar Caucus, 128

Boehner, John, 8

Bonica, Adam, 136

Boston College, 159

Bowdoin College, 159

Brady, Henry, 79

Broockman, David, 18, 41, 65, 103, 137, 144, 193, 282

Brosseau, Ruth Ellen, 120–21, 129, 154–55, 157

business regulation, 8; state legislative candidates' views of, 10–11

campaign advertising, 77

campaigning ability, 31, 40, 62, 86, 107, 146

campaign plans, 76–77

campaign spending, 132–33; growth of, 15–18, 21, 75, 77, 78, 81, 127, 137–38, 149, 155, 214, 218, 223, 226; personal finance vs., 82, 83; public financing of, 162–63, 170, 178–87, 201–2, 205, 206, 207; regulation of, 22, 26, 216–17, 218. *See also* fundraising

Canada, 154–55

Cancela, Yvanna, 195

Candidate Pipeline Project, 189–90

candidate recruitment, 18, 20, 22–23, 26, 74, 189–90, 205–6, 207–8, 218–19; cost of, 125, 126, 141, 157; historical data lacking on, 155; through interest groups, 19, 104–5, 112, 140, 219; through labor unions, 109, 139, 151–52, 219; logic of, 141–44; through networks, 122, 142–43, 149, 151, 153–54, 157; political scholarships combined with, 202–3; public campaign finance and, 184–85; from working class, 79, 99–118, 119, 122, 125, 126, 138–40, 144–51, 157, 161, 163, 165, 191–201, 210, 224

candidates: emergence of, 15, 75, 78–80, 82, 92, 191; entry process of, 34, 92, 126; training of, 22, 194–201, 207, 218–19

Carnegie, Andrew, 288n11

Castillo, Carmen, 209

Chamber of Commerce, 9, 137, 139, 197

city councils, 5, 12, 25–26, 52–54, 128, 130–32